3ds Max Speed Modeling for 3D Artists

Flex your speed modeling muscles using 3ds Max

Thomas Mooney

PUBLISHING

BIRMINGHAM - MUMBAI

3ds Max Speed Modeling for 3D Artists

First published: October 2012

Production Reference: 1111012

Published by Packt Publishing Ltd.
Livery Place
35 Livery Street
Birmingham B3 2PB, UK.

ISBN 978-1-84969-236-6

www.packtpub.com

Cover Image by Thomas Mooney (tomofnz@gmail.com)

Credits

Author
Thomas Mooney

Reviewers
Vincent Bourdier
Conor O'Kane

Acquisition Editor
Wilson D'souza
Pramila Balan

Lead Technical Editor
Pramila Balan

Technical Editors
Zinal Shah
Sharvari Baet
Manmeet Singh Vasir
Kedar Bhat
Merin Jose

Copy Editors
Brandt D'Mello
Insiya Morbiwala
Aditya Nair
Alfida Paiva
Laxmi Subramanian

Project Coordinator
Joel Goveya

Proofreader
Jonathan Todd

Indexer
Hemangini Bari

Graphics
Aditi Gajjar

Production Coordinator
Shantanu Zagade

Cover Work
Shantanu Zagade

About the Author

Thomas Mooney grew up in New Zealand. He now lives in a jungle with squashed frogs, mosquitoes, and regular thunderstorms and power cuts. He is a lecturer in design and also works as an artist. You can learn more about his work at www.tomofnz.com.

Tom tends to work, play, teach, and sit around all day with computers, and also likes to do comics, films, maps, screenplays, novels, storyboards, and iPad doodles.

His book *Unreal Development Kit Game Design Cookbook*, *Packt Publishing* was published earlier in 2012.

For my mother, a good, kind soul.

I would also like to extend a hearty back slap to all my students for being the subject of numerous tests (of patience mostly) during this book's development.

About the Reviewers

Vincent Bourdier is a twenty-six year old developer who is French with a passion for 3D. After self-learning 3D modeling and programming, he went to the University of Technology of Belfort-Montbéliard (UTBM) in 2003 and received an Engineering degree in Computer Sciences, specializing in imagery, interaction, and virtual reality. Passionate about computer graphics and image processing, he remains curious about existing and new technologies in a lot of domains such as AI, CMake, augmented reality, and so on.

He has been working as a 3D developer at Global Vision Systems (Toulouse, France) since 2008. He is now a Technical Leader on a 3D real-time engine.

Global Vision Systems (`http://www.global-vision-systems.com`) is a software developer and publisher offering innovative human-machine interfaces for aeronautics, space, plant, and process supervision.

I would like to thank my parents for their encouragement, even if they don't understand a word of my job, and my employers for the opportunity to live my passions and giving me challenges to meet.

Conor O'Kane is a game developer and teacher from Dublin. He lectures on game development at RMIT University in Melbourne, in courses covering game design, low-polygon art, character modeling, and iOS game development. He has worked as an Artist and as a Technical Artist for console game developers since 1999, and has been producing his own games independently since 2007, primarily with the Torque 2D engine. He currently develops games for Windows, Mac, and iOS platforms.

Conor lives with his wife and two children in Melbourne. When not making (or playing) video games, he enjoys practicing martial arts and learning to play the piano. You can download his free games and read articles and tutorials at http://cokane.com.

www.PacktPub.com

Support files, eBooks, discount offers and more

You might want to visit www.PacktPub.com for support files and downloads related to your book.

Did you know that Packt offers eBook versions of every book published, with PDF and ePub files available? You can upgrade to the eBook version at www.PacktPub.com and as a print book customer, you are entitled to a discount on the eBook copy. Get in touch with us at service@packtpub.com for more details.

At www.PacktPub.com, you can also read a collection of free technical articles, sign up for a range of free newsletters and receive exclusive discounts and offers on Packt books and eBooks.

http://PacktLib.PacktPub.com

Do you need instant solutions to your IT questions? PacktLib is Packt's online digital book library. Here, you can access, read and search across Packt's entire library of books.

Why Subscribe?

- Fully searchable across every book published by Packt
- Copy and paste, print and bookmark content
- On demand and accessible via web browser

Free Access for Packt account holders

If you have an account with Packt at www.PacktPub.com, you can use this to access PacktLib today and view nine entirely free books. Simply use your login credentials for immediate access.

Table of Contents

Preface

This book is aimed at artists who already know essentials of modeling and are considering modeling specialization. A big part of specialization involves seeking ways to streamline your work flow. Possibly you're a diploma student and want to level up your 3ds Max skills after a short course, or possibly you're self-taught and want to measure the skills you've obtained. The outcome of reading this book would be a thorough knowledge of the modeling pipeline from concept, base model, sculpted model, UV mapped model, textured model, to skinned and rigged model, allowing for high-quality rendering or export of a game engine-ready, animation-ready asset.

What this book covers

Chapter 1, First Launch: Getting To Know 3ds Max, covers starting from scratch with 3ds Max. This chapter should help you get up to speed. It covers the essential starting points for those making their first launch into 3ds Max.

Chapter 2, Model Shakedown: Make 3ds Max Work for You, examines model handling using readymade assets. The main asset is a rapidly constructed vehicle used for testing a prototype game. Our purpose is to cover the necessary model handling skills before we undertake actual modeling in the next chapter.

Chapter 3, The Base Model – A Solid Foundation in Polygon Modeling, covers getting started on a model, starting with a reference image. We'll examine the modeling skills needed to create a base model. It also introduces the challenge of constructing forms that match a design while keeping within the constraints of four-sided topology, with an eye towards surface-detailing requirements.

Chapter 4, Mod My Ride: Extending upon a Base Model, demonstrates ways in which various modifiers can be used to adjust modeled content quickly. The main emphasis is to provide alternative designs with little work by modifying existing content. We also cover basic concepts for soft-surface modeling, smoothing groups, and generating geometric models from shapes or curves.

Chapter 5, The Language of Machines: Designing and Building Model Components, demonstrates the usefulness of developing an internal library or vocabulary of visual memes for your tech, mech, and hard surface models. It is very difficult to make a fictional model of a man-made object without some familiarity with how real man-made objects get their look, especially in terms of fabricated or manufactured detail. In this chapter, we'll analyze some prevalent ideas about depicting 'sci-fi' tech along with time-saving methods for constructing parts to reference in models.

Chapter 6, The Cutting Edge: A Closer Look at 3ds Max Polygon Tools, examines newer features related to modeling in 3ds Max 2013 such as the Freeform tools, live cutting, edge loop modes, and some of the more peripheral modeling tools that are nevertheless really handy to know, such as working with Boolean compound objects.

Chapter 7, The Mystery of the Unfolding Polygons: Mapping Models for Texturing, demonstrates methods of UV Mapping and stresses the importance of becoming fluent in the process of preparing a model for texturing a stage, which bridges modeling and texture painting while calling on somewhat different skills. The challenge is simply to put a 3D surface onto a 2D image plane. 3ds Max's mapping toolset ensures the user is well-armed to meet the challenge.

Chapter 8, Custom Body Job: Painting using Viewport Canvas, shows how the extensive tools in Viewport Canvas can be used to directly paint on a model with texture coordinates, with many direct comparisons to Photoshop painting tools. We go through material and channel setup, brush settings and hotkeys, and approaches to importing layer content, managing custom brushes, and using layer masks to paint non-destructively.

Chapter 9, Go with the Flow Retopology in 3ds Max, shows different ways to get a highly detail model down to a useable polygon count without losing key detail from the original, primarily looking at the brush-based PolyDraw tools.

Chapter 10, Pushing the Envelope – Model Preparation for Animation and Games, walks you through the envelope weighting, paint brush weighting, and vertex weighting tools in the Skin modifier, which is used to bind a mesh to a rig. In this case, we use CAT to provision a rig and we use SkinWrap to match a low-resolution version of a skinned model to a higher resolution version.

Bonus Chapter, Containers and XREfs, discusses Xref and Containers. We will learn how to create and edit a Container. We will also learn how to use Xref and Xref scene.

You can download the Bonus Chapter from `http://www.packtpub.com/sites/default/files/downloads/Containers_and_ XRefs.pdf`.

What you need for this book

The following software are required:

- 3ds Max 2012 or 2013
- Adobe Photoshop or similar 2D image editor
- Optional: Pixologic ZBrush, Pixologic Sculptris, or Autodesk Mudbox for sculpting detail.

Who this book is for

This book will appeal to anyone interested in 3D modeling who wants to improve their speed modeling ability, particularly artists whose work is relevant to industries where hard surface modeling or model prototyping is required, such as games, films, or visualization.

Conventions

In this book, you will find a number of styles of text that distinguish between different kinds of information. Here are some examples of these styles, and an explanation of their meaning.

Code words in text are shown as follows: "You may like to try the `ModularToolbarsUI`, which exposes more than what the default UI does."

While there are very few cases where code is referenced, a block of code is set as follows:

```
FOR batch in selection DO
(
local newUVW = Unwrap_UVW()
addmodifier batch newUVW
newUVW.pack 0 5.0 true false false
)
```

New terms and **important words** are shown in bold. Words that you see on the screen, in menus or dialog boxes for example, appear in the text like this: "In the menu bar at the top of the screen, go to the Create menu and choose **Standard Primitives | Box**".

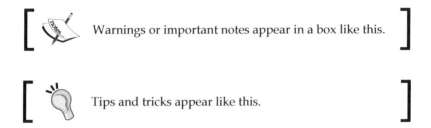

Warnings or important notes appear in a box like this.

Tips and tricks appear like this.

Reader feedback

Feedback from our readers is always welcome. Let us know what you think about this book—what you liked or may have disliked. Reader feedback is important for us to develop titles that you really get the most out of.

To send us general feedback, simply send an e-mail to feedback@packtpub.com, and mention the book title via the subject of your message.

If there is a topic that you have expertise in and you are interested in either writing or contributing to a book, see our author guide on www.packtpub.com/authors.

Customer support

Now that you are the proud owner of a Packt book, we have a number of things to help you to get the most from your purchase.

Downloading the example code

You can download the example code files for all Packt books you have purchased from your account at http://www.PacktPub.com. If you purchased this book elsewhere, you can visit http://www.PacktPub.com/support and register to have the files e-mailed directly to you.

Errata

Although we have taken every care to ensure the accuracy of our content, mistakes do happen. If you find a mistake in one of our books—maybe a mistake in the text or the code—we would be grateful if you would report this to us. By doing so, you can save other readers from frustration and help us improve subsequent versions of this book. If you find any errata, please report them by visiting http://www.packtpub.com/support, selecting your book, clicking on the **errata submission form** link, and entering the details of your errata. Once your errata are verified, your submission will be accepted and the errata will be uploaded on our website, or added to any list of existing errata, under the Errata section of that title. Any existing errata can be viewed by selecting your title from http://www.packtpub.com/support.

Piracy

Piracy of copyright material on the Internet is an ongoing problem across all media. At Packt, we take the protection of our copyright and licenses very seriously. If you come across any illegal copies of our works, in any form, on the Internet, please provide us with the location address or website name immediately so that we can pursue a remedy.

Please contact us at copyright@packtpub.com with a link to the suspected pirated material.

We appreciate your help in protecting our authors, and our ability to bring you valuable content.

Questions

You can contact us at questions@packtpub.com if you are having a problem with any aspect of the book, and we will do our best to address it.

1

First Launch: Getting to Know 3ds Max

This book is aimed at artists who already know the essentials of modeling and are considering modeling specialization. A big part of specialization involves seeking ways to streamline your workflow. Possibly you're a diploma student and want to level up your 3ds Max skills after a short course, or possibly you're self taught and want to measure the skills you've obtained. If you are starting from scratch, however, this chapter should help you get up to speed. It covers the essential starting points for those making their first launch into 3ds Max.

These are the areas covered in the chapter's topics:

- Quick start: Jump into making models
- Getting to know the User Interface
- Default and custom UI schemes
    - ° Switching UI presets
    - ° Making changes to hotkeys
    - ° Customizing the Quad menu
    - ° Making changes to the view layout
- Deciding on the best view navigation
    - ° Navigation with the ViewCube
    - ° Navigation with the Steering Wheel
- Displaying your model for modeling
- Setting scene units
- Searching for content in the scene

- Creating your own selection sets with Named Selections
- Common changes to 3ds Max default preferences
- Determining the hardware shading settings to use

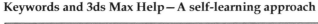

Keywords and 3ds Max Help – A self-learning approach

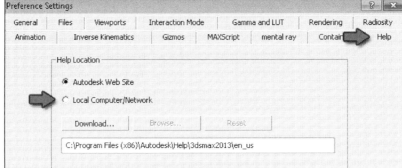

In this book, we indicate **menu**, **property**, and **tool** keywords in bold. Keywords in the book can be explored via the **Index** of the 3ds Max menu **Help | Autodesk 3ds Max Help** online. Offline documentation can be downloaded via an installer from the usa.autodesk.com under **Home | Support | Support and Documentation | Autodesk 3ds Max | Documentation and Help | 3ds Max 2013 Documentation** section under **3ds Max / 3ds Max Design 2013 Help Installer**, which you should then set active in 3ds Max via the menu **Customize | Preferences | Help | Local Computer/Network**, or you can simply **Download** it via a button there.

Quick start: Jump into making models

This quick start guide is a set of steps to go from a blank viewport to having a simple model you can edit at the **Sub-Object** level (meaning you can access the component parts it is made of and change the object directly), and access the **Editable Poly** tools.

These steps establish a geometric object you can extend upon polygon by polygon:

1. In the menu bar at the top of the screen, go to the **Create** menu and choose **Standard Primitives | Box**.

2. Notice that the **Create** tab ⚙ in the Command Panel on the right of the screen exposes the parameters for creating a new Box under **Geometry | Standard Primitives**.

3. In the **Create** tab parameters, you can also specify to set the **Length**, **Width**, and **Height** values, and also **Segments** to divide the box up in more detail. You can set these prior to creation, but it is easier to adjust them afterward.

4. Click in the view labeled **Perspective**. It gets an orange border to show it is active. Now click-and-drag in the **Perspective** view across the grid (*G* is the shortcut for toggling the grid visibility in any view). A planar shape will emerge, then when you drag up, you'll define its height as a box. We've created a box by specifying its length, height and depth. You can also, in the Creation Method section, click the radio button Cube. This will make a newly added box have sides of the same dimensions.

5. Having placed an arbitrary box in the scene via the Create tab in the Command Panel, we want to adjust or modify the parameters in the next tab ▨. There, set the **Length Segs**, **Width Segs**, and **Height Segs** to **3** each for the existing box. The settings will be kept for any future boxes made, until you restart 3ds Max.

6. Press *F4*. This will display **Edged Faces** on top of the shaded viewport render of the box. While the box is selected, it will have a white, highlighted wireframe.

7. If you create a box you don't like, click on it to select it and delete it by hitting the *Delete* key, or use the **Edit** menu and choose **Delete**.

8. To continue editing, right-click on the object to expose the **Quad** menu and go to **Convert To: | Convert to Editable Poly**. Editable Poly is a good type for modeling.

9. Don't choose **Editable Mesh**, which is a `TriMesh` object format type mostly maintained for legacy and compatibility reasons (and sometimes to speed up display of objects). There are more editing tools available for an Editable Poly than there are for Editable Mesh, and they work faster. Editable Poly is a Winged Edge polygon data structure. For the technically inclined, there is an exhaustively detailed discussion of what this entails on the CGSociety forums (`http://forums.cgsociety.org/showthread.php?t=146797`), but the main thing is the tools we'll be using for this book's lessons are exclusively for Editable Poly models.

10. Note that when you convert the primitive to Editable Poly, sometimes the quad menu extends available commands to the left side or right side, depending on where it is activated on the screen. This ensures a fit to the view. An example is shown in the following screenshot:

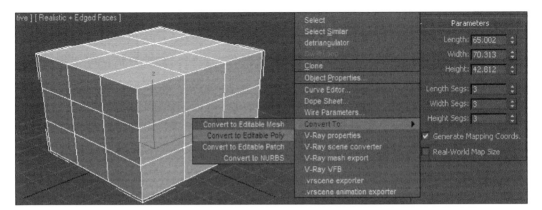

11. Right-click over the model and choose **Quad** menu | **Sub-objects** | **Polygon** in the **Tools 1** section, or press 4. This sets you into **SubObject** mode, editing **Polygons**, which are the components of the object surface. Now click on one of the squares that make up the top of the box. It will be highlighted in red. These squares are sometimes called polygons, sometimes quads, and sometimes faces (though strictly speaking, a face has three sides and quads are inherently composed of a pair of triangles).

12. Hold *Ctrl* and click on one of the polygons on the side of the box. It is added to the current selection. In earlier versions of 3ds Max, pressing *Ctrl* on an already selected polygon would deselect it, but lately this has been changed; now, only pressing *Alt* will deselect.

13. Right-click and choose **Quad** menu | **Extrude**. When you hover the cursor over the selected polygons, the cursor changes to show you are in **Extrude** mode. Drag on the faces and they'll push out, generating new geometry. Right-click to exit **Extrude** mode.

14. Besides the white wireframe, there is a white bounding box surrounding the model. Bounds show the widest range of the model in each dimension. This also helps you spot the object that is selected. You can turn it off if you press the [+] icon at the top left of the viewport, choose **Configure Viewports**, then turn off the **Selection Brackets** tickbox in the **Selection** section of the **Visual Style & Appearance** tab.

15. Now select just the top extruded polygon by clicking on it. Press the icon
    ▦ to enter **Move** mode (or **Transform** mode). You can also right-click and
    choose **Quad** menu | **Move**. An XYZ gizmo or guide appears. If it doesn't,
    try pressing *X*, which toggles transform gizmos on and off. Highlight the
    blue **Z** arrow and then drag the polygon upward.

16. The following screenshot, on the left, shows the extrusion results, and
    the image on the right shows the transform results, with the **XYZ** gismo
    showing the blue **Z** axis highlighted, which constrains movement to **Z**.

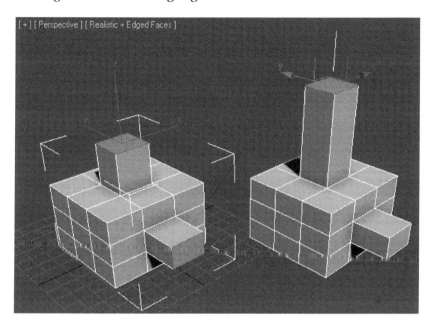

17. It is a modest start, but you've made an object, converted it to Editable
    Poly for editing, and added to the model and transformed part of it. These
    processes are simple, but you'll have to repeat them many times, and these
    tools alone can help you get a lot done.

18. To finish up, right-click on the model and choose **Quad** | **Top-Level** from
    Tools 2. This turns off the Polygon editing mode and lets us adjust the entire
    model at the **Object** level rather than the **SubObject** level.

19. Press *W* to enter **Move** mode if you aren't already in it (yet another way to
    do it), and then hold *Shift* and move the object, which is one way to produce
    a **clone** or copy of the model. Try using the same tools and processes you've
    just proceeded through to adjust other parts of the model.

20. Save your first creation by pressing *Ctrl + S* and choosing a path and a filename (`YourName_FirstModel_01.max`), which is a good convention because it informs us who made the model, what its subject is, and the iteration number for the piece. The extension `.max` is used by all 3ds Max scenes. The default path for 3ds Max scenes is `C:\Users\~\My Documents\3dsMax\scenes\`.

21. To export the model to a game engine like **UDK** (`.ase` or `.fbx`), or a sculpting program like **Sculptris** (`.obj`) or **Mudbox** (`.fbx` or `.obj`), you can choose the appropriate format under **File | Export | Export Selected**. The default path for 3ds Max to export to is `C:\Users\~\My Documents\3dsMax\export\`.

Getting to know the User Interface

First of all, it is useful to look at some of the conventions of the 3ds Max UI. While our goal at the moment is to get used to the patterns that windows, buttons, menus, and tabs follow in 3ds Max, some features of 3ds Max will surface along the way that we'll have to reserve discussing in depth until later.

For example, to edit objects, you can add **Modifiers** to them, and these can be added on top of each other as a stack. From modifier to modifier, the stack GUI arrangement is always the same. Here is what to look out for: any ◾ icon like the one next to **Editable Poly** in the following screenshot means you can expand it to view further parameters. Other editors in 3ds Max, such as the **Curve Editor**, share this convention. Shown on the **Bend** modifier in the following screenshot, an ◾ icon will collapse an expanded section back again. The little lamp icon 💡 for each modifier lets you enable and disable a given modifier temporarily, without losing its settings. Right-click on the modifier label (for example, Bend) to get further options such as **Delete**, **Rename**, **Copy**, **Cut**, **Paste,** and **Off in Viewport** (which disables a modifier in the scene until render time).

A menu item with a + icon, similar to the ones shown in the following screenshot, can also be expanded by clicking on its label. Once expanded, it can be closed by clicking on its label again. These menu items can be re-arranged by dragging them, as can modifiers in the Modifier stack. A blue line will highlight the position they will drop into.

The various sections of **Command Panel**, which can be extensive, can be scrolled using a hand cursor 🖑 that appears when you drag on empty space in the Command Panel. You can also use the slider down the right side. This is also true of the **Render** dialog (*F10*). The slider is quite thin, but is easy to use once you know that it is there. On the **Editable Poly** option, if you expand all the sections, you can see this slider. On a modifier such as **Bend**, which has few parameters, it isn't included.

Any icon that shows a text field with a downward triangle icon ⏷ means you can expand a rollout list, as is the case with **Modifier List** in the Command Panel. Likewise, any icon with a little black triangle in the corner can be held down to expand a **fly-out** revealing more options or tools that relate to it. An example is the **Align** tool: ▦.

Any numeric field can either accept type or be adjusted using a spinner on the right ⏺. Most spinners can be right-clicked to drop their value to zero or its lowest possible value; for example, a Cylinder primitive's **Sides** parameter can only go down to 3, or it would be a flat object.

Many text buttons and icons in 3ds Max, if you float the cursor over them for a short time, will display the name of the tool, and often a tool tip or instruction referring to the use of the tool. This is particularly true for the Ribbon tools, which often also display illustrations as they expand. An example of a tool tip is shown in the following screenshot:

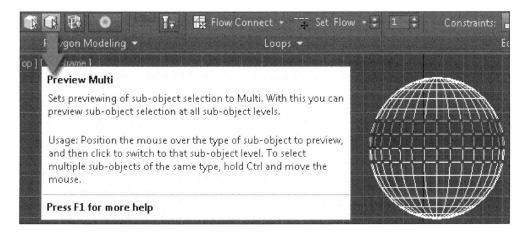

The icon ![icon], which resembles a pin in the modifier stack, lets you keep a pinned object's modifier stack displayed even if you select a different object in the scene. The icon ![icon], which resembles a pin in the Ribbon UI, lets you keep an expanded rollout menu from being reverted closed (while the current object is selected). This seems to work when you haven't minimized the Ribbon to one of its three minimized modes. In the following example, the **Teapot** primitive's modifier stack is pinned, so it shows even though the **Sphere** primitive is currently selected. Meanwhile, in the Ribbon UI, the extra tools of the **Geometry (All)** section have been expanded and pinned. This would remain so until some object other than the **Sphere** primitive was selected instead.

The Ribbon UI can be collapsed to a minimal set of headings by clicking on the upward triangle shown at the top of the following screenshot (and the tiny downward arrow next to that indicates there are some options for this collapse command). There is a strange redundancy to this set of options, as the option **Minimize to Tabs** seems just fine. While the Ribbon is minimized, all you need to do to access the Ribbon tool is click on the tab titles, which then expand out.

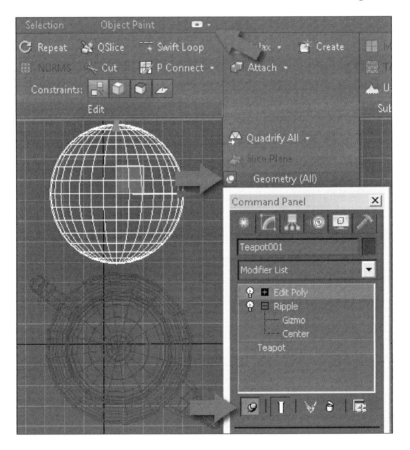

Similarly, if you are using the Ribbon, then you can drag the labels of each section to re-arrange them, as shown in the following screenshot. The example shows the **Graphite Modeling** tools, where the **Loops** section is being dragged next to the **Polygon Modeling** section. Note that the Ribbon menus change automatically depending on what is selected and the editing mode you are currently in (such as the **Polygon** mode or the **Vertex** mode).

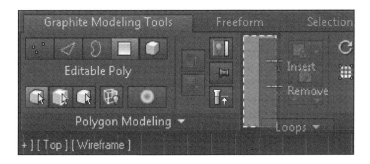

The next thing to get used to is accessing **Settings** of tools while editing. Any tool with a box icon ■ next to it, or exposed under it in the case of the Ribbon UI, opens further settings for the tool. In the **Quad** menu, shown in the following screenshot, many of the editing tools show this.

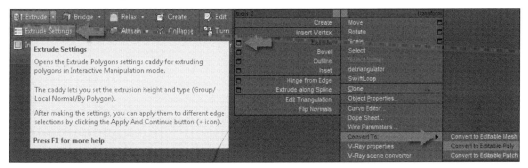

Right-click in a view with an **Editable Poly** selected to expose the major editing tools (tools 2). Also, a sideways arrow in the **Quad** menu, as in the case of **Convert To: | Convert to Editable Poly**, reveals options for a command. In the preceding screenshot, the **Extrude** tool is shown in **Polygon** mode. There are multiple ways to access the tool itself and its settings: you can do so via the Ribbon or via the **Quad** menu. You can also access the same **Extrude** tool and other editing tools in the **Command Panel** in the section **Editable Poly | Polygons | Edit Polygons**.

Command Panel has a couple of interesting features: it can be floated, and in versions from 3ds Max 2012, it can be minimized, a lot like the menus in ZBrush, off to the side and out of the way unless needed. By default, **Command Panel** is docked on the right-hand side of the screen. You can widen it to show several columns by dragging on its edges. Views can also be enlarged in the same way. You can float **Command Panel** by dragging on its top edge or by right-clicking and choosing **Float**. There is also the option to **Dock | Left**. There is also the option to **Minimize**, which lets Command Panel slide out of view off to the side when not in use. A vertical strip labeled **Command Panel**, if you roll over it, pops it back out. When the Command Panel is floated, you can drag it to either side of the screen to re-dock it there, or you can double-click on its label.

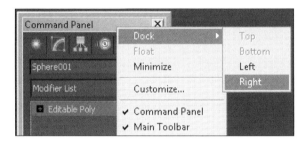

The label also has a [⊠] icon that lets you turn the **Command Panel** off. To reveal it again, go to the top row of icons—the **main toolbar**—right-click, and you can enable it from the list of menus there. If you happen to disable the main toolbar, you can get that back again if you go to the left side of the UI, just under the green 3ds Max logo , and right-click to expose a menu that lets you enable it again. Above the main toolbar are the main menu entries: **File, Edit, Tools, Group**, and so on. These can be hidden by clicking the down arrow icon and choosing **Hide Menu Bar**. To get it back, click there again and choose **Show Menu Bar**. The uppermost icons displayed are entries in the **Quick Access Toolbar**, which you can add your own entries to by right-clicking on a tool and choosing **Add to Quick Access Toolbar**. Here, I'm adding **Swift Loop**, a handy tool, to the Quick Access Toolbar from the Ribbon.

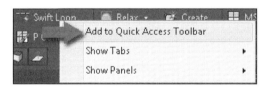

Unfortunately, such additions are per session additions. Next time you load up 3ds Max, they won't be preserved. The **Undo** and **Redo** buttons are there, with icons that let you access the available undo and redo history too. If you start to customize the **Quick Access Toolbar,** you will notice the option when you right-click to add a **separator**, which is a little dividing bar to space out menu items nicely. These are seen all throughout 3ds Max: in the modifier stack, in the various editor icon rows, and in the **Quad** menu.

> If you really get lost with missing windows you've closed, try going to the **Customize** menu and choose **Revert to Startup Layout**.

Default and custom UI schemes

In the current version, the UI is well-designed and visually appealing. The dark tones allow users to work without glare, and the icons are colored for easy spotting. There are still some legacy UI presets you can try out, including the 2009 interface that is used in many tutorials online. You can also save changes you make to the UI in an external file and set it as the default if you wish.

Switching UI presets

This quick demonstration shows two ways to change the presets for the user interface:

- One way to switch UI presets is to expand the **Customize** menu and choose **Load Custom UI Scheme**, which pops up a browsing window to locate a `.ui` file.

- Expand the **History** rollout at the top of this window to expose `C:\Program Files\Autodesk\3ds Max 2012\UI`. This path includes several options you can try out. `3Dsmax2009.ui` is nearly the same as the 2012 default except the views are toned much lighter.

By default, Custom UI files, including small changes you make to the default UI, are saved in `C:\Users\~\Appdata\Local\Autodesk\3dsMax\2012\64bit\enu\UI` (supposing you are using the 64 bit version).

There is another way to access UI presets, which is by going to the **Customize** menu and choosing **Custom UI and Defaults Switcher,** which has a slight advantage of including visual previews of each UI as you select it in the list. Here you can see a list of tool-based settings and a list of UI schemes (on the right). You may like to try the ModularToolbarsUI, which exposes more than what the default UI does.

Downloading the example code

You can download the example code files for all Packt books you have purchased from your account at http://www.PacktPub.com. If you purchased this book elsewhere, you can visit http://www.PacktPub.com/support and register to have the files e-mailed directly to you.

Making changes to hotkeys

Let's change the rather annoying **Selection Lock Toggle**. When turned on, this toggle prevents you from selecting anything else, which can be handy if you intend it to be on, but not so nice if you toggle it on by mistake. Since its hotkey is *Space*, you can imagine this to be easy to do. Setting it to *Ctrl + Space*, which is not assigned to a command, would be better, since it is less likely to be accidentally hit.

This is done as follows:

1. Go to the **Customize** menu and choose **Customize User Interface**. This window pops up with the **Keyboard** tab selected, so all we need to do is browse down the alphabetical list of **Actions** for **Selection Lock Toggle**, which also shows its icon (the padlock 🔒 found under the time slider).

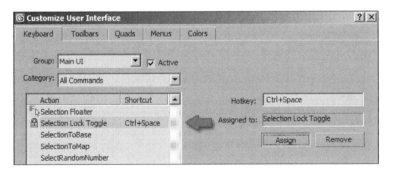

2. First, the hotkey *Space* will show next to **Selection Lock Toggle**. On the right, press **Remove** to remove it; then in the **Hotkey** field press *Ctrl + Space*, and click on **Assign** to commit it. Don't forget to press **Save** at the bottom of the window. You'll be prompted to save a .kbd file, which you can name yourname.kbd. It will be saved with the UI next time you save the UI, and 3ds Max does this anyway when you end the session.

3. Most commands in 3ds Max let you set a hotkey. You can view the assigned keys by browsing the **Shortcut** list. Or you can go to the **Help** menu and choose **Keyboard Shortcut Map**, which opens an interactive shockwave image that exposes main hotkeys as you roll over a diagram of a keyboard. Given the file type, your browser may not permit it to load, but you can find it here: `C:\Program Files\Autodesk\3ds Max 2012\hotkeymap.SWF`. Note that this handy utility only shows default hotkeys.

4. Not all the default hotkeys are as convenient as they could be.

5. The **Scale** command actually is a flyout with three options. On the keyboard Q stands for Select, W stands for Move, E stands for Rotate, and R stands for Smart Scale. Unfortunately, Smart Scale is not very smart, and often you'll only want to use the regular scale tool only to find you've actually cycled through to the Squash option. So, if we set R as Select and Scale, or just Scale, instead of Smart Scale, we avoid this oversight. You can always cycle through the three scale options using $Ctrl + E$, **Scale Cycle**.

6. There's a very handy shortcut called **Transform** tools. This tool can be found in the **Edit** menu, where it's called **Transform Toolbox**. It doesn't have a hotkey by default. This could be set to $Ctrl + T$, which is available. We'll discuss its functionality later on, and make frequent use of it as we model.

7. Another tool that is often used, which doesn't come with a hotkey, is the **Manage Layers** dialog, which is used for organizing scene content by layer and also for hiding and freezing content. Since I use this tool often, I've taken to setting it to *Space*, since it doesn't matter if I tap on it by mistake; it is easy to notice the dialog when it opens or closes.

As well as using the Layer Manager, you may want to get the free script Outliner 2 (which imitates the Autodesk Maya Outliner) from `http://script.threesixty.nl/outliner`. The link downloads a `.mzp` file that you can simply drag from Windows Explorer into the 3ds Max viewport to install. Once installed, this uses the hotkey H, which overrides the **Select By Name** tool's hotkey, so you may want to set **Select by Name** to another hotkey (or use a different hotkey for the Outliner). Note that content hidden by the **By Layer** option in the Layer Manager can't be unhidden by the Outliner if you are in Hierarchy mode. At the bottom of the Outliner there is an icon that enables Layer mode, a substitute for the actual Layer Manager.

Customizing the Quad menu

You may have noticed that when you right-click, a menu appears under the cursor with shortcuts to many tools distributed elsewhere in the 3ds Max UI. For instance, you can press the **Select** icon or press *Q* or you can right-click and choose **Select** from the **Quad** menu. This menu can be changed to suit your need, though part of its utility comes from memorizing its layout for speedy access, so making changes often may defeat the purpose. Still, there are a few tools that you'll regularly use that could benefit from being in the **Quad** menu.

> **Swift Loop** is a tool used to add additional edge loops to an **Editable Poly** model. We'll discuss its use later too, but in brief, you can add a box to your scene, right-click on it, and choose **Quad** menu | **Convert To:** | **Editable Poly**. Then press 2 to enter **Edge** mode, then go to the **Ribbon UI** | **Graphite Modeling Tools** and expand the **Edit** panel to expose the **Swift Loop** icon ⛏. Clicking this enters a mode whereby clicking on an edge will add a perpendicular loop to the model. Using the **Swift Loop** tool is very handy, but accessing it from the Ribbon time and again is frustrating. It would be better to add it to the **Quad** menu, where it is always right under the cursor.

The following demonstration shows how to add this commonly used modeling tool to the **Quad** menu:

1. Go to the **Customize** menu and choose **Customize User Interface**. Previously, we changed settings in the **Keyboard** tab; this time, skip over to the **Toolbars** tab to get the **Quads** tab.

If you're disinclined to add these additional tools to the menus, you can opt to press **Load** here and choose `\Packt3dsMax\Chapter 1\PacktUI.mnu` to do so automatically. Several common tools are arranged for easy, swift access. There is a version for both 2012 and 2013 version of 3ds Max.

2. There are four squares on the right side of the UI, with the **transform** section highlighted in yellow. Click on the lower-left square **tools 2**. Expand the entry **[+] Context Edit Poly Tools 2 FLAT**.

3. Highlight **Swift Loop** in the **Actions** list, then drag it over to the top entry of the **[+] Context Edit Poly Tools 2 FLAT** list, where it should be inserted above **Create (Poly)**. Of course, you can drop it where you like, but this is a reasonable location, and it will show up as shown in the following screenshot when you right-click to access the **Quad** menu. At the bottom of the window, press **Save** and try it out.

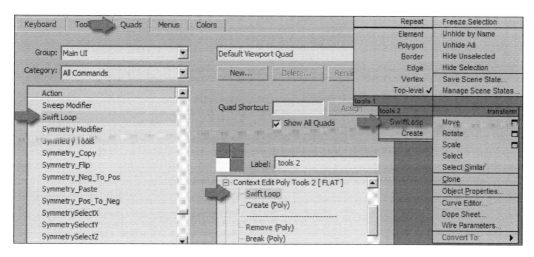

A preference you may want to set while in the **Quads** tab of the **Customize User Interface** dialog is to turn off **Show All Quads** option, via its tickbox. What this does is it only displays the part of the quad box that you highlight with the mouse. It uses less screen space as only a quarter of the menu is seen at one time.

Should you want to remove or rename an entry in the **Quad** menu, right-click on it to access a menu showing those options.

Note that there are contextual **Quad** menus depending on what mode you are working in, and you can edit these by expanding the rollout that shows **Default Viewport Quad**. In particular, it is useful to customize the **Unwrap UVW Quad** to access mapping tools faster. See *Chapter 7, The Mystery of the Unfolding Polygons: Mapping Models for Texturing*, for coverage of mapping processes.

Also, you will notice there are hotkeys to filter the **Quad** menu. For example, the **Modeling Quad** (*Ctrl + RMB*) only shows modeling tools. The **Snaps Quad** (*Shift + RMB*) lets you set the current snap type. This is quicker than moving the cursor up to the **Snap** icon ▒ to right-click and access the **Grid and Snap Settings** menu. The hotkey for entering Snap mode is *S* and it uses whatever settings you most recently set. Snaps are used for precision modeling, and snapping functionality is discussed further in *Chapter 5, The Language of Machines: Designing and Building Model Components*.

Making changes to the view layout

The most obvious way to change the viewports is to resize the default 4 x 4 panels by dragging their inner frame border. Each viewport has a [+] menu where the top entry is the **Maximize Viewport** or **Restore Viewport** command, *Alt + W*.

There are more controls for the view arrangement. If you press [+] in a view and choose **Configure Viewports** or right-click anywhere over the viewport control icons at the bottom right of 3ds Max or open the **Views** menu and choose **Configure Viewports**, you will get a pop-up window, **Viewport Configuration**, where the tab to open is called **Layout**, as shown in the following screenshot. Click this tab and notice the two rows of preset panel layouts. Click on any of them, and then click on the large panels that are labeled with the current setting. A list will appear with the available options you can set. This method is the only way to swap out a **Track View** option that has been set in a viewport, so keep it in mind if you do any animation.

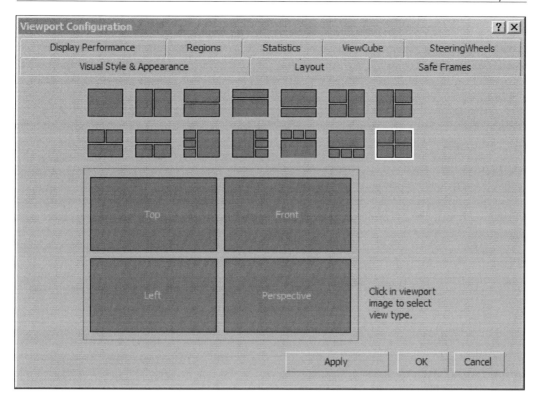

Deciding on the best view navigation

3ds Max is over 20 years old. Some of its navigation tools go way back to the early days, and over time some replacement navigation tools have been added. If you are used to an old navigation method, then a new one sometimes doesn't appear to add any advantage, whereas to a new user (or a user familiar with other applications using the same method), it can seem obvious to use the newer tool. We're going to evaluate all the methods to navigate the views, and you can decide for yourself which you prefer. Remember that if you use more than one 3D application, then it is always a good practice to use the same method in both cases, especially for scene navigation. Unfortunately, few applications share common UI defaults. 3ds Max is customizable in terms of hotkeys and menu items, and its navigation tools do have keyboard entries you can change.

Pan, Orbit, and Zoom

The quickest way to access Pan Mode in 3ds Max is to hold and drag the middle mouse button. You can also press the 🖑 icon or you can press *Ctrl + P* to pan. You will notice that the Orthographic views pan is less jumpy than the Perspective view.

The quickest way to access Orbit mode is to hold *Alt* and drag the middle mouse button. All the main navigation modes make use of the middle mouse button.

Zoom = **Middle Mouse Button (MMB)** *Scroll*. **Pan** = *MMB hold + drag*. **Orbit** = *MMB + Alt + drag*.

There are, however, other ways to orbit. *Ctrl + R* is the hotkey for Orbit and the equivalent icon is 🔄, and it gives you a circular yellow manipulator that allows some axial control for the orbit.

There are three common viewport navigation methods (**Zoom**, **Pan**, and **Orbit**) and some additional ones such as **Walk Through**, **Zoom Extents**, and **Zoom Extents Selected** (which equates to a frame object tool), and **Field-of-View (FOV)**, a camera control. Their functions will be discussed as we go through this chapter.

Open the `.max` file `\Packt3dsmax\Chapter 1\Begin.max`. You will see an assembly of un-textured models that form an industrial platform. We'll practice zooming around these, as having objects in the scene gives a more visceral feeling to the views than an empty scene does.

In the bottom-right corner of the UI there is a panel of viewport control buttons. In the following screenshot, these buttons are shown on the left for the **Perspective** view and are shown on the right for the **Orthographic** views (basically the same except for Region Zoom shown by default in Orthographic as FOV doesn't work in Orthographic views).

Zoom mode, if chosen here with the magnifying glass icon 🔍, permits a very smooth forward and backward motion of the virtual camera. The default hotkey for Zoom mode is *Alt + Z*. You can also zoom if you scroll the mouse wheel, but that is an incremental zoom. Next, we'll talk about how to adjust that increment, but it's handy to know that *Ctrl + Alt + MMB drag* (not scroll) allows you to zoom smoothly. This somewhat clunky key combo can be changed to suit in the **Customize | Customize UI Interface** dialog in the **Mouse** tab in the settings under **Category | Navigation**.

Go to the menu **Customize** and click on **Customize UI Interface**. This has several tabs at the top. Click on the one called **Mouse**. There is a panel under this tab called **Mouse Control** where you'll see two tickboxes for **Zoom Above Mouse Point (Orthographic**) and **Zoom About Mouse Point (Perspective)**. The default zoom uses the center of the active view. The zoom options just mentioned use the cursor location in the view.

Checking these two options lets you zoom into objects under the cursor more easily, without having to pan. Below this is a numerical input field for **Wheel Zoom Increment**. The lowest number it accepts is 0.01. Enter `0.01` and click on **OK**.

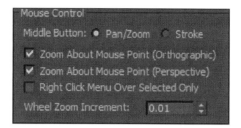

This scene has been scaled so that this value works well. In larger scenes, you may find the increment doesn't work so well. The thing to do is try out values until you're happy.

You can also select everything in the scene (*Ctrl* + *A*) and uniformly scale everything up or down accordingly, so you get an incremental zoom value that works well.

Notice as you zoom now with the mouse wheel in the Orthographic views (top, front, and left) that zoom has a different feel than scrolling in the Perspective view, which seems faster. If you over-zoom or get lost, you can use the hotkey *Shift* + *Z* to undo view changes. To reframe a view, if you are lost, it helps to select an object or polygon and press **Zoom Extents Selected**, discussed next.

Zoom Extents Selected is a command that goes hand-in-hand with Orbit (*Alt* + *MMB*). When you are spinning around an object, it frames the selection in the current view. The default for the flyout with the icon is **Zoom Extents**, which frames the whole scene, but I find that **Zoom Extents Selected** is much more useful because it lets us locate items we've selected by name. **Select By Name** (*H*) is a command that lets you choose objects from a pop-up list. We mentioned that the hotkey for Orbit (besides using the ViewCube compass) is *Alt* + *MMB*. You can also use the legacy Orbit command via its icon in the view controls panel.

This pops up a controller you can use to adjust the view, shown in the following screenshot:

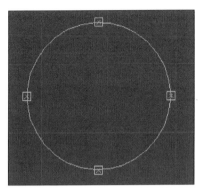

If you drag the crossed squares, the cursor changes to indicate that you'll be orbiting in one axis, either up and down or side to side. If you drag outside the circle, the cursor changes to indicate you'll tilt the view. If you drag within the circle, the cursor changes to indicate you'll make a free orbit in any axis based on the direction in which you move the mouse, much the same as with *Alt + MMB*.

The Orbit icon we mentioned, , actually has three settings. I find that almost always I use just one, but it isn't the default. If you click-and-hold the flyout icon, it reveals three options. Any icon in 3ds Max with a black triangle in the bottom-right corner has the same flyout options, a convention also seen in many other applications. The following screenshot shows the flyout buttons:

The uppermost option is **Orbit Scene**, the middle option is **Orbit Selected**, and the lowest option is **Orbit SubObject**. The last option works well when you are editing some small part of an object and want to orbit around that part, but it also works fine at any level of selection. Usually I set 3ds Max to use this and leave it that way.

Navigation with the ViewCube

The ViewCube is a tool introduced to many Autodesk products so they share a common basis for navigation. It is debatable how many people really use this tool, but for new users it is certainly a good way for learning how 3D space works. Power users will probably turn it off to save memory. Of course, it is possible many people love it.

There are four components in the ViewCube. The first is the Home button, which lets you store and return to a bookmarked view that you have set by right-clicking on the Home button .

The second component of the ViewCube is the cube itself. You can click on its faces, on its edges, and on its corners.

The third component is the **Tumble** tool that appears if you are viewing the face of the cube, which rolls the camera 90 degrees at a time when clicked.

The fourth component is the **Axial Orbit** tool shaped like a circular compass under the cube, which lets you spin the scene. It only allows one degree of freedom, unlike Orbit mode. If you like the ViewCube but don't like the compass under it, you can turn the Compass display off in its configuration.

Making adjustments to the ViewCube display

The following steps walk you through the use of the ViewCube in order to familiarize yourself with its settings, so you can decide which to opt for.

1. If you have the ViewCube exposed, right-click on the Home button and choose **Configure** or else click [+] in the view and choose **Configure Views** and click on the **ViewCube** tab.

2. There is a checkbox labeled **Show the ViewCube**, which you can turn off if you don't like the ViewCube. If you do like it, but want to work a little more efficiently, click the radio button **Only in Active View**. You can only use the ViewCube in the view you are currently in, so it saves a little memory to not have four of them spinning around at once.

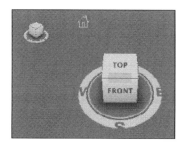

As shown in the preceding screenshot, you can diminish or increase the ViewCube size to taste. The left-hand side example is set to tiny, which is usable but problematic because the labels aren't visible, and the normal size is on the right. The large size is simply massive, and this is a case where small is probably better. No doubt the default size is too distracting to trouble with. You can also adjust how visible it is using **Inactive Opacity** in the same section.

In the viewport configuration options for the ViewCube, it is definitely a good idea to check the **Snap to Closest View** checkbox, to help keep the regular viewing angles lined up.

Clicking **Fit-to-View on View Change** means that whenever you change the camera using the ViewCube, you'll be zooming to the scene extents, which is probably not desirable unless you are editing only one model.

It definitely speeds up your work flow if you turn off **Use Animated Transitions** options when **Switching Views**. The transition is snappy, and you won't waste time waiting for the camera to animate through its turn.

Having the **Keep Scene Upright** checkbox checked is a good idea, just for stability in the view.

Navigation with the Steering Wheel

The **Steering Wheel** is an interesting but slightly twitchy tool introduced to 3ds Max in an attempt to provide game-like navigation, where you can fly or drive through the scene. New users, who will get used to this tool, will probably get a lot out of it, but users already familiar with the classic navigation methods already discussed will probably avoid it. Strangely, I like it when I remember to use it, but that is only in cases when I have to explain how viewport navigation can work. Still, there are a few features that are outstanding when using the Steering Wheel, in particular the **Rewind** and **Walk** tools.

The Steering Wheel shortcut is (supposedly) *Shift + W*, and I've noticed that *Shift + W* doesn't seem to turn anything on, which explains why I never really took up this tool. The reason is the hotkey is set in the context of the Steering Wheel group, not the main UI group.

The reliable way to activate the Steering Wheel is to go to the **Views** menu and choose **Steering Wheels | Toggle Steering Wheel** or choose one of the different modes it offers there. It is also possible to assign **Toggle Steering Wheel** as an entry in the **Quads** menu for speedy access. Look under **Group | Steering Wheels** in the **Quad** tab of the **Customize User Interface** menu to find it.

Using the Steering Wheel

In the following example, we will open the Steering Wheel and explore the methods it offers for scene navigation.

Open the max file `Packt3dsmax\Chapter 1\Begin.max`. You will see an assembly of un-textured models that form an industrial platform. We'll use this scene to drive around using the Steering Wheel to compare how it feels in comparison to the regular navigation tools.

For a scene like this, which is surrounded on four sides by walls, the Steering Wheel actually responds very nicely. The slight lag in getting it started is the only drawback.

There are four types of steering wheels. The default is the **Full Navigation Wheel**. The others are streamlined derivations of it. The mini wheels are smaller, and there are also the **Basic Wheels | View Object Wheels** and **Mini Tour Building Wheels** options. All of these can be accessed from the down arrow icon on the lower corner of the Steering Wheel, shown in the following screenshot:

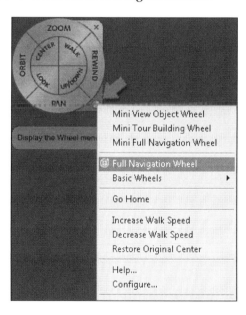

The **Look** command allows you to orbit around the camera's location, a lot like the 'look around' control in many 3D games. Try looking around the scene, and notice how it differs from the **Orbit** command, which turns around a pivot. After you have looked around, try using the **Rewind** command. This will present you with a filmstrip of prior views that you can slide along to choose among them.

The following screenshot shows the **Look** control highlighted. Each section of the wheel will be highlighted green, and then when you drag the cursor, the camera will act accordingly.

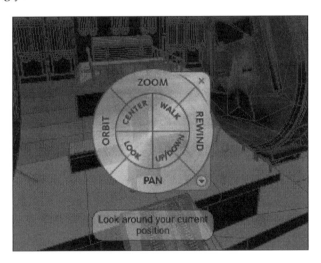

A tool tip appears underneath the **Look Tool** label, and a cursor replaces the wheel when it's being used.

When you are using the Steering Wheel's **Orbit** tool, a green pivot displays, and it is around this that the camera turns. This can be moved by pressing **Orbit** while holding *Ctrl*. Once you have moved the cursor where you want the pivot to be, as shown in the following screenshot, releasing it will allow you to orbit around the new pivot.

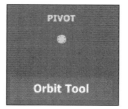

If you have set a **Home** bookmark from the right-click menu of the ViewCube's Home icon 🏠, you can choose the **Go Home** option from the Steering Wheel's menu too, shown in the following screenshot:

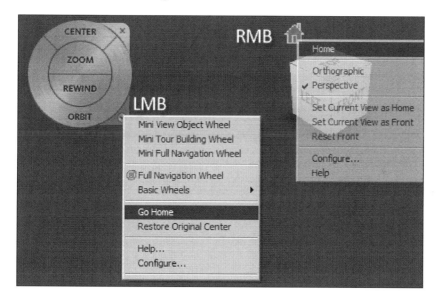

While the **Rewind** tool works very well, if you don't have the Steering Wheel active, you can use *Shift* + *Z* to undo viewport changes.

Displaying your model for modeling

There are several viewport display modes that can be accessed by the label in each viewport, shown in the following screenshot:

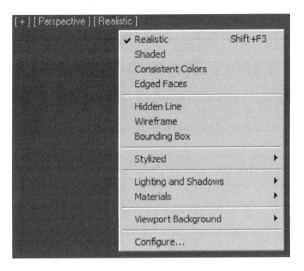

If you open a scene such as Packt3dsmax\Chapter 1\Begin.max, you usually see four views and the orthographic views are shaded differently to the **Perspective** view. This can be changed. Press *F3* in the **Perspective** view. The view changes to **Wireframe**. Press it again; the view changes back to **Shaded** mode. In **Shaded** mode, press *F4* to turn on and off **Edged Faces**. The following screenshot shows clockwise: **Hidden Line**, **Wireframe**, **Shaded**, and **Realistic**.

There are several intermediate ways to shade the view, including **Hidden Line**, which shows only the **Wireframe** directly facing the camera, culling the rest; and **Flat Shaded**, which removes any surface smoothing (so a Sphere's facets would all appear flat or faceted instead of round).

3ds Max 2012 introduced a **Realistic** shading mode that supersedes the **Shaded** shading mode in earlier versions. This is a technology update that allows faster shadow computation; therefore, faster view spinning, better texture resolution, and better lighting.

By default, views are lit using virtual, hidden lights you can't edit. Once you add your own lights (and in this scene there is a Daylight System), you can set the view to render those, which helps you design shadow casting and so on. To adjust this, go to the **View** menu and choose **Viewport Configuration** where the **Visual Style & Appearance** tab should be displayed (or you can swap to it). Look on the right-hand side to the **Lighting and Shadows** section. For the **Illuminate with** option, click on the **Scene Lights** radio button.

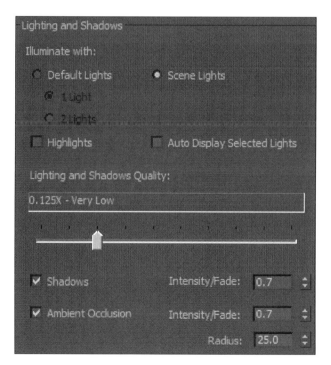

Here you have a few additional options. Turning off **Highlights** will prevent glare from glossy surfaces, so you can always see the edged faces on a surface. Sometimes it is nice to model with a glossy surface to help view the form changes, but often it means you'll not be able to tell what you are doing as the highlight eclipses the mesh wireframe. You can raise or lower the **Lighting and Shadows Quality**, where lower values calculate faster (often without an apparent drop in visual quality). You can also tick on **Shadows** and **Ambient Occlusion** checkboxes, and set their **Intensity/ Fade**, which works well around 0.7 so that shadows are not black.

Model display

Neutral, consistent colors tend to be the easiest to look at when viewing un-textured models. By default, 3ds Max applies random colors to each new model. The shaded surface and wireframe share this color. Sometimes, the viewport lighting causes surface shine to obscure some of the mesh edges, as shown in the following screenshot on the left-hand side:

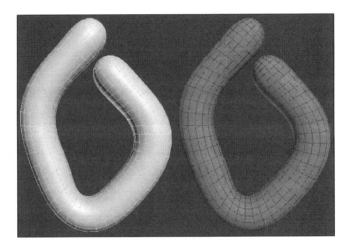

In this section, we'll change this so all models get the same wireframe color and have a neutral gray material, as shown on the right-hand side in the preceding screenshot:

1. Open the **Material Editor** (*M*). In 3ds Max 2012, you should see a version of the Material Editor called Slate. The legacy Compact Material Editor is still available, but for now Slate will do fine. Right-click in the **Slate View1** canvas and choose **Materials | Mental Ray | Autodesk Generic**. This assumes you have iRay set as your renderer, which is also the installation default. If not, you can set a Standard Material instead.

2. The **Autodesk Generic Material** defaults to a dark gray color, which is possibly a bit heavy. To change this, double-click on the **Material** node and notice that on the right the **Default Generic** properties display. In the **Generic** section, under **Color | Use Color**, there is a color picker and you can adjust it to a mid-gray: **Hue**=0, **Sat**=0, and **Value**=0.5. Click on **OK**.

3. Now you can assign the Material Model to objects in the scene when you press *Ctrl + A* in the scene, then right-click on the **Material** node and choose **Assign Material to Selection** or press the icon 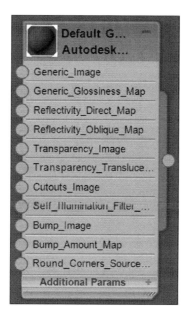 in the editor icon row. Materials that are assigned to a selected object are displayed in the Material Editor with white corners around the sample preview, as shown in the following screenshot:

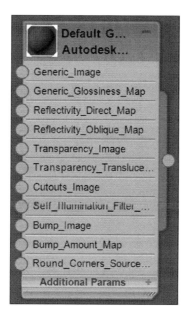

4. In 3ds Max 2013, dotted white edges appear around a node that is showing its parameters in the Parameter Editor panel on the right-hand of the Material Editor.

5. At the top of the Material properties panel, you can name this material Model in the text field. We'll discuss more about the Material Editor later in *Chapter 3, The Base Model – A Solid Foundation in Polygon Modeling.*

6. Although this material is a neutral gray, it doesn't affect the wireframe displayed; it can if you access the **Display** tab of Command Panel and choose **Display Color | Wireframe | Material Color**. A better way to display the model, however, is to have the surface shaded with the **Material color** and the **Wireframe** set to the **Object Color**.

7. Click on the **color picker** to the right-hand of the object name, which is Box001, and the following dialog will pop up:

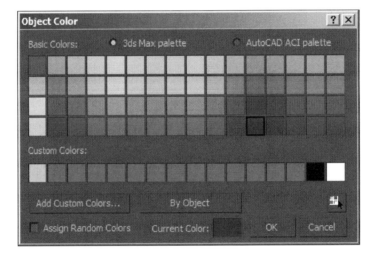

8. Choose a dark color, such as the blue color, as shown in the preceding screenshot, in the **Current Color** slot. A light color may reflect scene light and make it difficult to tell what is going on, especially when you are zoomed in on a model.

9. Uncheck the checkbox for **Assign Random Colors**, so that each newly created object gets the same color.

10. You can still change colors, but do so in a logical way. Set your own classifying criteria, such as all animated objects are dark green and all static objects are blue. This is easiest to set after creation.

Setting scene units

The way physical-based lighting performs when your scene renders is scene-scale dependent. Setting up scene units helps you to achieve real-world scale to your model. Sometimes, you may not want to work in real-world scale, especially if your objects have to match to the objects in another application when they are exported.

The following instructions show how to set custom scene units:

1. Open the .max file Packt3dsmax\Chapter 1\Begin.max. Every scene is saved with its own units of measurement. If your default scene has a unit setting different from the scene you're loading, you'll be prompted to choose the one that you prefer to use.

2. Go to the **Customize** menu and choose **System Unit Setup**, which pops up the following dialog box:

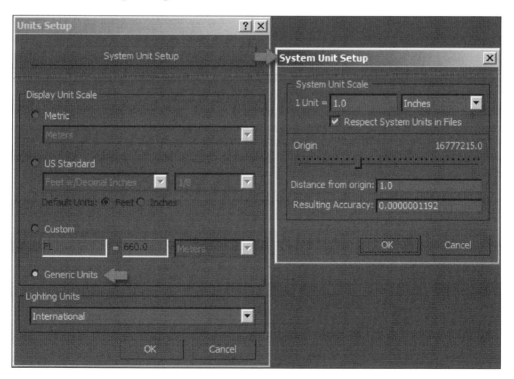

3. The **Generic Units** radio button is active by default, and the measurements for this are set via the **System Unit Setup** button at the top of the window, shown on the left-hand side. Click this to expose the pop up on the right.

Searching for content in the scene

In a scene with hundreds of models or model components, naming objects is probably the best way to keep content easy to access. There are a few ways to rename an object. One way is to type in the **Modify Panel**  the name you want in this field:

You can also rename objects by selecting them in the scene or highlighting them in the Layer Manager, and choosing **Rename Objects** from the **Tools** menu. Another way, if you are using the Outliner script we discussed earlier, is to double-click on the object label.

In the following steps, we will look for a single object amid hundreds using filters:

1. Open the `.max` file `Packt3dsmax\Chapter 1\Begin.max`. This scene is made of hundreds of objects mostly called `Object001` and `Part001` and so on.

2. You could use the **Select by Name** tool, and you could use the Outliner to browse the scene. Another way is to use **Tools | New Scene Explorer**.

3. In the **Scene Explorer** window that pops up, you get a list of objects rather similar to the Outliner script's **Hierarchy mode** list. At the top, there is a menu called **Select**. Open this and choose **Search** from the bottom of the menu, as shown in the following screenshot. You can alternatively click on the icon **Configure Advanced Filter** from the vertical icons.

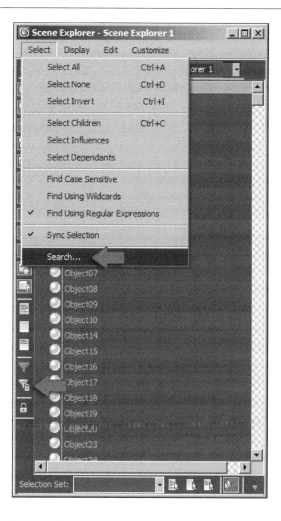

4. Another window will pop up called **Advanced Search** or **Advanced Filter** (depending on how you opened it), and this lets you filter the scene by numerous **Property/Condition/Reference** value combinations. For instance, expand the **Property** list and choose **Hidden**, and set the **Condition** to **Is** so that only hidden objects will be searched. Notice that the object **Skydome** is the only hidden object. It is highlighted in yellow. You can unhide it using Outliner or if you right-click in the scene and choose **Unhide All** from the **Quad** menu, then similarly freeze it.

5. In the **Advanced Filter** window, click on **Remove**. This clears the current filter.

Creating your own selection sets with Named Selections

In most scenes, you will have certain objects you select often. Quick access to these is very important. Also, some objects can be hard to directly select if they are surrounded by or covered by others.

By default, the *H* key is reserved for the **Select by Name** option, but if you take up the free script Outliner, you may have to change that. You can also use **Named Selections**, which lets you create a hot list of entries of your own. This rolls down from the main toolbar, as shown in the following screenshot, where it says **Sky**:

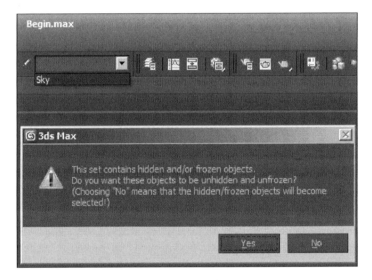

1. Open `Begin.max`, and go to the expand icon ▼ for the **Named Selection Set** list and notice there is an entry **Lines** and an entry **Sky**. Click on **Sky**. This is a huge sky dome that provides a background for the scene. When you launch, it is hidden and frozen, but when you choose it, you'll see a prompt checking whether or not you want to reveal it. This prompt appears because its hidden state is set for its layer.

2. You can either choose **Yes**, and the object will be revealed, or **No**, and the object will be selected but remain hidden. Its entire layer will be affected.

3. Add to the list of **Named Selections** by choosing some objects in the scene and then typing an entry in the **Create Selection Set** text field where **Sky** is included. After typing, be sure to press *Enter* to commit the entry.

4. Now you'll want to edit entries in the **Named Selections** list. Click on the icon ▧ next to the text field, or go to the **Edit** menu and choose **Manage Selections Sets**, which pops up the same window.

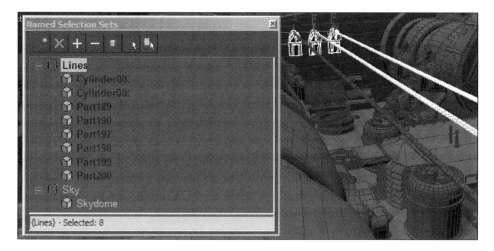

5. Let's add an object in the scene to the existing set of **Lines**. Select **Cylinder01** by using either **Select by Name** ▧ in the **Named Selection Sets** window's icon row, then press the **Add** icon ⊞.

The icons for managing objects include **Remove** ▧ (which removes a list or objects from a list; it doesn't remove them from the scene), **Select Objects in Set** ▧ (which works if you don't have them selected to start with), and **Highlight Selected Objects** ▧ (which shows in the list the items currently selected in the scene if they belong to a given **Named Selection Set**). They are highlighted in blue.

[Using a **Named Selection** is a good way to add a selection shortcut to each joint in a biped when you do character animation.]

Common changes to 3ds Max default preferences

Changes to preferences are quite subjective. There are many preferences in 3ds Max, but only a few that really make a big difference when starting to model. These include auto-save settings, the option to increment files when saving, levels of undo, whether to use large or small icons, whether to display certain warnings each time you take certain steps, and removing some small elements of clutter from the UI.

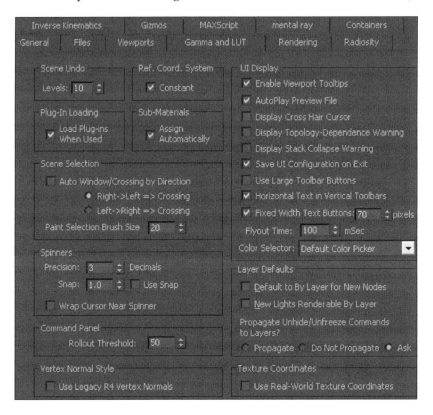

In the **General** tab, you can set the number of **Scene Undo** levels higher if you have a lot of RAM and think you might need more undo steps. Alternatively, you can reduce the number so your session has less overhead.

When you move objects you can set the transform gizmo to align with either the view grid, the local space of the object, or even another object. This is called the Reference Coordinate System. By default, when you swap from Move mode to Rotate mode to Scale mode, each has its own Reference Coordinate System. This can be annoying, since you have to track which system is active for which transform mode. The preference **Ref. Coord. System | Constant** checkbox keeps the system you set as current across all the transform types when you switch from one transform to another.

It is probably a good idea to turn off the **Use Large Toolbar Buttons** checkbox; it allows a little more screen space for the viewports, and also you can fit more icons in the toolbars.

The next few options are for reducing pop-up warnings that, if you know what you are doing, are somewhat distracting.

The first is the **Display Topology-Dependence Warning** checkbox. If it is checked, it will tell you whether a Modifier you're collapsing would depend on a **SubObject** selection (points, edges, and so on) from below in the Modifier stack, or when you change the **SubObject** selection while other Modifiers are using that selection.

The next is the **Display Stack Collapse Warning** checkbox, which occurs when you use the option to collapse modifiers, essentially merging their result.

Also, you have three choices for how to deal with unhiding content on layers that are hidden. The setting is called **Propagate Unhide/Freeze Commands to Layers?**. By default, you're asked if you want to unhide the layers and the object (**Ask**). You can set it so that the layers are always unhidden too (**Propagate**), or the layers are never unhidden too (**Do not Propagate**).

In the **Files** tab, if you are doing modeling work, it is handy to set **Increment on Save** checked, so that every time you press *Ctrl + S* to save, you won't write over the same file but add a new one like this: `file001.max`, `file002.max`. It requires some housekeeping occasionally but is a safe option, since if you save over your work or something else goes wrong (computers!), then you won't lose anything; alternatively, you may want to develop a habit to increment the number of file saves using *Ctrl + A* instead of *Ctrl + S*.

When you save a maxfile, it includes properties, the schematic view, and a thumbnail image for the browser. You may feel that this is unnecessary information, and those can be turned off individually.

If you are opening a very old maxfile from earlier versions, sometimes an obsolete file, a message will appear warning you to re-save. This can be turned off here by ticking off **Display Obsolete File Message**.

In the **Viewports** tab, there is nothing much to change. **Set Display World Axis** should be unchecked. This gets rid of the tiny, slightly obtrusive axis in the corner of each viewport. Of course, if you like it there, you can leave it on, but if you want to check which way the world X axis is, for instance, create a Box and enter Move mode with the **View** or **World reference coordinate system** active.

Finally, the number of auto-backup files and the duration that they are saved is set at the bottom of the **Files** tab, in the **Auto Backup** section. Backup files are kept in c:\users\~\documents\3ds max\autoback. Once you've written the amount of files that you've set as the number to save, they'll start saving over each other, starting with the oldest. Broadly speaking, if you set 10 backups at 10-minute intervals, that is enough to provide you with 100 minutes of continual work that you can look back on if you decide you need to go back in time.

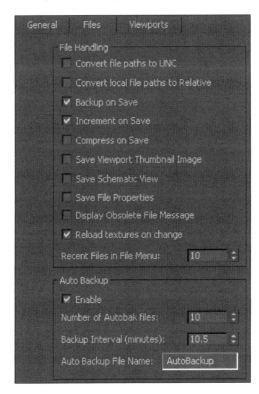

Determining the hardware shading settings to use

The default views in 3ds Max 2012 and 2013 are driven by a newly introduced technology called **Nitrous Accelerated Graphics Core**, which is designed to allow larger sets of assets to be handled in real time with a better quality visual appearance.

You can revert your display settings to **Direct3D** alone, or to **OpenGL**, or even **Software**, but it depends on what hardware you are using, particularly your graphics card. If you are using a laptop with an integrated graphics card, you may be best off with Software or OpenGL rendering, but this will likely not be very fast or look as good. Nitrous views depend on access to the GPU (graphics card cores) to provide a responsive, high-quality viewport shading, and this is what gives you real-time ambient occlusion (soft shadows) and accurate shadow casting and reflective, transparent surfaces in the viewport even with unlimited lights.

You can read more about hardware concerns for 3ds Max in The Area — Discussions community — which you can access from the 3ds Max **Help menu | 3ds Max on the web | The AREA**. Also, you can obtain a report on 3ds Max's view of your GPU: **Help | Diagnose Video Hardware**.

Summary

By now you should be progressing with view navigation and have gained a feeling for just how much functionality is packed into the menus and dialogs of 3ds Max. You'll quickly find that what you're unfamiliar with at first, in the topics we've covered in this chapter, becomes intuitive with practice. By the end of the next chapter, no doubt you'll be flying around views, panels, tabs, and menus without thinking, ready for the next challenge.

We've covered a few niche methods of navigation as well as the main methods, and you'll be able to decide for yourself whether you want to use the middle mouse navigation method and hotkeys, or ViewCube and Steering Wheel. You may also want to experiment with new device-driven navigation, such as the Wi-Fi and touch-based **CAD Control** iPad app for 3ds Max by Maide Inc (and other Autodesk products), available on iTunes.

Besides navigation, we also considered ways to begin to customize the look of 3ds Max and make tools accessible based on your own preferences. It takes time to decide which tools are best to use and where to place them. Do you use the Quad menu, keyboard shortcuts, a toolbar, or mouse click to the default locations? Each user will develop a different preference. I've provided a complete UI preset that I like, which has most of the day-to-day modeling tools set in the Quad menu. At first it took a while for me to get used to this streamlined layout, since I was more used to the regular tool layout, but it didn't take long before I was enjoying a faster working speed. The UI preset can be found in `Packt3dsMax\UI Settings\PacktUI.ui` and can be loaded via the **Customize menu | Load Custom UI**. There is a version for 2012 and 2013. In later chapters, this UI will be referenced often, but the commands are also described in terms of their default layout in case you prefer to work with a "fresh install" style UI. One benefit of only using 3ds Max in its default state is that whenever you set it up, you're always going to be in a familiar place. However, the `Packt3dsMax\UI Settings\PacktUI.ui` can be set up with one command, and you can always revert back to the defaults the same way.

In the next chapter, we will look at general considerations for model handling, supposing you may want to work with an already built model. The main thrust will be toward ensuring you use 3ds Max's scene organization, visibility, and collaboration tools well. The next chapter's topics include importing of content, rendering basics, scene transforms, and setting object properties.

2
Model Shakedown: Make 3ds Max Work for you

This chapter examines model handling using readymade assets. The main asset is a rapidly constructed vehicle used for testing a prototype game. Our purpose is to cover the necessary model handling skills before we undertake actual modeling in the next chapter.

The following are the topics that will be covered in this chapter:

- Setting filters in the Display panel
- Object Properties – Show Frozen in gray
- Object Properties – Animation trajectories
- Object Properties – Render properties
- Moving and rotating objects using pivot controls
- Local, Screen, and Pick spaces
- Cloning objects: Instances, References, and Snapshots
- Adjusting modifiers in the viewport
- Organizing a scene using Groups
- Importing models
- Using a template scene including lighting, camera, and render settings
- NVIDIA iray ActiveShade rendering

Setting filters in the Display panel

This topic introduces the **Display** panel, which lets us filter certain categories of objects to prevent clutter in the view. As an example, we will show an air bike for a single rider, and toggle the display of elements in the scene to provide a clearer view.

Display panel filters

The **Display** panel lets you control objects by hiding and freezing them. This section shows you how to control display of objects based on their type:

1. Open the scene `Packt3dsMax\Chapter 2\BikeStart.max`.

2. Orbit (*Alt + MMB*) the scene to familiarize yourself with its contents, then press *Alt + W* to restore four views.

3. The Command Panel icons are as follows; click on **Display** ⬜:

4. After clicking on **Display**, look at the **Hide by Category** section. Click on **None**, and notice that a few already hidden categories (**Shapes** and **Helpers**) that were ticked are now not ticked. The **All**, **None**, and **Invert** buttons override any of the ticked categories.

5. Further down, there is a customizable category panel showing the **Bone**, **IK Chain Object**, and **Point** entries. **Bone** at the moment is `blue`, which means it is hidden.

6. Click on **Point** to deactivate **Bone**. You will notice that every object in the scene that is in the **Bone** category will be displayed, revealing a biped driver.

7. Within **Bone**, click on **Add** to add extra entries to the list, including specific primitive types.

8. From the **Add Display Filter** pop-up list, scroll down to the bottom and add **mr Sky Portal**. This will hide two local lights in the scene linked to the HUD elements of the bike. If you press *Ctrl + LMB* (left mouse button) on the entries here, you will append them to the active hidden list.

9. You could also click on the preset **Lights** category to hide those two objects, but that will also hide the **Daylight** system, which we'll import later on.

   Importing objects when their category is hidden can be distracting since they will be in the scene but not viewable until you enable the category.

10. Ensure the biped rig `Bip01` is unhidden.

11. On the top of the biped's head there is a little green **Helper** object called `HeadNub`, also called a **Dummy**. In the **Command Panel | Display | Hide by Category**, toggle the **Helpers** checkbox to hide it. There are also two small helpers on the biped's fingertips.

 Helpers are non-rendering objects that can serve many purposes. In this case, they are the end of the bone chains and are used under the hood by the biped system.

Hiding and freezing objects

This section shows you how you can freeze sets of objects in more than one way.

1. Under the **Hide by Category** section there is a **Hide** section, which you can expand to reveal commands such as **Hide By Name**, **Hide by Hit**, **Hide Unselected**, **Hide Frozen Objects**, **Unhide All**, and more. These are also found if you right-click in the scene via the **Quad** menu in the **display** quad.

Similar commands are there for the **Freeze** section. When I first learned 3ds Max, I used this method a lot. Later, I more often used the **Quad** menu, and eventually I got in the habit of using the **Manage Layers** menu's **Hide** 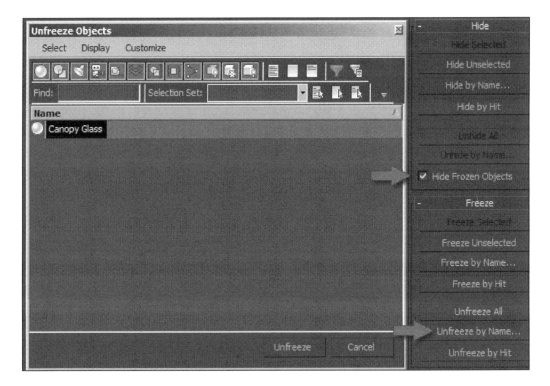 and **Freeze** commands. It is good to learn all the available routes to these commands, and just use the closest, or the most suitable, as the occasion dictates.

2. In the scene there is a frozen object, which you can't move or see right now. It is the glass part of the canopy over the bike rider, and it is linked to the Canopy frame. By default, **Hide Frozen Objects** is disabled, but in this scene it is enabled. So expand the **Freeze** section and click on **Unfreeze All** (or **Unfreeze by Name...**) to expose Canopy Glass. You could also simply toggle off **Hide Frozen Objects**. The state of this toggle is saved with the scene.

Display Properties

The **Quad menu** lets you access **Object Properties**. The **Display** panel also lets you access this menu, as given in the following steps:

1. Under the **Hide** and **Freeze** sections is a section called **Display Properties**. This is only active when you select scene objects; so open **Layer Manager** ⬛ from the main toolbar, and highlight the `Biped` layer in the list. This layer includes all the Biped components.

2. Click on the ⬛ icon to select all the layer contents at once.

3. Go back to **Command Panel | Display | Display Properties** and check the **Display as Box** option. This substitutes the biped geometry (which itself is simplified) for an even more simplified object.

4. Observe the difference, then uncheck **Display as Box**, and instead check the **See-Through** option. This adds viewport only transparency filtering to the object. It won't affect rendering. **See-Through** display is great when you are editing objects that are inside other objects. The hotkey is *Alt + X*. Below this, the **Never Degrade** option is for when you orbit the scene and want to keep maximum display fidelity. The hotkey to toggle that is *O*.

By default, 3ds Max drops out detail on models from highest to lowest display quality, in order to keep the display running smoothly. You might want to force key objects to display at the best resolution, in which case you'd enable **Never Degrade**. The global icon for toggling **Progressive Display** ⬛, also known as the **Adaptive Degradation Toggle**, is in the status bar at the bottom of the UI, next to **Add Time Tag**.

It should be noted that the **Display Properties** section is mirrored in the **Object Properties** section of every object, which can be accessed in the **Quad menu**

Object Properties – Show Frozen in Gray

Object Properties were mentioned in the previous section, in relation to **Display Properties**. In the next few sections, commonly used toggles for **Object Properties** will be discussed.

Freezing objects via Object Properties

This section describes how to access **Object Properties** to find display controls set for each object individually:

1. Under **Command Panel | Display | Hide By Category**, ensure **Shapes** is not turned off, and make sure the toggle previously discussed, **Hide Frozen Objects**, is toggled off.

2. Press *H* to search for the shape called `Canopy Guide`. This object helps to indicate the limits of the canopy's rotation; it is bright pink in color.

3. With `Canopy Guide` selected, right-click and go to **Quad** menu | **Transform | Object Properties**. In a custom quad entry this will show only as **Properties...** which is how it will appear in `PacktUI.ui`. You can also access it via the **Edit | Object Properties** menu.

Note that in the **Interactivity** section, there are **Hide** and **Freeze** toggles. These are a little redundant unless you already have this window open. What is more important is the checkbox **Show Frozen in Gray**. For the shape, as it is pink, it will turn gray when frozen. Usually this is good, as it provides a visual cue to what you can't select. What often happens though is you want to freeze objects that are either color coded deliberately, like this one, or are displaying a reference texture in the view. In order to maintain the pink color, turn off **Show Frozen in Gray**, click on **Freeze** (or freeze it later), and then click on **OK**.

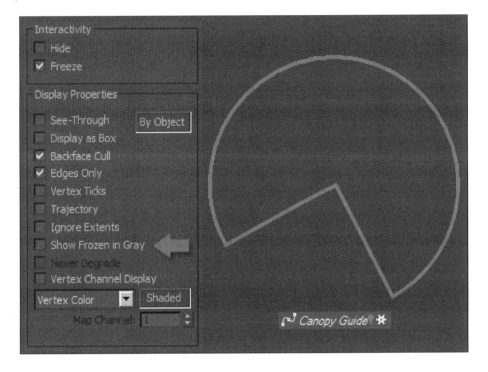

The result should be as shown in the previous screenshot, where the shape `Canopy Guide` shows **Frozen** ✳, but is still pink.

Object Properties – Animation trajectories

A further display property that we can achieve per object is the trajectory or motion an object has over time. A trajectory is a 3D curve that visualizes the motion of the object in parallel with the keyframes in the timeline.

Toggle trajectory

When an object moves, its path can be traced as a line called a **trajectory**. The following steps show how to expose this in the viewports:

1. In the scene, there is a HUD panel in the bike's canopy that follows the animation of the canopy itself — they are linked. The canopy simply rotates, so it has no trajectory, but the panel, while not animated directly, gets its motion from its parent, like chewing gum stuck on the spinning wheel of a bike. The trajectory display is already on in the scene.

2. Press *F3* to view this more clearly in the wireframe:

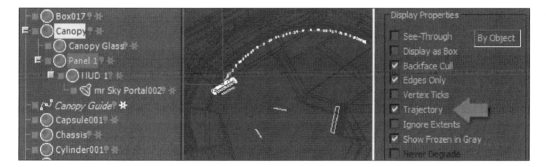

3. The trajectory displays even when the object is not selected. To turn it off, use the **Named Selections** list to select `Panel 1`. Right-click on it and select **Object Properties**. In the **Display Properties** section, turn off **Trajectory**. You can also access the **Trajectory** checkbox in the **Display** section ▣ of the Command Panel.

4. In this case, it doesn't matter if we see the trajectory or not. However, when you are animating, it is extremely useful to see it. This works for all moving objects, except biped rigs. For biped rigs, joints have their own **Trajectories** toggle ▲, found in the biped **Key Info** settings in the **Motion** panel ◉.

The trajectory in the viewport is a 3D curve, the combined result of the X, Y, Z curves. Animators can edit curves in **Curve Editor** (accessed in **Quad menu** or from the menu bar **Graph Editors | Track View – Curve Editor**). It's out of the scope of a modeling book to discuss the **Curve Editor** in depth, but it doesn't take very long to figure out how it works. A good guide by 3DBuzz is shown at `http://youtu.be/XZMLm0P-KLM`.

Object Properties – Render properties

Besides viewport display properties, you can set render properties in the **Object Properties** dialog. We'll look at the following examples: turning off **Cast Shadows/Receive Shadows**, and making an object visible or renderable, or invisible to the camera.

Disabling shadow casting

This section shows how to turn off the cast shadow displayed at render time for a given object selection:

1. In the scene, search for and select the `Chassis` object. This is the largest part of the vehicle.

2. Right-click and go to **Quad** menu | **Object Properties**.

3. In the **Rendering Control** section, set the first channel, **Visibility**, from 1 to 0.5. This equates to the **See-Through** viewport display setting (*Alt + X*), but applies at render time as well as in the viewport. It is not the same as setting the object to use a transparent material, which is discussed later. It simply fades out the object (in the viewport and at render time).

4. Click on **OK** to view the difference and then set the visibility of the `Chassis` object back to 1. Changes here are not tracked by **Undo** (*Ctrl + Z*).

If one object is linked to another, it inherits the visibility (**Inherit Visibility**) of its parent, by default. This can be toggled if needed. A quick way to set **Visibility** to 0 is to instead use the **Renderable** or **Visible to Camera** toggles; but those can't be animated whereas **Visibility** can be. **Renderable** works in all cases, and just turns off the object. **Visible to Camera** and **Visible to Reflection/Visible to Refraction** work with **MentalRay** (which is active in the current scene) and **Default Scanline Renderer**, but do not work properly in iray. Its main feature is that while the object won't render, its shadow and reflection will.

As an example, a large Sphere primitive was added to the scene up in the air, and its **Visible to Camera** setting was disabled. Then the vehicle had its **Cast Shadows** and **Receive Shadows** setting disabled. So only the Sphere primitive's shadow hits the ground. This makes the plane appear to have a simple blob shadow (a blob shadow is often seen in games, where calculating character or vehicle shadows onto the environment in real time per polygon would be slow. You can even use a texture shadow on a single plane instead of a cast shadow). Of course, the shadow is by no stretch adequate for the shape of the plane, but it just illustrates the use of the **Rendering Control** settings in **Object Properties**. The softness in the shadow casting comes from the use of a **mr Sun**, with **Shadow Softness** ramped up, and a **mr Sky** with the **Haze Driven** property set. These are found in the modifier panel with the Daylight001 object selected.

 Don't be tempted to render yet; that comes a bit later. At present the BikeStart.max scene has no lighting, except the two small HUD displays; so the scene will render very dark. Later in the chapter, we'll import and adjust a background template to achieve a nice look. A **Daylight** system is included with that.

Refer to the following note to know more about lighting:

 Lighting isn't extensively covered in this book as our goal is to handle modeling; instead we provide a solid, globally lit scene in which any model will situate well with minimal adjustment. If you want to light and present models, it is worthwhile to check out *Marmoset Toolbag*, an application for focusing on real-time game model presentation (www.8monkeylabs.com/toolbag).

Moving and rotating objects using pivot controls

This topic covers a very simple operation that you'll use every day. Selecting several objects and moving them around at once presents a few variables, such as the location of the selection's pivot, or whether the transform is local to each object, or based on the entire selection set. There's no setting that works in every single case. You have to flexibly jump back and forth depending on what you are trying to do.

Pivots

A pivot is the point around which, or from which, an object transforms. There are three ways to reposition an object's pivot in 3ds Max. You can do so by moving it manually in XYZ, or by using the align tools, or by sticking the pivot on an object's surface. There's more than one way to align a pivot too, as the steps following the next paragraph will show.

3ds Max offers a tool called a **Working Pivot**. It lets you set, per transform, a temporary pivot of an object that you can reset later. It works in 3D space. The 3ds Max Working Pivot lets you temporarily stick the pivot on a surface, and has a **Reset** button to send the pivot back home, so let's take a look at how it works:

1. Open `BikeStart.max` and select the editable poly's object `Tail_R`, which is the rearmost part of the vehicle. The nature of the object requires that it rotate around a hinge, but right now it has its pivot at its center. You could handle this by linking it to a hinge object at the correct location, or you could just move the pivot (either permanently or temporarily).

2. Right-click and go to **Quad** menu | **Isolate Selection** to hide away other objects apart from the selected one, `Tail_R`. The object will be framed in the view. A pop up will show **Exit Isolation Mode**, which releases this mode.

3. In the Command Panel, click on the **Hierarchy icon** and expand the **Working Pivot** section. Click on **Edit Working Pivot** and you should see the pivot of the object highlighted with a special helper, shown in the next screenshot.

Note that since this is a helper, if you had the **Display | Hide By Category | Helpers** option checked, it will automatically reveal all the scene's helper objects too. If you don't want to see the additional helpers, you could select **Exit Isolation Mode**, reselect `Tail_R`, then right-click and go to **Quad menu | Isolate Selection** again.

4. When you click on **Edit Working Pivot**, you can only move the Working Pivot.

5. In the **Place Pivot To:** section click on **Surface**, as shown in the following screenshot. Move the cursor over the backend of the object, as shown in the following screenshot, and click. Note that the pivot aligns to the view. This is because **Align to View** is ticked. Turn this off, and move the guide gizmo over the polygons. Notice that it follows their surface normal (the direction they face). Click on the polygon again, and note the pivot aligns to the surface, not the view.

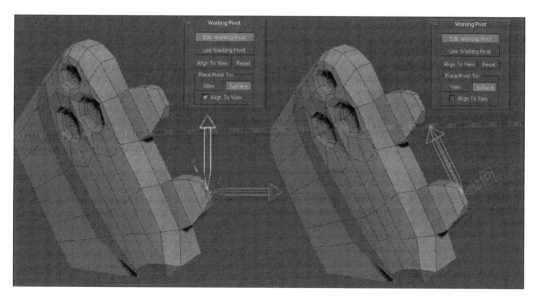

6. If you turn off **Edit Working Pivot**, the pivot of the object will jump back to its original position. Click on **Use Working Pivot**, and then it will jump back to where you placed it. So, in a sense, you've now got two pivots assigned to the object.

7. In 3ds Max 2012, you would click on **Exit Isolation Mode** in the **Warning: Isolated Selection** pop up to revert to normal working mode. In 3ds Max 2013, you just right-click and toggle off **Isolate Selection** where you enabled it. An optional, legacy-style script is available for those who want it at `http://www.scriptspot.com/3ds-max/scripts/isolate-selection-legacy-mode-for-2013`. There is also an icon toggle at the bottom of the 3ds Max UI, as shown in the following screenshot:

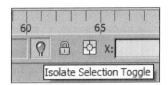

8. Ensure `Tail_R` is selected, then click on **Rotate** in the main toolbar. Notice that the **Ref. Coord. System** option at the side is set to **Working**, not **View**, or **Local**. Rotate in **Y** to check the motion of the tail flap.

9. The downside of using the **Working Pivot** is that we can't convert this over to be the absolute pivot of the object. If you click on *N* to enter the **Autokey** mode for animating the tail flap rotation, you'll notice the **Working Pivot** keeps its orientation, but the pivot position jumps back to the center of the object until you press *N* again.

10. Undo the rotation of the object and then turn off **Use Working Pivot**.

11. To manually move the absolute object pivot, click on the **Hierarchy** icon in the Command Panel, and go to **Adjust Pivot | Affect Pivot Only**.

12. You can then slide the pivot using the **Move** gizmo to the location where we placed it on the polygon in the previous steps. Remember, we're moving the actual pivot of the object, not the temporary Working Pivot.

13. Having repositioned the pivot, turn off **Affect Pivot Only**, then switch to **Ref. Coord. System | Local**, and click on **Use Pivot Point Center** . This should mean the pivot is now in the same position and orientation as the Working Pivot, though the facing direction of their X axis may differ. Rotate either pivot 90 degrees, until their facing axis is the same.

14. Now you've set the local pivot of `Tail_R`, delete the existing `Tail_L`.

15. With the **Ref. Coord. System | View** option active, select `Tail_R`, then use the **Mirror** tool in the main toolbar with its **Clone Selection** radio button set to the **Copy** option, to create a flipped copy. Name it `Tail_L`. If `Tail_R` is positioned on the X axis at `-10.0`, then `Tail_L` should be positioned on the X axis at `10.0`.

In the following screenshot, the result shows that you can now rotate either side with its **Ref. Coord. System | Local** option set to active, and suitably reversed.

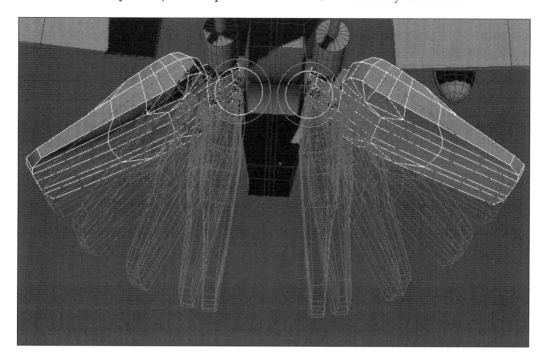

The previous screenshot shows a rotation over five frames of a rotation around 70 degree in Y axis. Ghosting has been turned on by going to the **Views** menu and checking **Ghosting**. This viewing option assists animators by showing a representation of onion-skinning. It can be set in the **Customize | Preferences | Viewports | Ghosting** section. You can ghost ahead, backward, or either side of the current frame in increments of your own choice.

When you are moving a pivot around by hand, you may want to enable **Snap to Vertex** (which snaps the pivot to a nearby vertex) or **Snap Tangent** (which helps line up the pivot with the side of the object). Also, you can go to **Edit | Transform Toolbox**, and work with the commands in the **Align Pivot** section. Let's consider the following example:

1. In the scene, select Stand_Front, one of three objects that make up a proxy for the vehicle's landing gear. Open the **Transform Toolbox** option from the **Edit** menu.

2. Click on the **Align Pivot | Center** button (not the radio button **Center**). The radio button **Min** means one side of the selection, **Center** means the middle of the selection, **Max** means the other side of selection, and **Origin** means 0,0,0 in the 3ds Max scene. The **Center** radio button is used when you just want to center one axis at a time.

3. Click on the **Min** radio button, then click on the **Z** button. Note that the pivot jumps to the bottom of the stand. This would be good if you wanted to line the stand up with the ground:

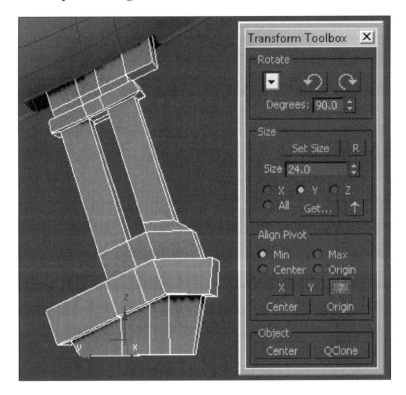

4. Click on the **Max** radio button, then click on the **Z** button. The pivot jumps to the top of the stand, which would be good if you were going to retract the landing gear into the fuselage.

5. If you click on **Origin**, the pivot will move to the world center 0,0,0. You can also move the object itself to 0,0,0 by clicking on **Object | Center**.

6. If you want to commit the change of pivot, click on the **Size | R (Reset XForm)** button. After you click on the **Reset XForm** button, you will also be able to set the size of the object numerically using X, Y, Z, or All filters for the axis you are setting the size for. The **Get** button returns the current XYZ dimensions for the selected object.

Local, Screen, and Pick spaces

Let's consider the ways in which you can situate and face the axis of the transform gizmo. Think of a tree growing on a flat ground, among a row of trees. One tree is out of line from the rest, growing at a 45 degree angle. For all the trees, if you scale them up in the **View** space (aligned with the ground), they will grow straight up. If you scale them up in **Local** space (aligned with their own axis), the 45 degree tree will shoot upwards at a different angle to the rest.

Changing the axis direction of the gizmo

Sometimes the facing direction of a mesh and its pivot don't agree. Here's how to adjust the pivot to face a given direction based on its local space, or view space, or to use the facing direction of another object in the scene.

1. Changing **View**, **Local**, and **Working Pivot** space only changes the orientation of the transform gizmo accordingly.

2. In order to change the option that is active, go to the main toolbar, where there's a rollout with the **Reference Coordinate System** tool tip.

3. Select Clamp_01 in the scene, a small feature we're going to distribute copies of around the cockpit wheel. With **View** chosen, the transform gizmo aligns to the grid (G), and with **Local** chosen the transform gizmo aligns to the object's original length, width, and height space.

4. When you create objects, such as Cylinder primitives for instance, their local axis often begins aligned to the grid. It is only when you rotate them that a difference becomes apparent.

5. The following screenshot shows the difference between the **View** and **Local** space for the object Clamp_01:

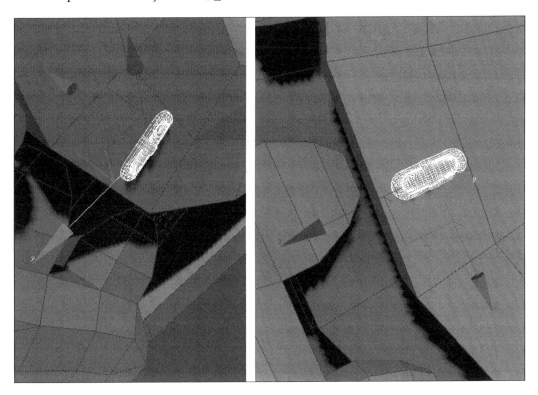

Note that in local space the **Z** axis orients to the object's length.

6. Suppose we wanted to place clones of Clamp_01 around the circle, followed by the vehicle's canopy when it rotates. We could do so using **Move** and **Rotate**, if we were patient and didn't mind small discrepancies of angle and position.

7. We could measure the distance across the circle wherein the canopy rolls around, and move the pivot (as discussed in the previous topic) until it was halfway across that distance. Otherwise, we could use the **Ref. Coord. System | Pick** option to select the Canopy object, and temporarily borrow its pivot while producing copies.

8. With Clamp_01 selected, click on **Rotate** (*E*).

9. In the **Ref. Coord. System** rollout, select **Pick**. In the view, a dotted pick line will appear, which connects from `Clamp_01` to any object you click on. We could use this method, but it would be more reliable to click on **Select by Name** , with **Pick** as active and highlight `Canopy`. After highlighting `Canopy`, click on **Pick** to close the dialog:

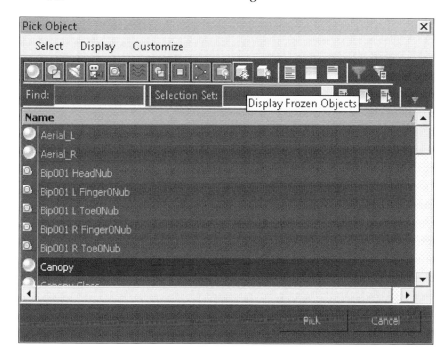

10. This next part can be really confusing when you first encounter it. You've just set `Clamp_01` to rotate around the `Canopy` object, but the pivot hasn't changed. Why? We also need to access the **Use Pivot Point Center** flyout (which is still set on the object) and instead change it to the third option, **Use Transform Co-ordinate Center** :

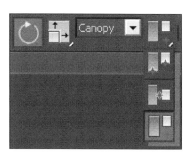

Having changed this, you'll see the pivot jump from `Clamp_01` to the middle of the **Canopy**.

11. Press *A* to enable **Angle Snap**, which defaults to a 5 degree rotation step.

12. Hold down the *Shift* key and rotate `Clamp_01` so it generates a copy of 5 degrees around the X axis, using the picked pivot of the `Canopy`.

13. When you let go, a pop up will ask you for cloning options. In the **Object** section, click on the **Copy** radio button. This means that the cloned object won't share any changes to the original. Click on **OK**.

14. The new object is selected after creation. Select `Clamp_01` again, and in the **Graphite Modeling Tools** in the Ribbon under **Geometry (All)** or in the **Command Panel** under **Edit Geometry**, select **Attach** and click on `Clamp_02`.

    This combines the cloned object into the first object as an element of it.

15. Turn off the **Attach** mode, then hold down the *Shift* key, and rotate `Clamp_01` exactly 30 degrees in the X axis, using `Canopy` as the **Ref. Coord. System** (and with **Use Transform Co-ordinate Center** ▦ active).

16. When you release the *Shift* key, you'll be prompted for cloning options, and this time select the **Instance** radio button in the **Object** section. This means that the cloned object will share changes made to it with the original, and vice versa.

17. Also set the number of copies to 11. Why 11? Since we're making a full rotation around the canopy at 30 degree spacing, that divides to 12, but one instance, the original, is already there. So if we set it to 12, the final clone would overlap the original object.

> If you are not good at dividing 360 degrees, in the pink **Listener** field at the bottom left-hand corner of 3ds Max, type 360 divided by the angle you want to rotate, and you will get the amount of copies you'll need. For example, 360 / 30 returns 12.

18. Some of the clones slightly overlap the cover of the `Canopy`. To fix this, we can scale the objects all together. There are two ways to scale them—one is by their own pivot center and the other is by the selection center.

19. Click on **Select by Name** ▦, or press *H*, and type `Clamp` in the **Find:** field. All the cloned `Clamp` objects will be selected in the scene.

20. Return the **Use Transform Co-ordinate Center** ▦ flyout to the first option, **Use Pivot Point Center** ▦. Set the **Ref. Coord System** option to **Local**. The pivot will appear over whichever member you roll the cursor over. Now scale the objects in Z axis so they are a bit smaller. Make sure you keep the objects selected.

21. Set the **Use Pivot Point Center** ![icon] flyout to the second option, **Use Selection Center** ![icon]. Change the **Ref. Coord System** option to **View**.
The pivot will jump to the middle of the selection.

22. Scale the objects so they cross the outer lip of the canopy circle, as shown in the following screenshot:

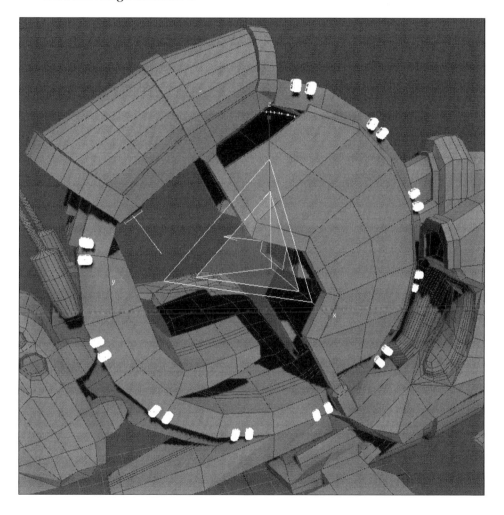

The previous example shows how simply switching the active **Ref. Coord. System** option and the center for the transform lets you create diversity when scaling and rotating objects based on a flexible pivot. Incidentally, another way to achieve this would be to create a Circle shape, use it as the path element in a **Path Constraint**, and then duplicate the Clamp objects at 12 percent steps around the path.

Cloning objects: Instances, References, and Snapshots

This section is an extension of the previous section where we made multiple copies of a part on the vehicle. You chose between the clone types **Copy** and **Instance**. In this section we'll explore the ramifications of that kind of choice.

A **Copy** is independent of its source, but gets all the modifiers and properties the original one has. They don't share any changes down the line. An **Instance** maintains a connection between the original and the duplicate, and changes down the line to either will be shared. A **Reference** shares changes, but modifier level changes added on top of it aren't shared. A **Snapshot** is an extracted copy of a mesh, which rebuilds it as an editable mesh in its current state. It is used to get the state of a mesh resulting from the effects modifiers have on it. A good case for using a Snapshot would be to extract the expression or pose the result derived from combined Morph targets and Skinning.

Adjusting Instances

Instances are clones that change with the original (and also affect the original if changed). The following example shows how to deal with this:

1. Under the vehicle, attached to its wing, is a Capsule primitive `Tank1`. Select it and center its pivot (**Edit | Transform Toolbox | Align Pivot | Center**), then press *Ctrl + V*, which is equivalent to "paste a copy here". In many applications, *Ctrl + C* is often a hotkey for copy, but in 3ds Max that will generate a Camera in the scene that matches the current view. Just click on *Ctrl + V* with something selected in the viewport. Of course, to copy numerical values and strings of text in fields, copy and paste shortcut keys work as usual.

2. You'll be prompted to select **Copy**, **Instance**, or **Reference**. Select **Instance**.

3. Move the new object across to the next mounting, `TankGrip2`.

4. In the Command Panel, click on **Modify**. Then in the **Modifier List** select **Taper**. Notice that the modifier is added to both Tank objects.

5. In the **Taper** modifier, set the **Taper | Amount** value to -0.2, and the **Taper Axis: Primary** to X.

6. Delete `Tank2`. We're going to explore other possibilities; this time, select `Tank1`, hold the *Shift* key, and move it over to `TankGrip2`.

7. Select **Reference** when prompted for the cloning options.

8. For `Tank1`, add a modifier called **Relax** and push its **Iterations** value to `5`. This will propagate to the reference copy.

9. For `Tank2`, add another modifier called **Push**. Set its value to `0.55`. This modifier will not propagate back to the original. Notice how the modifier stack looks for the Reference.

10. To revert **Instances** to unique objects, click on **Modify | Make Unique** . Instanced texture maps use the same concept, and there's an equivalent command in the Material Editor .

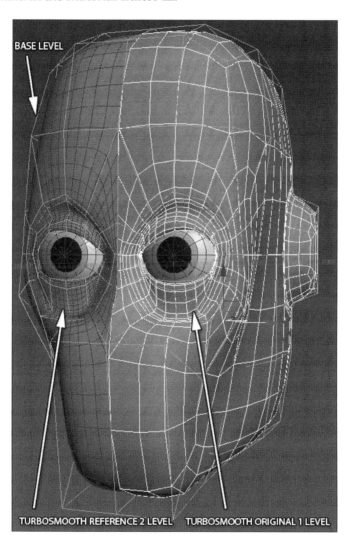

A Reference copy with a Symmetry and **TurboSmooth** modifier is well suited for use alongside a low-poly base mesh as you edit it as a half. This allows you to work on the easy-to-edit base mesh while viewing the extrapolated result of the model with the finishing modifiers on it, without having to worry about adjusting the modifier stack. An example is shown in the earlier screenshot, with the levels of subdivision noted. The current level is the orange cage (on the original), which shows up on the mirrored copy as well.

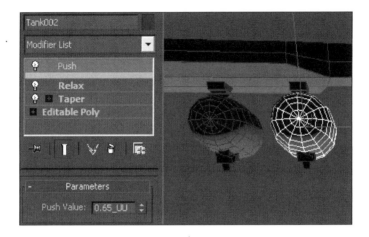

The thick gray divider line below the **Push** modifier helps demarcate what is going on with the Referenced clone in relation to its original. Modifiers below this gray divider are shared with the source model, and modifiers above are limited to the Reference copy.

11. Add an **Edit Poly** modifier above the **Relax** modifier, but below the gray line. Press 4 to enter the **Polygon Sub-Object** level, then select the triangular polygons on the front of Tank2.

    Select just one of the triangle faces and then click on **Grow**. Then use *Alt + Marquee* to deselect the additional three polygons.

12. Right-click over the selected tip of Tank2, and go to **Quad menu | Extrude** to push the selection inwards, generating a cavity. Notice both Tank models are affected.

13. Turn off the **Polygon Sub-Object** level, and highlight the **Edit Poly** modifier you added.

14. Drag the modifier upward above the **Push** modifier until a blue guideline shows above **Push**. When you release the **Edit Poly** modifier, which is now appearing above the gray line on the **Reference** won't be shared anymore to Tank1.

15. Finally, select both `Tank1` and `Tank2`, click on **Mirror**, and select **Instance** as the clone option. Then move the copied objects across to the other side of the plane so they line up with the `TankGrips` there.

Capturing a Snapshot

A **Snapshot** is a model with its modifiers collapsed in its current state. Select a model, go to the **Tools** menu, and click on **Snapshot...** to open the **Snapshot** dialog. The **Clone Method** options are the same as in the previous example, with the addition of the **Mesh** option. This is the default method for this tool, and is what collapses the existing modifiers in the copied object.

Try this out using `Tank1` or `Tank2`, and verify if the cloned mesh has its modifiers collapsed. Note that it is generated as an **Editable Mesh**, not an **Editable Poly**. When you perform the **Snapshot**, the clone is produced at the same spot. The original model remains selected.

You can also **Snapshot** the state of a model over the duration of an animation, by switching the default **Single** radio button over to the **Range** radio button, and then setting **From**, **To**, and **Range** parameters.

In the following screenshot, the right-hand side model is a snapshot of the model on the left-hand side, which has a **Bend** modifier set to 90 degrees:

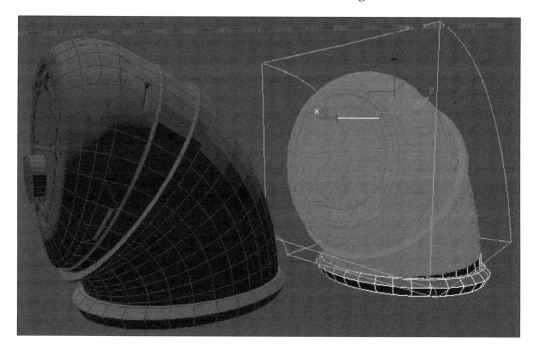

Adjusting modifiers in the viewport

In the previous section, we dragged a modifier in an object's modifier stack to shift its order. In this section we will introduce handling modifiers across several objects. Mostly, this is done by right-clicking on a modifier to show its contextual menu, and you can use the **Copy**, **Cut**, and **Paste** commands for modifiers from there. We're going to examine ways to control a selection of modifiers to affect their active state in the view, so that you can toggle one modifier and all its instances in one go, and also enable modifiers to perform differently in the view and at render time.

Assigning a single Turbosmooth to all your models

In the following steps, we'll look at how to use one modifier to affect many objects, for easier toggling of its result while working:

1. Open the \Packt3dsMax\Chapter 2\BikeFinish.max scene.

2. None of the objects in the scene are smoothed. In the main toolbar, find **Selection Filter flyout**, as shown in the following screenshot, which is currently set to **All**. In the drop-down, change it to **Geometry**.

3. Press *Ctrl + A* to select all. Only the geometry objects will be selected.

4. In the Command Panel go to **Modifier List**, select **TurboSmooth**. A warning will show about instanced objects receiving the same modifier; you can ignore it.

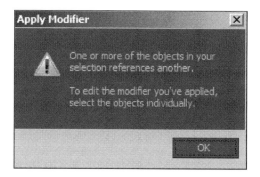

To delete a modifier per object, right-click on the modifier and select **Delete**, or you can click on the trashcan icon at the base of the modifier stack.

> Note that there is a black horizontal bar below it that lets you resize the stack.

When you right-click on the modifier, you will also see the option **Rename**, which will help you rename a modifier—this is a fairly unusual operation, since if you rename a modifier you might forget what its function is. A good solution to ensure changed modifier names remain functional is to keep their title and append the renamed part.

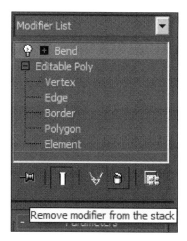

Selecting objects that have a certain modifier

Once you have more than a handful of objects that share a modifier, removing the modifier requires access to all of them at once or you'll be there all day. There is a script by Jordan Walsh called *Modifier Modifier Zorb*, which handles this really well. It can be found at `http://www.scriptspot.com/3ds-max/scripts/modifier-modifier-zorb`.

Installing it is just a matter of extracting the download file to the 3ds Max main folder so the `\Script` and `\UI` folders get merged in. Then you go to **Maxscript | Run Script** and browse to `C:\Program Files\Autodesk\3ds Max 2013\Scripts\Zorb\` and click on `Zorb-Modifier Modifier 2.mse`. You can customize access to it by looking for **Zorb Tools** if you want to assign it a keyboard shortcut or add it in the Quad menu.

When you run the script, the following screenshot will be displayed.

Highlight the **TurboSmooth** entry (given that you had added TurboSmooth previously to all the geometric objects in our scene `BikeFinish.max`). The entry now has 47 members. Right-click and select **Delete**, or one of the other options:

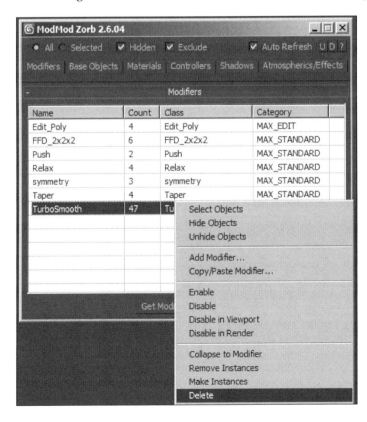

At the top, on the right-hand side of the window, is a **U** button, which updates the list of entries. At the bottom of the window, if you click on the **Get Modifier Properties** button, you can access parameters of the highlighted entry in another dialog.

One of the nicest features of Zorb Tools is you can show all the modifiers in the scene, independent of what is selected, and even use it as a search tool to select all the modifiers with a given modifier. Zorb Tools isn't limited to displaying modifiers. It has tabs that filter base objects, materials, controllers for animated objects, and a few others.

The major benefit of this tool is that you can work in 3ds Max in a "class-centric" way rather than a per-object way.

Setting different modifier attributes for views and rendering

Using **Zorb Tools | Get Modifier Properties** for a selection of modifiers, or right-clicking on the modifier in the modifier stack, you can set **TurboSmooth** so the **Render Iterations** (or subdivision) is higher, say 2, and the **Viewport Iterations** are lower, say 1. You can also right-click and select **Disable in viewport** if you don't want to see the subdivision while working, but still want it active during render time.

Organizing a scene using Groups

Groups associate several objects together without actually making them a single object. The area where groups are particularly useful is when you clone sets of objects that you need to keep together per copy. Groups are managed under the **Group** menu in the main toolbar. There are just a few tools, and if you use groups a lot, it is handy to put the **Group** tools into the **Quad** menu.

A group can be animated as a root of the objects it collects together. The idea of a group precedes the idea of an assembly, which precedes the idea of an XRef, which precedes the newer, more elaborate **Create | Helpers | Container** concept. Consequently, groups are simplest. Groups are stored locally in the scene, not externally as a file. Containers are saved to a file. You can find a PDF supplement on *Containers and XRefs* in the provided content for this chapter.

Group functionality

This section looks at simple manipulation of objects via a group and ways to control the group itself:

1. Open the scene `\Packt3dsMax\Chapter 2\BikeFinish.max`. Press *Ctrl + A* to select all the objects.

2. Click on the **Group** menu in the main toolbar, and select the **Group** command.

3. At the prompt enter a name, such as `Vehicle`. It can help to append a prefix to group names, though groups can be identified by the fact that their names are shown in bold in lists. In hierarchical lists, the icon for an *object* is ◉, and for a *group* it is ▣. In some cases the latter icon is also used for representing Shape objects, such as in the **Select by Name** dialog.

   When groups are created from a selection they are automatically put into a closed state where you can't access the individual elements. In order to control a group, use the **Group** menu. The available commands are **Open** and **Close**, **Group** and **Ungroup**, and **Explode**.

   > You may also notice **Assembly**. Assemblies are for creating convenient lighting rigs and are not covered in this book. The main difference between an assembly and a group is that an assembly gets defined with a head object to control properties of the lights it includes. Consult the online documentation via the **Help | Autodesk 3D Max Help** menu. In that, look up **Managing Scenes** and **Projects | Using Assemblies**.

4. Go to **Group | Open**, and notice the pink bounding box around the grouped object.

   This pink box represents the group itself, and can be selected, moved, animated, and hidden. It displays even when you have **Display Selection Brackets** toggled off in the viewport configuration options.

With the group open, you can select, manipulate, and edit any component object in the group. In order to close the group again, you can select any object and select **Group | Close**.

To extract an object from the group, such as the two **mr Sky Portal** objects for example, select the objects and go to **Group | Detach**.

You can add objects to an existing group using the script Outliner, by dragging them into the group in the hierarchy list. Another way to do this is to ungroup the grouped objects, add the objects you want to include in the selection too, and then recreate a fresh group with the same name (or a new name).

The **Ungroup** command will maintain any groups inside the selected one. The **Explode** command will ungroup all groups inside the selected one as well.

Make a group from the two **mr Sky Portal** objects, and then select everything else as well and create another group called Vehicle—you will get a nested hierarchy.

First try using Ungroup, to expose the **mr Sky Portal** lights again, with the objects still grouped. Revert the changes using **Undo**, then try using **Explode** to expose everything, this time with the objects ungrouped.

The way that groups inside groups form a hierarchy is similar to how linked objects work as parent-child using the **Link** 🔲 and **Unlink** 🔲 commands.

Parent-Child relationships can be viewed in the **Schematic** view. It is very handy for navigating the scene's hierarchical layout. The following steps show how to create a **Schematic** view:

1. Click on a viewport's label, for instance, **Top**, and select **Extended Viewports | Schematic View | New** from the drop-down menu.

   The initial appearance of the view gathers the entire scene, so it just looks like a bunch of markers.

2. Instead of displaying **Reference** mode 🔲, switch to **Hierarchy** mode 🔲 and scroll the mouse wheel to zoom in.

3. Open the **Schematic** view's **View** menu, and toggle **Show Grid** (G).

In **Schematic** view, groups show as green labels, as in the following example, with their contents nested below. Selected items are displayed with white labels and select the content in the scene:

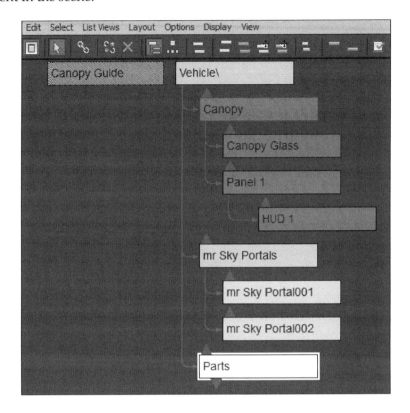

Importing models

Quite often you will be working with outsourced models, downloaded models, models by colleagues, royalty-free models that come with 3D magazines, or models you began in a sculpting application such as Forger (iPad), Pixologic Scultpris (free), ZBrush, Autodesk MeshMixer (free), or Mudbox, or even models exported from Unreal Development Kit, or another game editor that you might use as reference guides for detailing work.

If your content is an `.obj`, `.fbx`, `.3ds`, or `.dwg` (or another generic model format), to import a model go to **File | Import | Import**.

If your content is another `.max` scene, to merge a scene go to **File | Import | Merge**.

If you have a model whereby the content you'll import will replace an existing model or selection of models with the same name, go to **File | Import | Replace**. This could be the case if your scene is populated with Cylinder primitives that represent trees and you use **Tools | Rename Objects...** to call them all `Tree`, without numbering. If the target high-resolution tree model is also called `Tree`, then you can quickly repopulate an entire scene.

Different model formats (`.obj` or `.fbx` for example) have their own import dialog feature in which you can specify the properties of the model you want to preserve, such as Texture coordinates, Topology, or Smoothing Groups. In the `\Packt3dsMax\ Chapter 2\` content folder, there are two models; import each one and observe the options for each:

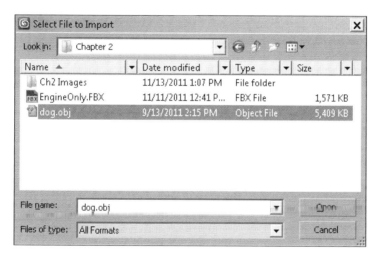

There are many peculiarities of file imports, in terms of the properties to select, and the majority of these are to do with materials that the object had in the original case but no longer has. Most models only save their mesh definition, but some can embed textures or tag the files alongside during export in a subfolder. Most modeling applications apply a default material to the object so you can see what you are doing, and this has to be replaced by the user when you swap applications. Textures, however, can sometimes be automatically exported with the asset and applied again. Normally, doing this yourself will help you verify all the required textures are in place once you've assigned a new material. Sometimes, the problems that occur when importing are more esoteric.

With Pixologic Sculptris, for instance, handling a model exported from it, when you import it to 3ds Max as `.obj`, you must click on **Import as single mesh** in the **OBJ Import Options** window, even though only one mesh is listed in the dialog. This is because if you don't select the option (and you were using symmetry in Sculptris), you get an **Invalid Vertex Index** error message caused by the symmetry line in the source mesh, and it refuses to import.

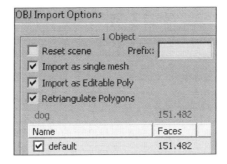

With many imported OBJ models, the surface smoothing calculation in the original application doesn't cross over to the smoothing groups that 3ds Max understands. So, it is necessary to add your own or the model surface will be faceted. Adding the **Modifier Smooth** setting to the imported model will usually handle this issue well. You just have to set the **AutoSmooth** option checked, and then set a high smoothing threshold value (around 90 degrees is normally fine). The following screenshot shows the difference this makes:

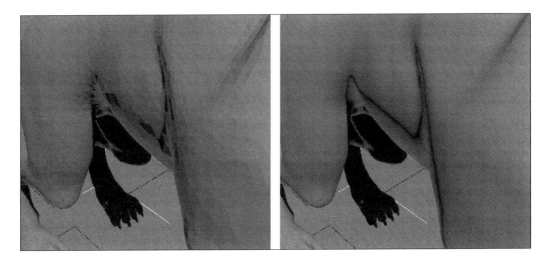

With `.obj` import, you can set the **Smooth** option enabled in the import options, if the mesh has smoothing data. You'll see a green dot next to the data the model contains, and a red dot if that data isn't included.

Using a template scene including lighting, turntable camera, and render settings

When you are modeling, a lot of time is wasted to construct a suitable scene for each model to show against, to light the model, and to set up a camera turntable. Using a template scene that provides those things is useful as a stand-in until the model is totally finished and can be either handed off to a colleague for their tasks, or presented professionally in a custom setting.

There is a nice template scene that ships with 3ds Max: `C:\...\3dsMax\scenes\Studio_scene_share.max`. This reproduces the look of a small photographic studio, with moveable light rigs. The ceiling light is fixed in place, but we've provided a version where you can move the light rigs and the area lights follow at `\Packt3dsMax\Chapter 2\Studio_scene_share_mod.max`. The rigs can be grabbed via the **Named Selection** entries, and the scene is set up for rendering with **Mental Ray**.

Just import your content from a model or scene file, and align 🔲 the content to the `Dummy01` object positioned on a stand with cameras facing it, then scale it to suit.

For the vehicle used in this chapter, an additional template scene has been created for a turntable animation—a 360 degrees spin around the model—which is a classic way to show off the asset. The scene includes a slightly reflective ground, a skydome, and lighting and exposure settings that work well with both **Mental Ray** and **NVIDIA iray**.

1. Open `\Packt3dsMax\Chapter 2\Bike.max`, and go to **File | Import | Merge**.

2. In the **Merge** dialog, click inside the **History:** field, use the drop-down list to go to the shortcut `\Packt3dsMax\Chapter 02\` folder, and select `TemplateBackdrop.max`.

3. In the **Merge** dialog, click on **ALL** to select all the objects, then click on **OK**.

4. After merging, press *C* to jump the view to the existing `Camera002` view. Pressing *Shift* + *F* shows the actual gate of the film, or the aspect ratio of the render.

5. There are six selected entities after the merge (unless you click on something). Raise these 20 units in Z axis to fit with the vehicle model.

   You may want to group them as `Backdrop` first. If the imported objects don't line up to the ground level, then to offset the group, right-click on the **Move** icon ⊞ to access the **Transform Type-In** dialog, which offers XYZ fields for absolute word position and an offset position.

6. This scene has a turntable animation already animated for `Camera002`. It is currently 100 frames, or about 4 seconds. Click on **Play** ▶ to view it. The hotkey for Play is /.

7. To scale the animation's duration longer hold *Ctrl + Alt + RMB*, and drag on the frame range of the time slider towards the left. This adds time to the end of the frame range.

8. Right-click on the timeline and ensure that **Configure | Show Selection Range** is ticked:

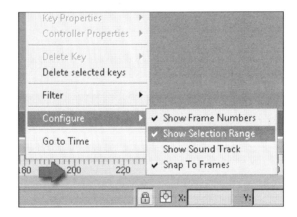

You should see a black bar under the selected object's keys.

9. Drag a Marquee selection over all the keys in the timeline so that they are highlighted in white. Now scale the animation to the end of the adjusted timeline by dragging the right-hand end of the black selection range bar, which has a white handle:

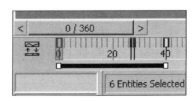

10. Alternatively, you can click on the **Time Configuration** icon ⬛, click **Re-Scale Time**, and adjust the **Length** value shorter or longer to suit.

In order to animate a camera turntable yourself, make sure the camera target, as well as the object you want to turn around is centered to 0,0,0. Click on **Link** ⬛ to link the camera head to the camera target. Press *N* for **Autokey** mode, then rotate the camera target in Z to any amount at frame **100**. Right-click on the key created for it, and select **Camera.Target:Z Rotation** from the drop-down menu. A pop up will appear showing its frame number, rotation value, and interpolation type.

Set the rotation value to **360** (and 0 at frame 0), and the interpolation type to **Linear** at the end and first frame, as shown in the following screenshot. There are **Go To Frame** arrows in the top left-hand corner of the dialog:

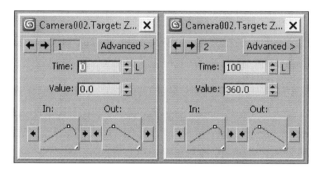

NVIDIA iray ActiveShade rendering

While final rendering is generally the area for a specialist, you can achieve a pretty good idea of the final look of the lighting and materials in your scene using **ActiveShade**, which is getting faster and faster year by year, particularly on robust machines (mostly through the uptake of NVIDIA's CUDA technology and OpenCL). You can read about this at http://blogs.nvidia.com/2011/08/nvidia-photorealistic-rendering-technology-demo-at-siggraph-2011/.

In order to enable NVIDIA iray as an ActiveShade renderer, perform the following steps:

1. Press *F10*.

2. Scroll down the **Common** tab of the **Render Setup** dialog.

3. Click on the **...** button (select **Renderer**) next to **ActiveShade**.

4. Select **NVIDIA iray** renderer from the options available. Do the same for the **...** button (select **Renderer**) next to **Production**.

Enabling NVIDIA iray for ActiveShade depends on having a version later than the Subscription Advantage service pack 2 for 3ds Max 2012. For 3ds Max 2013 it is in-built.

To start it up, click on *Shift + Q*, or click on the **Camera** view label and select **Extended | ActiveShade**. The iray renderer should kick in; you can also select the flyout icon .

To start with, it is a good idea to set the properties for the **ActiveShade** renderer, in the **Renderer** tab, so settings are minimal. For example, 30-second time to complete and four bounces rather than unlimited bounces.

> Find out more, particularly about the iray material plugin, at `http://blog.irayrender.com/`, which has been aggressively developed by Autodesk, but many users still prefer an external renderer or integrated third-party renderer.
>
> For comparison's sake, Arion "real-time photography" by Random Control (`http://randomcontrol.com/arion`) allows you to specify how the GPU and CPU will be assigned for rendering frames—a foreshadow of NVIDIA's *Project Maximus* (pushing towards controlled leverage of CPU and GPU). It can even offload rendering load to another machine, while you keep working on the scene. Recent additions (support for 3ds Max in v1.5.1 are participating media (fog and smoke) and real-time sub-surface scattering, a feature of materials such as wax, quartz, raspberries, and so on), which is generally computationally heavy to achieve.
>
> An expensive alternative to iray is Chaos Group's mature product *Vray* and *VrayRT*, which have been leading renderers for many years (`http://www.chaosgroup.com/en/2/vray.html`).
>
> There are similar products all over the place, and a promising one is the relatively cheaper *Octane Render*, which has recently been released for internal 3ds Max rendering too. Refractive Software aims to offer automatic translation of materials from different renderers so they parse through its renderer (`http://www.refractivesoftware.com/forum/viewtopic.php?f=7&t=9692`).

You can use the `Studio_scene_share.max` scene to try out ActiveShade with iray, of which an example using the floating viewport option is shown in the next screenshot. You can set it to display in one of the views, but the floating viewport is a better option since it allows you to push it off onto a second monitor, and five views are better than four.

Don't forget to watch the **Render Message: iray Renderer** dialog for warnings and information about your machine's processing power, and progress reports.

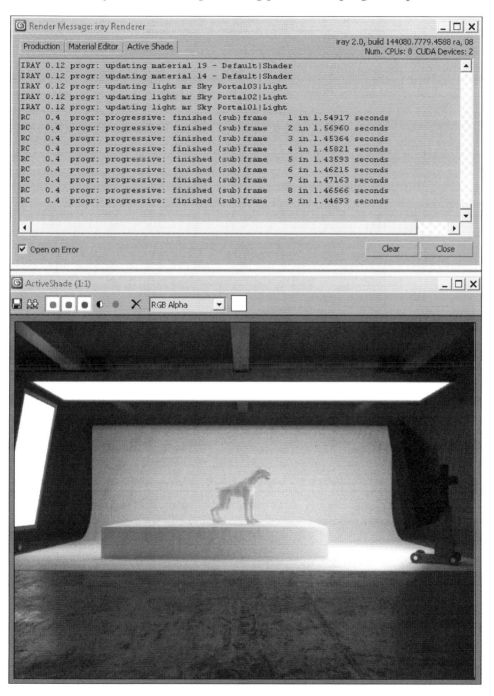

Summary

This chapter covered a lot of ground concerning model handling. A key idea that was introduced is that using a template for a background in which to place models saves a lot of time setting up lighting. It's easier to adjust a preset lighting situation than to create a lighting situation from scratch every time you want to preview and render a model. Instead, you want to save that time for working on the model.

In our supplementary content, we also cover some collaboration tools such as Containers and XRef scenes and objects. Besides enabling content sharing and content protection while collaborating, these let you organize large volumes of data more efficiently. This is particularly important in scenes where you are using many copies or instances of objects (such as scattered trees or buildings) that you don't need to display all the time.

I predicted at the end of the previous chapter that you'd become progressively more comfortable with the 3ds Max UI and accessing tools. Hopefully, you notice this progress too. By now you'll be more familiar with adjusting the pivot of a model and transforming it, understanding the model's relation to the world space, and keeping content organized within the scene. In the next chapter, we'll begin looking at methods to directly edit a polygon-based model.

3
The Base Model – A Solid Foundation in Polygon Modeling

This chapter covers getting started on a model, starting with a reference image. We'll examine the modeling skills needed to create a base model. It also introduces the challenge of constructing forms that match a design while keeping within the constraints of four-sided topology, with an eye toward surface-detailing requirements.

The following topics are covered in the chapter:

- Introducing the project
- Adding image reference
- Viewport image planes
- Forming the base model
- Quad menu's editable poly tools
- Setting values with the Autodesk style caddy
- Fitting the model to the artwork
- Generating round forms from quad-based geometry
- Detaching and attaching parts of a model
- A preview of sculpting workflow

Introducing the project

In the previous chapter we handled an existing model. The circumstances were akin to what you'd expect to deal with when working with another artist's model. In this project, we'll make a model from scratch to about the same level of finish as a game prototype model for a vehicle.

The design for the vehicle is a cabin that sits atop a robotic six-legged crawler, shaped somewhat like a crab or spider. The cabin is all we'll build in this chapter, but we'll see the walking crawler later on, provisioned with a CAT rig (**CAT** is a skeletal system that ships with 3ds Max and allows Skin-driven animation of a mesh. **Skin** is a modifier, which binds a mesh to an animation rig or skeleton based on vertex weightings).

Adding image reference

The reference images for this project are found in the content files for the book under `\Packt3dsMax\Chapter 03\`, where there is a front view (`Front.png`) and a side view (`Side.png`).

1. Open the \Packt3dsMax\Chapter 03\SceneStart.max scene, which is a template scene with NVIDIA iray settings provided. It includes a camera, ground **Plane** primitive with an Autodesk **Generic Material**, and a **Daylight** system overhead with appropriate exposure applied in the **Environment** settings (press *8*). The scene objects are frozen and on a layer ⬚ of their own called *Basic Elements*.

2. Open the Material Editor (press *M*) and make sure that **Slate Material Editor...** is the active option through the **Modes** menu.

   In our template scene, NVIDIA iray is set as the renderer for previewing what we're going to make. So we need to use appropriate materials. For example, NVIDIA iray accepts mental ray materials and not the Standard materials designed for the default scanline renderer. A model destined to live in a game will have its material asset set in the game editor, but you'll first need to preview your work in progress inside of 3ds Max.

3. In the **View1** area, right-click and go to **Materials | mental ray | Autodesk Generic**.

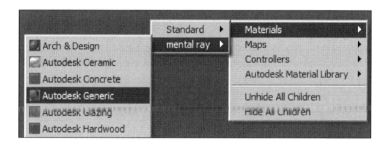

4. Double-click on the material node, and on the right-hand properties panel in the top textfield call the material Front (a unique and clear name).

5. In **View1**, from the **Generic_Image** nub of the material node you added, drag a wire out and you'll be prompted to select a map to add. Go to **Standard | Bitmap**. You could also click on the **Image | None** button on the right-hand panel in the properties for the **Autodesk Generic** node.

6. Immediately, you can browse for a file to set in the **Image** channel. The reference images for this project are found in \Packt3dsMax\Chapter 03\ where there is a front view (Front.png) and a side view (Side.png). Click on Front.png and double-click on the image preview for the map to enlarge it.

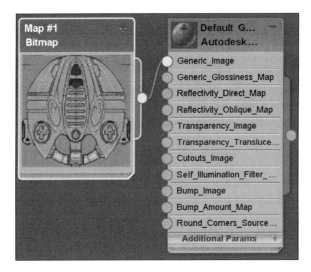

7. Hold *Ctrl* and left-click on the Front material node and its **Map** node to select both. You could also drag a rectangular marquee around them to select them.

8. Hold *Shift* and drag these to make a copy of them.

9. Double-click on the new material node (which was automatically assigned a unique name) and call it Side.

10. Double-click on the **Map** node for the **Image** channel of the material Side. In the **Bitmap Parameters | Bitmap:** channel, change the image file used from Front.png to Side.png.

    Now you have two materials representing front and side views for which we're going to build reference planes next. But first you'll need to know the size of the two images.

11. Click on the name of the file assigned to the **Image** channel in its **Bitmap Parameters** entry. This opens a browser to assign a file, and for the selected Front.png file, its **Statistics** and **Location** are displayed in the dialog, including its dimensions. In this case, 460 pixels wide and 374 pixels high.

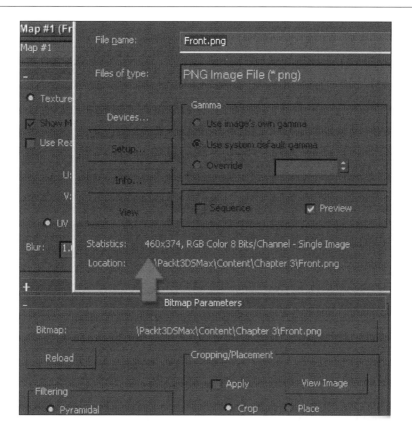

Viewport image planes

For the following steps we'll construct front facing and side facing planes in the views and assign and show the materials for the modeling reference, so that as we build the model we can closely match the geometry to the design. You can also do this directly in the viewport background by pressing *Alt + B* and assigning an image in the **Background Configuration** dialog. It is debatable as to whether planes offer the more flexible approach or background images. In teaching, I've noticed students often have some trouble getting used to the view fitting options for the background image method.

1. Go to **Create | Standard Primitives | Plane** and drag the cursor diagonally anywhere in the **Front** view (since now we're going to establish a front facing reference image). The size doesn't matter now since we'll set it in the **Modify** panel to fit the image dimensions. Name the plane PlaneFront.

2. Click on **Modify** 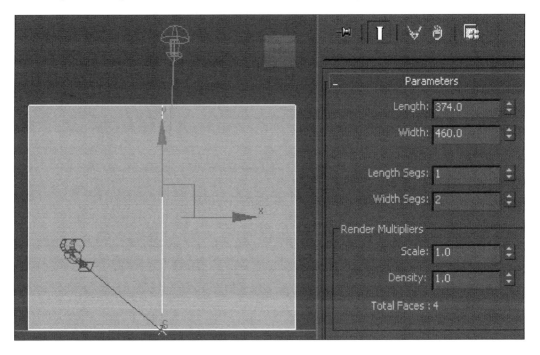 and for the **Width** parameter of the plane, match the width of the `Front.png` image, which in this case is `460.0`. Do the same with the **Length** parameter of the plane to match the height of the image, which in this case is `374.0`. Also, set **Width Segs** value to `2` and **Length Segs** value to `1`. The default plane has 4 x 4 segments, which we want to simplify down, preserving a center line, as shown in the following screenshot:.

3. Press *A* to turn on **Angle Snap....** This is because when you rotate a model you can hit 90 degrees or 45 degrees quickly instead of shuffling around 90.03 and 89.92, for example. The default angle snap value is 5 degrees, and you can change it by right-clicking on the **Angle Snap** icon and changing the **Angle** value in the **Grid and Snap Settings** dialog.

4. Press *E* to enter **Rotate** mode, and hold the *Shift* key and turn the plane 90 degrees in Z to produce a copy (a straight copy not an instance) facing to the side. It doesn't matter which direction you rotate it, since you can always mirror it using the **Mirror** tool to find the best axis once the image is applied to it. Name the new plane `PlaneSide`.

5. In the Material Editor (press *M*), right-click on the `Side` material and select **Assign Material to Selection**. Then right-click again and select **Show Standard Map in View**. If you wish, you can instead select **Show Hardware Map in View**. Click on `PlaneFront` in the view and assign the `Front` material to it in the same way.

If you find your image is showing white, it could be that the view is using hardware lighting and the scene is too bright. The fix for this, for each view, is to click on the view label [+] and select **Configure Viewports...**, and click on **Default Lights** in the **Lighting and Shadows** tab.

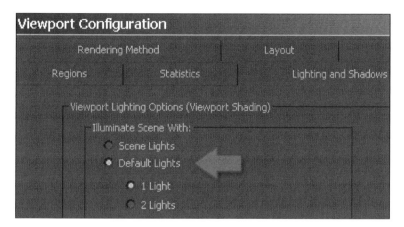

On the other hand, If your image plane shows as black, it probably means you are facing it from behind. You can flip it with the **Mirror** tool , setting the appropriate axis. Also, make sure the side view image does not face toward the front image, as shown in the next screenshot. By default, 3ds Max shows the **Left** view in the 4 x 4 views split. It may be more pleasant to model with the **Right** view active instead. While you can switch to the left view by pressing *L*, the right view has no shortcut (since the *R* key is reserved for **Scale**). So you need to right-click on the view label to swap the view.

6. At the moment your planes will be crossed (as shown in the following screenshot on the left). Move them so they are spread apart, as shown in the following screenshot on the right:

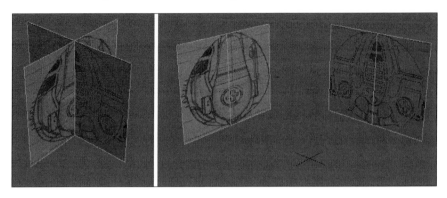

7. Also move the planes up so they sit on the ground. The best way to do this is to click on **Edit | Transform Toolbox** and with the planes selected change the pivot to **Min Z**. Then you can change the Z value for both planes to 0.00.

8. It is vital to make sure that PlaneFront is centered to X = 0.000 in the world also. Symmetry that we'll use later is much easier to control if it is mirrored from the world center.

9. PlaneSide is too wide, since it is a copy of the front plane, so set its **Width** value to 300 to match the reference image, in the same way we discussed earlier. You can get the dimensions for Front.png and Side.png from the **Bitmap** file information after you add it to the material in the Material Editor, or in Windows Explorer by highlighting the file and looking at the status bar at the bottom.

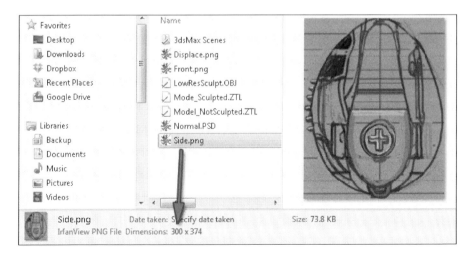

10. Select both planes. Right-click and select **Object Properties**. Set the **Display Properties** option **Show Frozen in Gray** such that it is unticked, so when we freeze the object it still displays the bitmap assigned to it. Click on **OK**.

11. In the scene, click on the **Manage Layers...** icon 🔲 and click on 🔲 to add the two planes to a new layer. Call the new layer Ref and click on **Freeze** alongside that layer. Note that when you create a new layer it becomes the active layer, so if we were to add a new object it would also go on the frozen layer Ref. For this reason there is a little tick mark next to the layer that is active. Move this to the 0 (default) layer, as shown in the following screenshot:

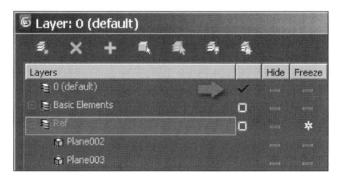

Now would be a good time to save the scene as MyModelStart.max. Our image reference is sufficiently prepared, and we can start to concentrate on building the basic form of the model.

> The method discussed previously will serve for most models, though you may need to extend it to include a top or back view. To this end, you can grab the free Maxscript Blueprint Manager from Studio 75ive at http://75ive.com/tools/#blueprint_manager.

Forming the base model

If you are working to a set scene scale in order to match your model with other models, you can scale your reference planes once you have set their relative size. Scale using **Local** transform and set **Use Pivot Center** 🔲 and the two planes will scale individually from their pivots.

A starting scene ModelStart.max is provided in the next section, which has been scaled down to about one-third of its original size, to better fit the model's export scale, to the game level it is intended for. It continues from the point where the last section finished.

From this point on I'm going to assume you're using the preset UI `\Packt3dsMax\UI Settings\Packt2013_UI.ui`. You can load it from **Customize | Load Custom UI Scheme**.

To get started on modeling, for this model, we should probably start with a box rather than a sphere, even though the general form is spherical, because of the way that a sphere's edges gather into triangles at the top and bottom into a pole. Triangles, especially those joining into a pole, don't subdivide well compared with a grid-like topology. A box with a **TurboSmooth** modifier applied will tend to smooth into a spherical shape while keeping quad polygons.

1. In the **Front** view, create a Box primitive that has 2x2x2 segments. Press *F4* so you can see the model edges, and in the front and side views toggle *F3* so the views are shaded. Call the Box `VehicleShell`.

2. Make sure `VehicleShell` is lined up so its X position is **0.00** in the world, to line up with the `PlaneFront` reference image. Once you have done this you may want to set the pivot to **Min Z**. Also ensure the box lines up to the middle of the `PlaneSide` reference image.

3. Add a **TurboSmooth** modifier to the box, and notice its form rounds off considerably and that its segments are subdivided. Each polygon is divided into four smaller ones. Within the modifier settings set the **Iterations** value to 2. The modifier also has a **Smooth Result** setting that removes the six smoothing groups on the sides of the box, which keep its edges sharp.

4. This soft box is kind of hard to edit, having so many edges. Let's selectively remove some edge loops. Right-click on the model and select **Convert to Editable Poly**.

5. Press 2 to enter Edge Sub-Object mode or right-click and select the **Edge** mode.

6. Press *Ctrl + LMB* on the edges shown in the next screenshot. Then right-click and go to **Quad menu | SelectEdgeLoop**.

The steps continue in the next section, now we've selected the edges. We'll start to operate on selections using the Editable Poly modeling tools.

The Quad menu's editable poly tools

The `SelectEdgeLoop` command is part of the provided preset UI `\Packt3dsMax\UI Settings\Packt2013_UI.ui` presets that you can load by choosing **Customize | Load Custom UI**. For this command you can also click on **Loop** in the Command Panel under **Modify | Selection**, or go to the **Graphite Modeling Tools** tab on the Ribbon and go to **Modify Selection | Loop**.

This section covers some of the common editing tools that have shortcuts from both the Ribbon and the Command Panel in the Quad menu's editable poly region.

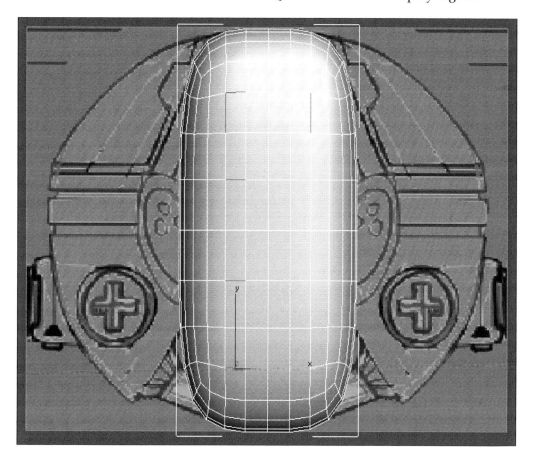

1. Right-click to expose the **Quad** menu. Press *Ctrl* (not beforehand) and then click on **Remove** in the **editable poly** quad. If you press *Ctrl* first and then right-click, you will expose the **Modeling Quad** menu variation instead.

   You need to press *Ctrl* because otherwise you will only remove edges, not the associated points that go with them. Discarding edges but not points too will make it very hard to edit the model. In the preset UI \Packt3dsMax\ UI Settings\Packt2013_UI.ui, I've also added **Remove** (edge) and **RemoveLoop** to the **Modeling Quad** menu (press *Ctrl* + *RMB*) to alleviate any confusion. It is the only Quad menu command that requires holding the *Ctrl* key. **Removeloop** doesn't require you to select an edge and then click on **Loop**. It selects the loop for you, but it is probably a good idea to select the loop yourself to confirm that you'll remove what you intend.

The following screenshot compares the effect of pressing *Ctrl* + **Remove** (left) and **Remove** (right) on the model:

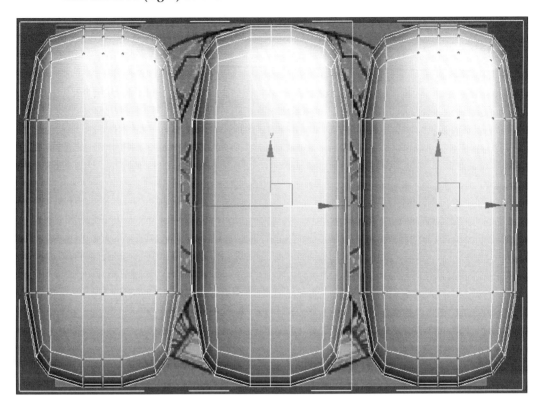

2. In the side view press *1* to enter the **Vertex** mode. Now, Marquee select around the top part of the model and scale in the horizontal axis so that it fits, as well as you can manage, the drawing's outline. See the next screenshot; we'll make improvements later. Do the same for the middle section, which is the widest, and the lower section. The only tool you need to do this is select and scale, selecting groups of points at a time.

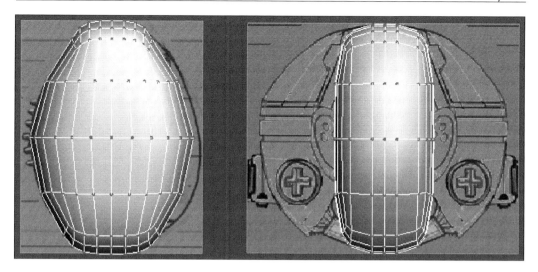

You may start to feel as you follow these steps that you can't see much of the reference art. There are a few ways to get around this. One way is to press *Alt + X* to toggle See-Through mode for the model, as shown in the next screenshot. The other way is to copy out another plane with the image reference on it, so you can see it off to the side.

3. Continue using the Marquee select tool to select and move parts of the model to better fit its profile. Remember not to directly select points. You want to select the side of the model facing you, and also the side of the model on the far side.

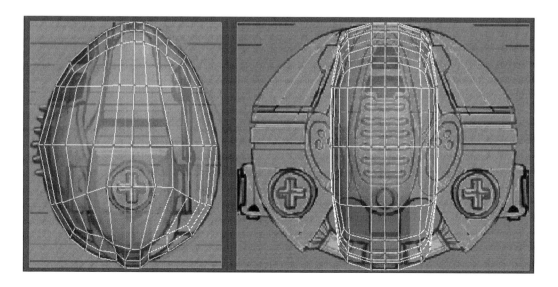

Even though there are not yet enough segments in the model to create edge loops that flow perfectly with the drawing's contours, it is always worthwhile to try at every stage you've added geometry to get the wireframe as optimal as possible before adding still more.

4. Right-click and select **SwiftLoop**, then add three edges as shown in the next screenshot. If you hold the *Shift* key when clicking to add the edge loops, the added loops should adapt to approximate the averaged curve better. Without pressing the *Shift* key, the edges will be added in a linear fashion.

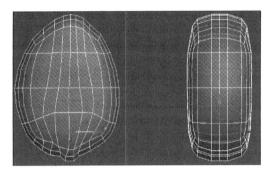

5. So far the Front view of the model is under-represented. Still, just using select and scale and select and move, you can easily adjust the model in vertex selections to fit the drawing contours. I have shown using red polygon selections the major areas of the model to address.

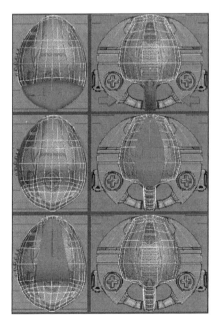

6. A challenge that often arises is when one view's selection appears to be in the right place while the same selection in the other view seems out of place. This is the case in the previous screenshot with the middle section, which looks fine from the front (it covers what will eventually be a hatch in the vehicle), while in the side view it doesn't appear deep enough. Let's adjust this and then we should be ready to start adding more geometry to flesh out the basic form in the area highlighted in the bottom image shown in the previous screenshot. Again, as much as possible, when moving edges try to find a suitable match with the design's contours. You'll frequently notice a ripple-down effect as one change leads to another as you balance the mesh up.

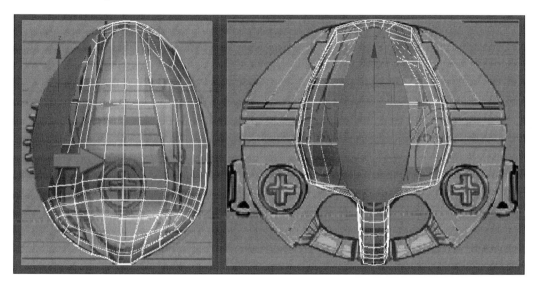

7. Since we'll start using tools to add geometry, it would be faster to work on half the model and then flip our changes across to the other side. To facilitate this, select half the model in polygon Sub-Object mode. While in this case you could just Marquee select half of the model in the **Front** view; you can also go to the Ribbon and click on the **Selection** tab. Then under **By Half | X**, click on the **Select** icon 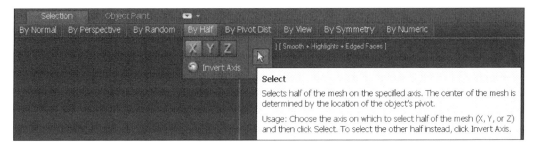. Hover the mouse over this to get a handy rollout usage tip.

8. Press the *Delete* key and then right-click and select **Top-level**.

9. Add a **Symmetry** modifier.

   Generally speaking, if you delete the negative X side of the model, the **Symmetry** modifier will flip the positive content as desired, but sometimes the deleted side will flip, in which case you get nothing. You can click on **Flip** in the modifier parameters to fix this.

10. You can't edit the model while you have the **Symmetry** modifier highlighted in the stack, but when you go down the stack to the **Editable Poly** level to keep modeling you can't see the symmetry you've added. To resolve this, click on the **Show End Result** icon 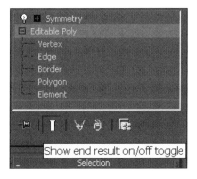 shown so that you can see both levels at the same time.

This icon is mirrored in the **Graphite Modeling Tools** part of the Ribbon interface.

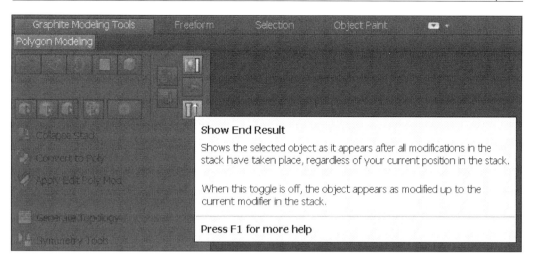

Show End Result

Shows the selected object as it appears after all modifications in the stack have taken place, regardless of your current position in the stack.

When this toggle is off, the object appears as modified up to the current modifier in the stack.

Press F1 for more help

11. Now make a polygon selection matching the one shown in the next screenshot. Right-click and select **Extrude Settings** in the Quad menu. The selected polygons will grow outward by a default amount.

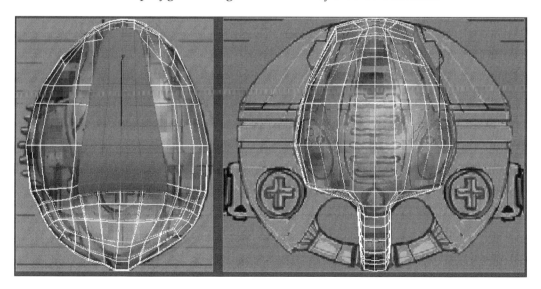

Setting values with the Autodesk style caddy

When you use polygon editing tools, there's often a **caddy** that pops up in the view allowing you to set variables for the edit. The first bar in the caddy has info about its components as you roll over those, and you can drag the top bar to place the caddy anywhere in the view.

For an interminable read on "Caddies versus the old Dialog Box" method of editing, look at the **Area** forum threads about caddies after they were introduced. There are some hacks to subvert caddies back to the older editing methods, but they come with serious caveats.

In essence, the design of the caddy is intended to match related Autodesk products to generate better interoperability.

Caddies all follow a similar layout so it isn't too difficult to get used to them. Any value will provide a spinner if you mouse over it, and you can click on the number to enter it numerically.

You can hold *Ctrl* to increase or hold the *Alt* key to decrease the sensitivity of the caddy spinners while dragging them to change a value.

Pressing the *Enter* key will save you from clicking on the **OK** icon ▣, and pressing *Ctrl + Enter* will save you from clicking on the **Apply and Continue** icon ▣, and pressing the *Esc* key will save you from clicking on the **Cancel** icon ▣. Any icon with a small downward triangle is a rollout, which lets you choose other states for the tool, such as in the case of the **Extrude Polygons** tool, **Group**, **Local Normal**, or **By Polygon**.

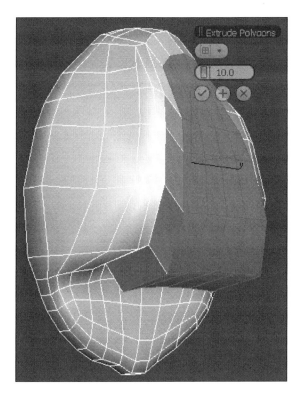

If you are unfamiliar with the idea of extruding faces on a model, try out these three settings to see the difference. **Group** extends the polygons out a single angle, while **Local Normal** extends them based on their individual facing directions. **By Polygon** extends every face outward separately, as a unique extrusion.

The following steps continue our modeling task from the previous section:

1. For the extrusion's **Amount** value, what you set will be remembered for further use next time. In this case, it doesn't matter what value you enter since you can just move the result by hand afterward. Select **Group** as the extrusion type and press the *Enter* key to commit the result and close the caddy.

2. Move the extruded polygons until they touch against the reference image, as shown in the following screenshot:

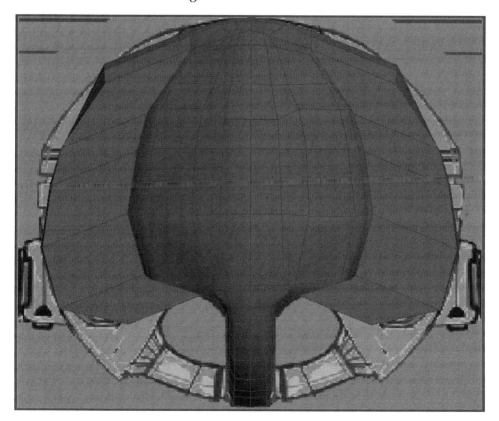

Also note, at this point it would be good to place an **Autodesk Generic** material on the model with a gray diffuse color, and set the wireframe color to be darker. The assigned yellow color in the previous images at some angles has a sheen that makes the selection wireframe, which is white, hard to see.

Fitting the model to the artwork

Once again we need to go through the easy but repetitive task of fitting the vertices and edges to best match the drawing using select and move. Between the extruded faces and the original faces, you can **SwiftLoop** in another loop. As you tidy the point distribution, you'll see opportunities to insert more loops to help match the model to the drawing.

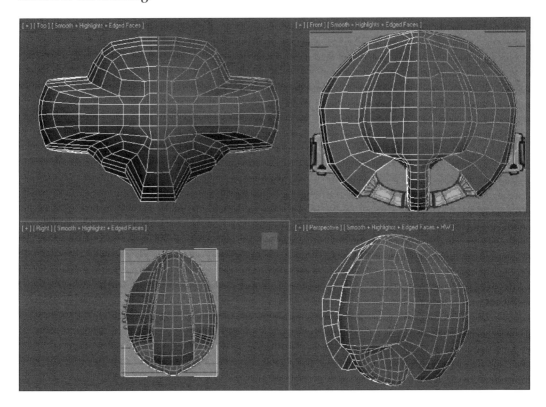

The following steps involve extending smaller forms on the model, and to do this, in any model, it is helpful if the current base mesh has a wireframe distribution to support the part to be extruded outward or cut away:

1. Select polygons as shown in the next screenshot, then right-click and select **Inset**. This tool lets you push polygons inward on a surface and is helpful for creating a framing prior to extruding. The settings allow you to control the amount numerically, which helps prevent unwanted overlap of polygons.

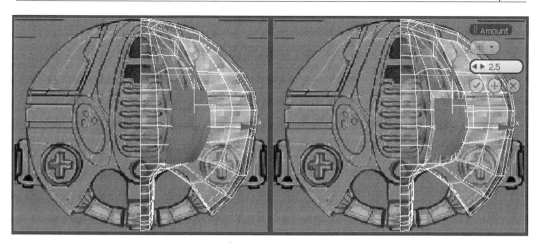

2. The shape we inset needs to be adjusted into a more oval shape, prior to extrusion, but we want to keep the points stable on the object surface. To ensure this we can look in the Command Panel, under **Edit Poly**, and select one of the **Constraints** radio buttons; in this case **Face**. This will allow points to slide on the current face while you arrange them to fit the oval shape in the drawing. You can also access **Edit | Constrain to Face** in **Graphite Modeling Tools**, as shown in the next screenshot. Don't forget to set this back to **None** when you are done.

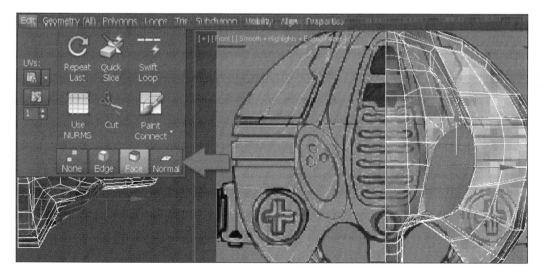

3. Extrude the oval selection of polys with **Group** set as the extrusion type. Then move and scale them to match the smaller inner oval, and also make sure they extend only as far forward as shown in the `side.png` reference image. At the base of the extrusion and at the end, add loops using **SwiftLoop** to keep the projected form sharp.

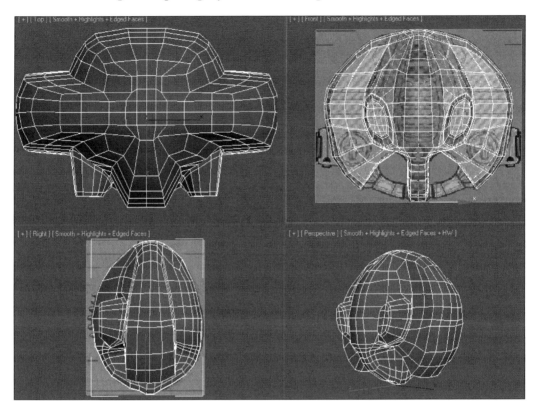

Generating round forms from quad-based geometry

Our model is made of quad-based geometry, but there are several round forms such as cylindrical shapes and tube shapes in the design. This section shows ways to handle the problem of fitting a square peg into a round hole, so to speak.

It is always best to work from large features to small, so the next important form to address would be the chubby circular cylinders that protrude on both sides of the chassis. The intention is that these are all similar on the front side and back, so we'll just make one, then copy and paste it around where needed, and then weld them onto the chassis.

1. As we did earlier, start by using inset polygons to make a framing device, and adjust the inset polygons to be as circular as possible. The circular shape will be best approximated as an octagon, with a clear cross of mesh edges through the center, as shown in the next screenshot. Avoid the temptation to rotate the circle to line up with the cross drawn in the reference image. This can be done after extruding the form. Inset an inner and outer ring.

2. To correct the cross through the middle we'll introduce a new tool, **Cut**. First, select the lines crossing the extruded circle and right-click and press *Ctrl +* **Remove**. Press *1* to enter Vertex Sub-Object mode, and right-click and select **Cut**. **Cut** by itself works well, but is greatly helped by working in the **Snaps** mode. Press *S* or click on the **Snap** icon .

3. The default snap is set to the view grid, but we need to snap to points on the model. Therefore, press *Shift* and right-click and click on **Grid and Snap Settings** (or right-click on the **Snaps** icon). This exposes options for snapping, and in the first tab you can turn off **Grid** and turn on **Vertex**. Also turn on **Midpoint** for future convenience. These settings will be conserved until you later have cause to change them.

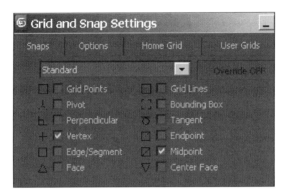

4. In Vertex Sub-Object mode (press *1*), using **Cut**, and with **Snaps** active, add edges across the circle, as shown in the following screenshot:

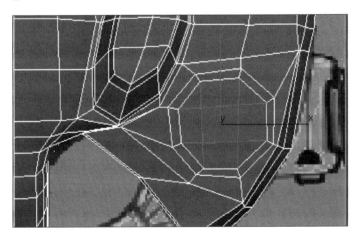

These cut-in edges introduce triangles into the model for the first time. This is not necessarily a terrible thing, but we can easily keep the model in quads (which makes for cleaner subdivision later on).

5. To do so, in Edge Sub-Object mode (press 2) highlight the four edges as shown in the next screenshot. Then right-click and go to **Quad menu | editable poly | ConnectEdgesOptions** (or the options icon next to **Connect** in the default UI). For this case no options need to be set, so you can then press the *Enter* key to commit the edit straightaway. Afterward, scale down the resulting edges a bit so the result looks as shown on the right of the following screenshot:

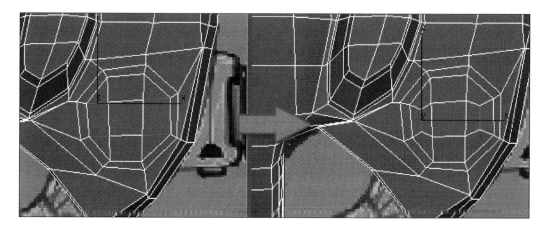

6. Repeat the same select, **Connect**, and scale step with the top and bottom edges. You may notice that five-sided polygons are created here. A solution for this is shown later in this chapter.

7. Extrude the circle you've made and the edge content within it forward about as far as the shape protruding from the side of the chassis in the previous screenshot, about 7.5 units.

8. Now we're going to copy and paste this extrusion to save having to rebuild the edges where this structure repeats. Enter Polygon Sub-Object mode (press 4) and click on the polygon in the middle of the extruded part, using **Grow** selection (*Ctrl + Page Up*) to expand outward, as shown in the following screenshot:

9. Add **SwiftLoop** around the base of this selection, which you can do while still in **Polygon** mode, where it joins to the rest of the model.

10. Right-click and select **Move**, and hold the *Shift* key and drag on the selected polygons to pull a copy of them away from the rest. You'll be prompted to select whether you want the copied objects to become a new object altogether or a new **Element** (or part) within the current object. Select **Clone to Element** and click on **OK**.

11. Move, rotate, and scale the new part to fit to the side of the model, and make sure it lines up with the details in the drawing you can see in the `PlaneFront` reference. The part may overlap existing polygons, so to fix this right-click and select **Borders** Sub-Object level (press 3), and click on the open edge of the new part. Move this out from the side so it doesn't overlap, as shown in the following screenshot:

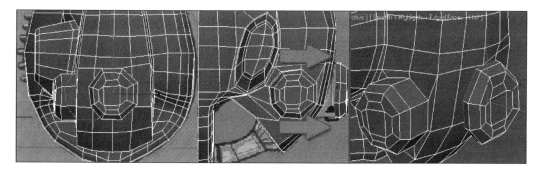

12. To connect this part back to the main model, we should construct a fitting frame of edge loops (again in a circle with eight sides) to fit it neatly. In this kind of situation, you'll normally find it necessary to select and move existing points and edges to make some room to add additional edges. To add edges, right-click and use **Cut** to add the framing loop, and **Connect** the corners of the added loop so the object maintains a quad-based structure, as shown in the following screenshot:

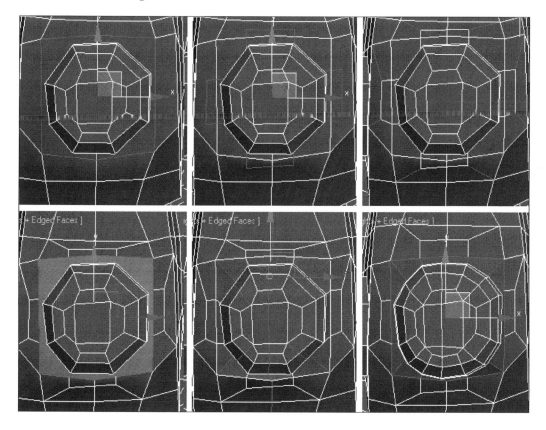

Using the **Bridge Edges** tool will allow you to close the gap between the deleted polygons (shown in the previous screenshot on the lower-left).

On the first extruded circle, the one in the **Front** view, there is a section of polygons that is five-sided, which is fixed in the previous example for the side circle by blending into the surrounding mesh. Let's fix the front now.

13. Navigate to the polygons shown in the next screenshot on the left (the first in the sequence of screen captures) and enter the **Vertex** mode (press *1*). Holding *Ctrl + LMB* points to the next image in the sequence. Now right-click and select **Connect Vertex**. Then select edges as shown in the next screenshot and right-click and select **ConnectEdgesOptions**, producing what's shown in the middle image in the sequence.

14. Click on **Graphite Modeling Tools** in the Ribbon. Now go to **Geometry | Relax**. This softens the created edge result.

15. For the diamond pattern, shown in the next screenshot (second from the right), you can dissolve it out in two steps. First, enter the **Polygon** mode (press *4*), select the diamond polygons, and press the *Delete* key. Second, enter the **Vertex** mode (press *1*), then right-click and use **Target Weld Vertex** to create a loop, as shown in the following screenshot in the final image of the sequence:

16. As we did earlier, select the circular protrusion and hold the *Shift* key and drag a copy by selecting the **Clone to Element** option, and this time fix the new part on the back of the model, much the same as it fitted on the side. To place it at the back you will need to rotate it 180 degrees.

17. The remaining form to complete on the model is the tube on the underside. Again we need to create an eight-sided shape that's more or less circular to frame the new form, paying attention to its size relative to the image reference.

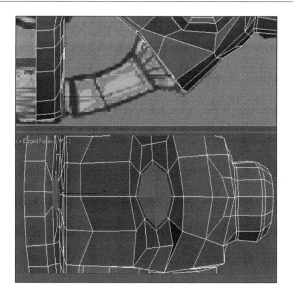

18. To span a gap between two polygon islands you can use the **Bridge** tool. This is found under **Graphite Modeling Tools | Polygons | Bridge**. In the preset UI `\Packt3dsMax\UI Settings\Packt2013_UI.ui` UI, this tool has been added to the **Quad** menu as **Bridge Settings**.

By default the new polygons will create a direct span, but in the settings you can add **Segments** and even bulge and taper the new geometry. In our case, rather than add segments, we can use **SwiftLoop** to add them selectively, after completing the bridge operation, as shown in the **Front** view of the entire model so far.

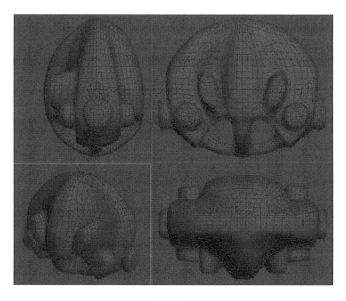

Detaching and attaching parts of a model

The model's upper half includes a cockpit and two unfolding engine covers. In this section, we'll cover how to isolate and detach polygon sections to generate new models based on the existing form.

In the next screenshot, an additional polygon loop has been added with some slight vertex nudges to provide a stable frame for the engine cover. To select any loop you can click on a polygon and then hold the *Shift* key, then click on another polygon in line with it. This also works for edges and points. A new feature in 3ds Max 2013 is that you can also simply double-click on an edge to select the loop to which it belongs.

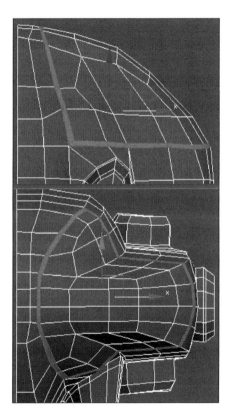

The polygons inside of this loop are the ones we'll detach.

1. In the **Front** view, Marquee select the polygons inside the edges shown in the previous screenshot. In the **Named Selections** field, type `CoverPolys` and press the *Enter* key to commit this selection to memory. For this, in the Ribbon, you can also use the buffer tool at **Stored Selections** | **Store 1** in the **Selection** panel.

2. With the same bunch of polygons selected, right-click and select **Detach** in the Quad menu (for the preset UI \Packt3dsMax\UI Settings\Packt2013_ UI.ui) or in the Ribbon go to **Graphite Modeling Tools | Geometry (All) | Detach**. In this case we'll keep the original polygons, so in the **Detach** options click on **Detach as Clone**. Call the detaching piece Cover and click on **OK**. After this you may also want to name the main object Body.

3. The original polygon selection should remain selected, not the new object, since we're still in Sub-Object mode. For now, right-click and select **Isolate Selection**. This temporarily shows only the current object. You could alternatively use **Hide Unselected** from the Quad menu.

4. Right-click and select **Extrude Settings**. Ensure **Group** is the active extrude method via the caddy and set a fairly small value. The value doesn't matter too much since the next step is to **Scale** the selection and move it down, as shown in the following screenshot:

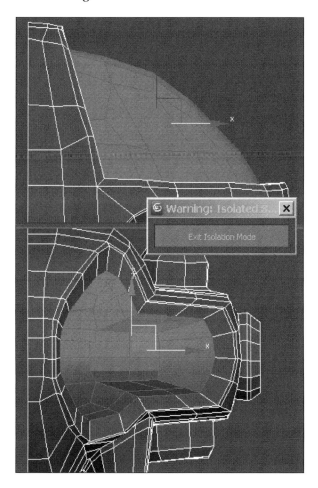

5. Still with the scaled polygons selected, right-click and select **Detach** using **Detach as Clone**. Name it `CoverInner`. This will gives us a second element for the `Cover` piece. Now click on **Exit Isolation Mode** in 3ds Max 2012 or toggle **Isolate Selection** so that it isn't ticked in 3ds Max 2013 (or **Unhide All**), and right-click and select **Top-level**.

6. Press *H* and select in the list `Cover` and `CoverInner`. Click on **Hide Unselected**, then orbit the Perspective view to show both the pieces clearly. Click on `CoverInner` and enter **Polygon** mode (press 4) and then press *Ctrl + A* (**Select All**). These polygons should face downward, not upward. To flip them go to the Ribbon and go to **Graphite Modeling Tools | Polygons | Flip**, as shown in the following screenshot:

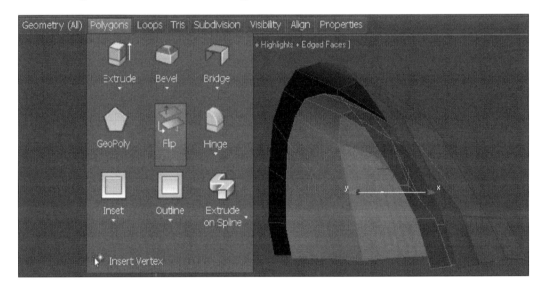

7. The two pieces, `Cover` and `CoverInner`, need to be joined into one. Go to **Top-level** for `CoverInner`, then click on `Cover`. Starting from `CoverInner` to `Cover` means we don't have to change its name, as we would need to if we attached `Cover` to `CoverInner`. Right-click and select **Attach**, or from the Ribbon go to **Graphite Modeling Tools | Geometry (All) | Attach**.

8. Enter Borders Sub-Object mode (press 3) and drag a Marquee over the object to select its open edges. Then right-click and select **Bridge Settings** (`\Packt3dsMax\UI Settings\Packt2013_UI.ui`) or go to the Ribbon and go to **Graphite Modeling Tools | Borders | Bridge** (for settings, click on the rollout below the **Bridge** icon). In the options, set the **Segments** value to 2 and then press the *Enter* key.

9. In **Edge** mode (press 2), select the loop you added via the bridge polygons segments and select **Chamfer** from the **Quad** menu. Push the divided loop so it lies closer to the top and bottom of the piece as shown in the next screenshot. These additional loops will help keep the edges of the form tight when it is later subdivided.

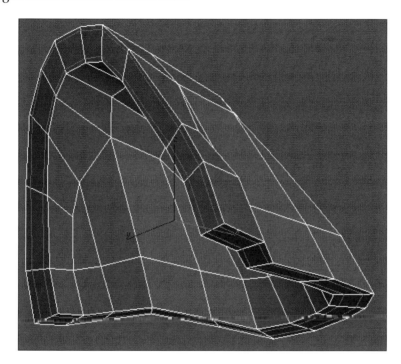

10. Right-click and select **Top-level** editing mode. Right-click and select **Unhide All**, and then go to the Body object and copy **Symmetry** and **TurboSmooth** as instances one at a time to the Cover object. Being instances, they will toggle on and off together. Within the **TurboSmooth** modifier, tick on **Isoline Display** so that only the structural wireframe of the model is shown, not all the subdivided edges.

The process of creating the cockpit hatch on the front of the model would be rather similar to what we did for the cover, except for the additional challenge of working down the model's **Symmetry** modifier mirror line. Generally, if you extrude a polygon on the symmetry line there will be one side of the extrusion facing inward that you should delete. Often an extrusion off the center line will have a little drift away from X = 0.00 that you can manually check and correct point by point. You can often do this quickly by selecting the border on the symmetry line and scaling it flat in X and moving it back to X = 0.00 after scaling.

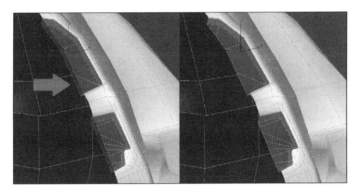

An example model representing the process covered in this chapter is provided in the content files for the book under \Packt3dsMax\Chapter 03\FinalBaseModel.max.

The rest of the detail on this model could be added as surface detail by sculpting in an application such as ZBrush or Mudbox. Even though it follows our design, this base shape can be modified in many ways to generate alternative designs, as we'll see in the next topic.

First, very briefly, the next section highlights features of the sculpting steps by which we could quickly create a textured detail level to map onto a model derived from this one. Some of these steps are expanded upon in later chapters, such as UV mapping, assigning a material, and exporting a model.

A preview of a sculpting workflow

The modeling steps we've already been through can be leveraged further to add more fine detail to the model, but to demonstrate this all the way through to complete realization of the design drawing would take many more pages of rather similar operations. Instead, it would be more instructive to show a few features of a sculpting workflow, which can be used to obtain detail from a high-resolution model for texture mapping onto a low-resolution model.

The steps for sculpting an existing model begins with creating texture co-ordinates.

UV mapping (texture co-ordinates) flatten the model's 3D polygons into a flat square. **U** refers to horizontal texture space, and **V** refers to vertical texture space. This space easily matches the width and height of a Photoshop document. The classic concept of UV mapping is to imagine the surface of a dice (3D) being unfolded into a single flat surface (2D), so each facet can be painted with unique features. Details of the **Unwrap UVW** modifier in 3ds Max are discussed in *Chapter 7, The Mystery of the Unfolding Polygons: Mapping Models for Texturing*.

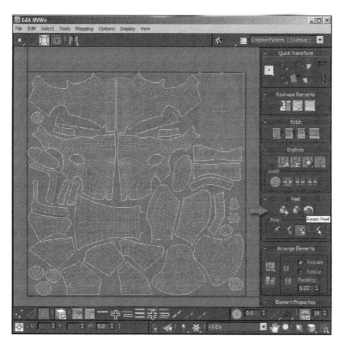

Once the model has texture co-ordinates, it can be exported to an `.obj` file for sculpting in ZBrush (or Mudbox or a similar sculpting package). This is not a ZBrush tutorial, so if you want to pick up ZBrush, visit `www.pixologic.com` and Eat3D in particular for DVD demonstrations, or see *ZBrush 4 Sculpting for Games: Beginner's Guide, Manuel Scherer, Packt Publishing*. For advanced users, also consult *EAT 3D: ZBrush Hard Surface Techniques 1* and *2* at `http://eat3d.com`.

In ZBrush parlance, the object we import becomes a **Tool**, and once loaded is set in the **Edit** mode (press *T*) on the canvas, adjusted, and then sent out again as an object. There is also a native "ZBrush to 3ds Max" command in ZBrush called **GoZ**, which automatically transfers content between the two applications. You can go both ways too, but it must be first initiated from within ZBrush before it installs the **GoZ** icon in 3ds Max on the Main Toolbar.

In ZBrush, it is handy to go to **Polygroups** and click on **Auto Groups with UV**. You can then toggle *Shift + F* to view the UV islands to confirm they are all good. The **PolyFrame** view of the imported 3ds Max model is shown in the following screenshot with one Polygroup unmasked:

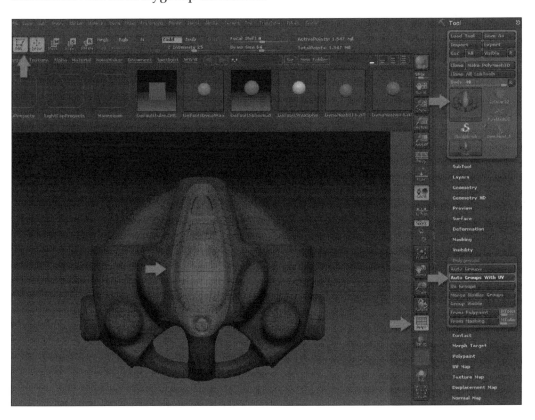

With clever masking of areas of the active Tool you can apply **Deformations** such as **Inflate** to get controlled form changes. Brush and cursor-driven edits can be moderated from a powerful **Stroke** menu. This lets you set perfectly circular or square mask. Its **Lazybrush** and **Backtrack** options help to ensure your strokes follow a curved or straight **Path** without wobbling. An example is shown in the following screenshot:

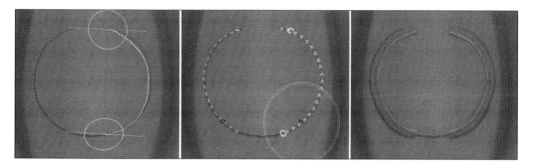

ZBrush requires geometry to be subdivided to obtain high resolution for brushwork. This is done through the **Geometry | Divide** commands. You can either **Smooth** your subdivisions, which softens the surface, or subdivide exactly. ZBrush's dependency on subdividing the entire model means that the base model should be composed totally of four-sided polygons or quads.

After detailing the model, you can extract the normal or displacement map using the **Normal Map** or **Displacement Map** menu. Before you begin, slide the **Geometry | Sdiv** slider to its lowest level. You can also click on the **Lower Res** button. You can only extract textures off the model at the base division level.

In the **Normal Map** menu, generally it is not a good idea to generate a normal map with **SmoothUVs** and **SNormals** turned on, since this changes the shape of the UV projection. When you click on **Create NormalMap** the application takes a little time to calculate a result. The size of the texture created is determined by the **UV Map Size** set in the **UV Map** panel. You may want to turn on FlipV for use in 3ds Max so you don't have to flip the UVs in 3ds Max later or flip the generated texture in Photoshop. Once the normal map has been generated, click on **Clone NM** so it will appear in the **Texture** library (on the left of the screen). You can then click on the **Texture** library icon and click on **Export** for the cloned normal map, which saves it to the disk. For displacement, it is much the same, except you use the **Displacement Map** options.

1. Having generated a normal map containing the sculpted detail, back in 3ds Max, go to **File | Import** and browse to your exported OBJ file. This likely differs a lot in form from the original OBJ file you exported to ZBrush. In the import options, be sure to set **Import as Single Mesh**.

2. You can test the normal map and displacement map by enabling the mental ray renderer. Press *F10* and go to the **Common** tab and scroll down to find the **Assign Renderer** section and there, click on the three dots to the right of **Production**. After that assign a **Standard** material to the imported OBJ model via the Material Editor.

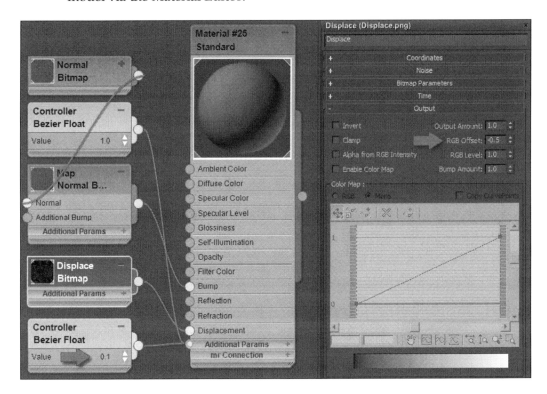

3. For a normal map, you should add a standard **Normal Bump** map to the **Bump** channel of the **Standard** material. You should set its contribution value from 0.3 (or 30 percent) to 1 (or 100 percent) to accurately reflect the texture. The **Normal Bump** map's **Normal** channel takes a **Bitmap** map in which you can assign the texture file you generated and exported from ZBrush. Again, .tga and .png are recommended formats. For displacement, you should check the **RGB Offset** value for the displacement map offset so that its black and white values correctly calculate to mid gray, as shown in the previous screenshot on the right. ZBrush defaults to a "mid gray equals no displacement" setting, where black displaces inward and white displaces outward.

If you use a **Standard** material with NVIDIA iray, it won't display a texture, since NVIDIA iray is oriented toward materials such as the **Autodesk Generic** type. You have to make sure that **Enable** is checked in the **Generic** material's parameters dialog for the **Bump** channel if you want to leverage it, even after you assign a bitmap to it. The **Generic** material has no channel for displacement. Instead you can use an **Arch and Design** preset. An example is available from CG Cookie at `http://vimeo.com/34604143`.

Of course, if your goal is to use assets in a game editor, you'll probably wind up finalizing settings for bump and displacement in the game editor rather than in 3ds Max, or in a specialized real-time asset previewing tool, such as Marmoset Toolbag (`www.marmoset.co`).

4. In the next screenshot, I've shown my ZBrush sculpt alongside the low-resolution model rendered using only the normal map. You can see that the small-scale detail is better preserved than large-scale changes in form. For this reason it is better to model large features in 3ds Max and do small, surface details in ZBrush. To preserve the large form details faithfully, one has to either reduce the polycount in ZBrush using the **Decimation Master** Zplugin or retopologize the mesh by hand, for which there are various methods, as we'll see later in *Chapter 9, Go with the Flow Retopology in 3ds Max*.

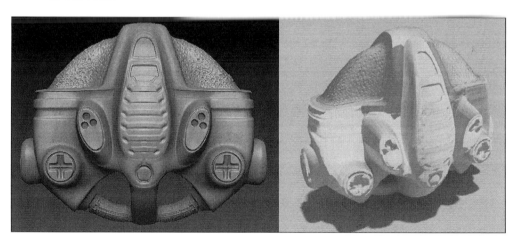

Summary

In summary, throughout this chapter you've built up fine control of modeling tools and should understand the various ways to access those tools, namely the Command Panel parameters, the Ribbon, and the Quad menu. We considered the separation of processes that contribute to a base model for the processes that contribute to surface detail on a model. For the base model, the repeated use of a few tools underlies most modeling procedures, and hopefully you'll be able to achieve the insight into determining which tools to use in a given situation, and the fluency to work through the base modeling process quickly.

In the next chapter, we continue to explore elements of model construction using the same Robot Spider we've built, adding legs and other features, particularly focused on deriving curved surface geometry from 2D Shape objects.

4

Mod My Ride: Extending upon a Base Model

This chapter demonstrates ways in which various modifiers can be used to adjust modeled content quickly. The main emphasis is to provide alternative designs with little work, by modifying existing content. We also cover basic concepts for soft-surface modeling, smoothing groups, and generating geometric models from shapes or curves.

These are the topics covered in the chapter:

- Marking poly loops
- Soft modeling
    - ° Modeling with Soft Selection
    - ° Modeling with Shift brush
    - ° Modeling with Free-Form Deformation (FFD) modifiers
    - ° Relaxation techniques

- Using Poly Select to apply modifiers to Sub-Object selections
- Generating shapes from edge selections
    - ° The Lathe modifier process
    - ° Shape construction and interpolation

- Comparing the Sweep modifier with the Loft object
- Smoothing Groups
- Generating forms using Cloth

Marking Poly Loops

A **poly loop** is a loop of polygons that can be colored to mark prominent features in a model to guide animators or orient the modeler. They can be used to help indicate key forms. In our case, we'll isolate some selections in the body of the vehicle:

1. Open the downloaded scene \Packt3dsMax\Chapter 04\BaseLegs.max, upon which you'll be confronted with the creepy crawly seen in the following screenshot.

   The legs were mocked up very quickly and aren't articulated. This will be added later. The design of the legs is based on the feet having a flexible, large surface area for traction, and spikes that can assist navigation, a feature one often finds with insects. In the scene, you will notice gaps between the legs and the body, which aren't shown below, because we're going to create a model to fill this gap so that the legs can be instances.

2. Select the Body object and press *F4* to show edged faces. Note that the model displays blue **Map Seams** to landmark the UV islands used for texturing. Some of these lines will be convenient to mark with poly loops, as seen in the following screenshot:

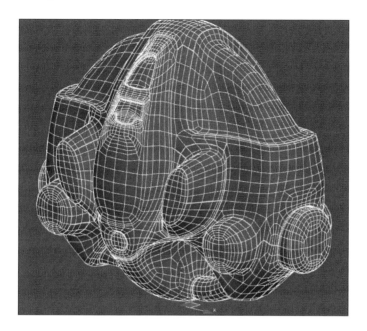

3. Convert the Body object to an **Editable Poly** object. This will collapse the **Unwrap UVW** modifier into the model data. Press *4* to enter the polygon Sub-Object mode. Around the forward bulge of the cockpit, select polygons using the left-click on one, then hold *Shift + LMB* on another one next to it. Doing this will select a loop.

4. Press *M* to open the **Material Editor** and hold *Shift* + *LMB* to drag the existing **Autodesk Generic** material in the **Slate** canvas to produce a clone of it. Double-click on the copy and rename it Loops. In its properties, below **Color | Use Color**, change the gray swatch by clicking on it to have a different color (refer to the following screenshot). Right-click on the material and choose **Assign Material to Selection**. In the view browser, toggle with *F4*. Repeat this for similar loops that might help define key structural forms in the model.

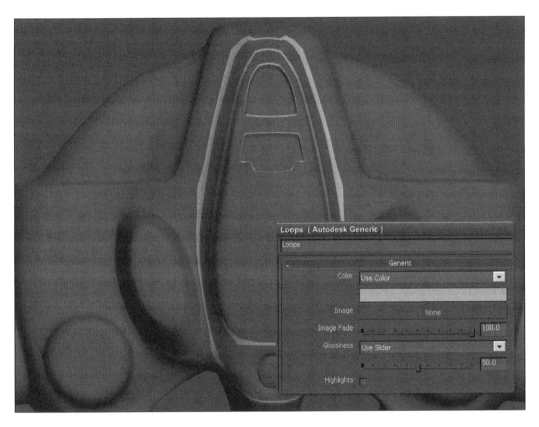

5. In the previous screenshot, which shows a wide loop where the cockpit bulges from the main body, the top is slightly kinked where the polygons run in a loop, but not quite smoothly. This could be a good target for reflowing the edges that exist in the model so as to give the loop a better shape.

6. The following screenshot shows this alteration, after using the **Cut** and **RemoveLoop** tools. The colored loop is now a lot better. The changed loops and the additional ones can be viewed by opening `\Packt3dsMax\Chapter 04\BaseLegsLoopFix.max`.

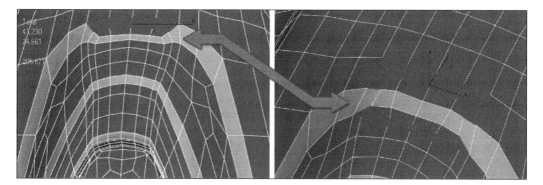

Soft modeling

There are quite a few ways to deform a section of the model in a way that includes a soft falloff from the location of the edit.

1. Open `\Packt3dsMax\Chapter 04\SoftSelectionStart.max` and search for Leg01. The other legs for the spidery vehicle are instanced clones, so a change to this will affect the others equally. Right-click and choose **Hide Unselected**. In the **Front** view, press the **Zoom Extends** icon to frame the object.

2. In the **Modify** tab , disable the **TurboSmooth** modifier by double-clicking on the light bulb icon for that modifier, or else right-click on it and choose **Off**.

Soft modeling with Soft Selection

Soft Selection is a method of transforming a Sub-Object selection with a falloff, to produce gradual deformations. There are three ways to enable **Soft Selection** for Sub-Object transforms. You can use the Ribbon under **Graphite Modeling Tools |**

Polygon Modeling, where there is a **Use Soft Selection** icon  that displays a help illustration if you hover the mouse over it. Clicking this icon opens a section on the Ribbon that shows parameters for the tool. This can either be floated or dragged by its upper-left corner to where you would like to see it on the Ribbon.

The primary parameter to set a value for is **Falloff**. This sets the influence, via a gradient from red (strong) to blue (weak), of the current selection on the surrounding area.

- Select a group of vertices on the top part of the leg and toggle **Soft Selection** on and off to see the difference. Also, adjust the **Falloff** value to see how its influence spreads. Move (then undo) the points to see the effect this has.

In the Ribbon, the **Soft Selection** parameters include an **Ignore Backfacing** toggle which, if not active, prevents the far side of the model from indirectly following the selection transformed, facing the camera. When it is active it highlights in blue. This would normally be enabled, but if you were to edit, say, a model of a decorative plate, and want to protect the bottom polygons from the changes to the top part, it would make sense to turn **Use Backfaces** off. This option can be found in the Command Panel, in a checkbox called **Affect Backfacing**.

Since the **Falloff** shape is radial, you may at times want to moderate its effect. To do so, you can use the **Paint Soft Selection** brush in the Ribbon or modify the **Falloff** shape using **Pinch** or **Bubble**, which influences the falloff graph's tightness and spread. Another option is to use **Edit**, a mode that lets your mouse movements shape the falloff degree. The following screenshot shows how the cursor changes to a circle, and dragging it vertically in the view increases or decreases the falloff radius.

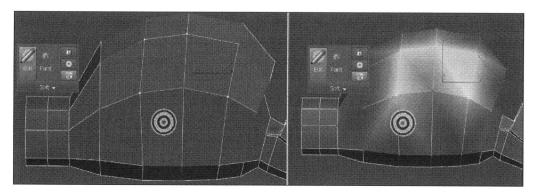

Also, as shown here, you can shade the falloff using the **Soft Selection** parameters in the **Modify** panel  within the editable poly itself. The tools already mentioned in the Ribbon have analogs there.

By default, the **Falloff** region spreads over the surrounding geometric structure even if the polygons are not contiguous. A good example is fingers, where falloff from polygons selected on one finger can affect those of its neighbor. You can use the **Edge Distance** parameter to limit the falloff spread only to the surface contiguous with the current selection.

A final way of evoking **Soft Selection** is by assigning it to the **Quad** menu; this has already been done in `Packt3dsMax\PacktUI.ui`. Personally, I like to fit the floated **Soft Selection** tools into the empty gray space at the very top of the 3ds Max window.

We can transform the selection with falloff and use this method to make adjustments more readily to complex curves. Bear in mind that the transform done can include rotating and scaling, not just moving. Be sure to check how changes you make to the leg look with **TurboSmooth** turned back on.

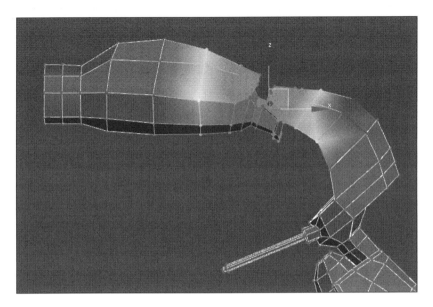

Soft modeling with the Shift brush

You will find the **Shift** brush menu in the **Freeform** tab of the Ribbon. The **Freeform** tab is next to the **Graphite Modeling Tools** tab that is exposed in the UI by default, as shown in the following screenshot:

The **Shift** brush allows you to paint deformations in the view's **Screen** space. **Screen space** is where the XY axes are aligned with the current view, so no matter how you orbit the scene, the XY axes are realigned to the view.

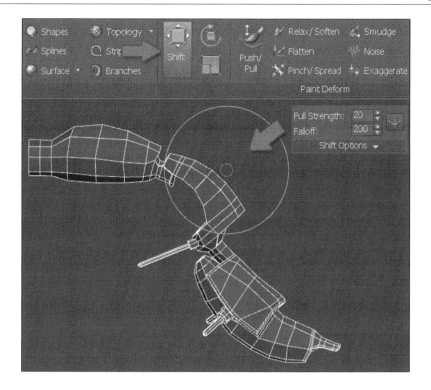

This tool can be used with a **Mirror** axis via the [▦] icon, which turns blue when active. Its settings dialog box lets you set the **Mirror Axis** value.

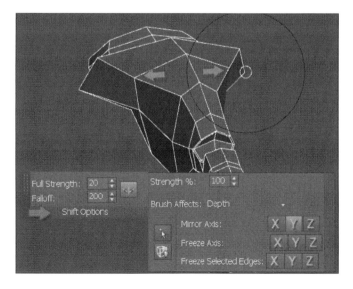

Soft modeling with Free-Form Deformations

Another way to apply gradual deformations to a model is to wrap it in a bounding lattice of control points and adjust the control points—a lot like the Warp tool in Photoshop, except in three dimensions. Free-Form Deformations come in the form of modifiers either based on boxes or cylinders. For this example, we'll use the **FFD(box)** modifier, which lets us set the number of control points manually for each axis. One nice feature of the FFD modifiers is they can be applied to several objects at once.

1. Open \Packt3dsMax\Chapter 04\SoftModelingFFD.max, click on the **Named Selection Sets** rollout in the Main toolbar, and choose *All Legs* from the drop-down list. This selects the legs, and you will notice in the **Modify** tab ▨ that they are instances of each other.

2. Go to the **Modifier List** menu and choose the **FFD(box)** modifier with all the legs selected. It will apply a default 4 x 4 x 4 control lattice to the selection. In the parameters for the modifier, click on **Set Number of Points**. **Length** is the depth of the model, **Width** is the distance across the model in the front view, and **Height** is the distance from top to bottom. You could confirm this by setting **Length** = 2, **Width** = 3, and **Height** = 4 and observe the result. A value of 2 is the minimum value you can enter, and it gives you points at each end of the control box, as shown in the following screenshot:

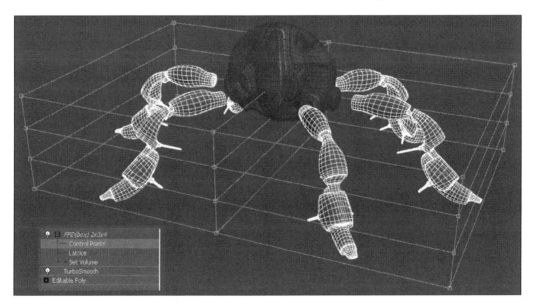

3. To select the control points, expand the + icon next to the modifier's name, then click on **Control Points**. Now you can Marquee select them in the viewport.

4. Set the **FFD(box)** to 3x3x4, click on **Control Points** so you can adjust them, and then select the two middle rows of control points in the **Front view**. Scale these inward, and then move them down slightly in Z. After that, Marquee select the three lowest rows and scale them inward using the uniform scale, as shown in the following screenshot. Turn off **Control Points** when this is done.

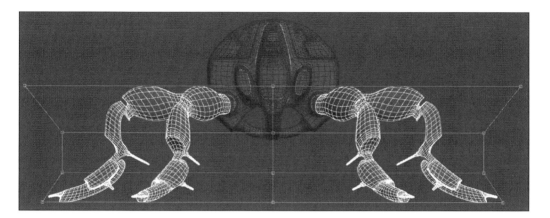

5. In the **Named Selection Sets**, choose Body and apply an **FFD(Box)** to the selection. Set the **Control Points** to 3x3x3, then click on **Control Points** so you can adjust the model. Freely rearrange the lattice to try and make a more interesting shape. It usually helps to first select entire rows of control points to make broad changes on, and then adjust individual points afterward.

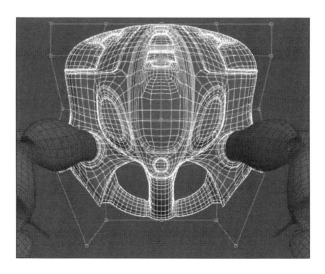

6. Don't forget to turn off **Control Points** when you are done.

Relaxation techniques

What **Relax** does is average the area of a selection of polygons, so larger polygons get small and small polygons get bigger. This often has the effect of smoothing the flow of edges in a model. It is a very simple tool, but has a huge impact on workflow.

In 3ds Max, **Relax** functions tend to shrink the object. To avoid this, it is worthwhile to use the third-party **TopoRelax** plugin, which provides a modifier that relaxes an object without changing its volume. It is written by Marius Silaghi and can be purchased at www.mariussilaghi.com/toporelax.htm.

An example of using **Relax** within the **Edit Geometry** section of an **Edit Poly** modifier is shown in the following screenshot. You can also find it in the Ribbon under **Graphite Modeling Tools | Geometry (All) | Relax**. The **Amount** value for **Relax** is iterative. **Relax** can be applied as a modifier too, which is helpful when working on multiple objects.

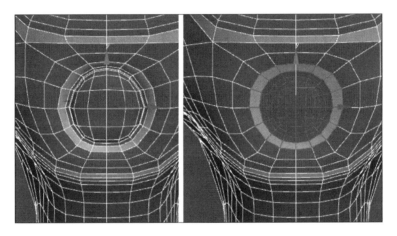

Using Poly Select to apply modifiers to Sub-Object selections

Normally, a modifier is applied to an entire object. You can apply a modifier to a Sub-Object selection (vertices, edges, or faces). For this to work as you continue editing, you have to retain the Sub-Object selection at all times or the result will change. This can be a problem if you are going back and forth between objects and up and down the layer stack, and in particular it is a problem if you happen to deselect the Sub-Object components that the modifiers above were depending on. The **Poly Select** modifier helps avoid this problem, because its only purpose is to demarcate a Sub-Object selection for its use up the stack. **Poly Select** also works on primitive objects or shape-based objects that have not been converted to **Editable Poly**.

A video demonstration by 3DBuzz on topology dependency issues while working with Sub-Object selections and modifiers can be found at http://www.youtube.com/watch?v=plhrkCB0GVA. We can add some additional utility to this in the modifier.

In the following screenshot, we see that if we add a **Relax** modifier to a Sub-Object selection, it applies only to that selection. Then, if we change the point selection below, the **Relax** modifier is upset by this (unless we reselect the same points again).

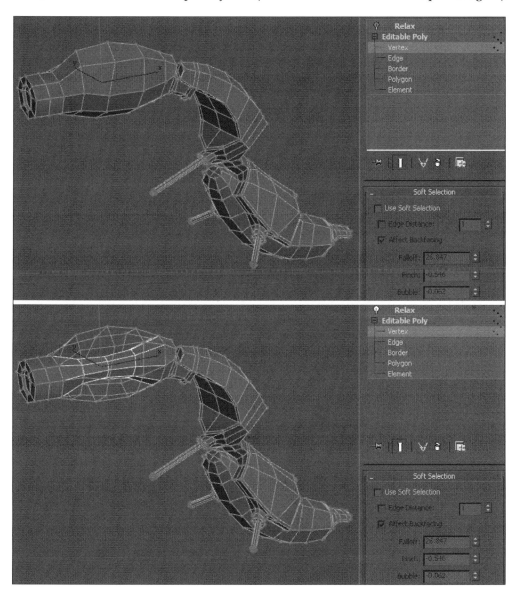

Note that the **Show End Result** icon 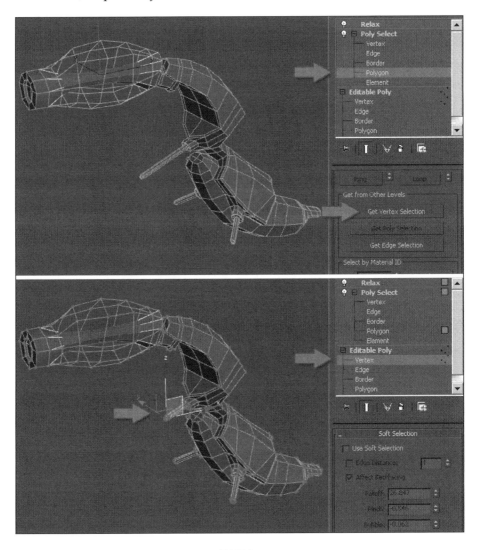 is toggled active for the screenshot.

If we keep the vertex option selected and add a **Poly Select** modifier, we can click on either **Vertex**, **Edge**, or **Polygon** mode in the modifier and directly select components in the view. As shown in the following screenshot, I chose the **Polygon** mode and then **Get Vertex Selection**. This acquires the current selection from below in the stack. This can be used to convert a selection from one Sub-Object mode to another (remember when you collapse the stack to **Editable Poly**, each Sub-Object selection remains current for its type). This is a little complex, so a better way is to right-click in the view and from the **Quad** menu choose **Convert to Vertex**, **Convert to Edge**, or **Convert to Face**, respectively.

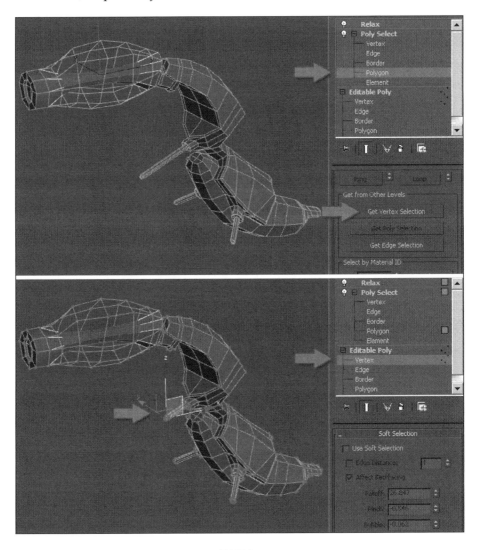

The previous screenshot shows one benefit of using **Poly Select**. Once you set a selection in the modifier for the **Relax** modifier to operate upon, you can go down to the editable poly level (or some other modifier below, such as **Edit Poly**) and adjust things as you wish without having to worry about messing up the Sub-Object dependency.

Generating shapes from edge selections

Any edge selection can be converted to a Spline. Splines have several uses. They can be rendered as wire-like volumes. They can be used as guides for animation, for polygon extrusions, and even UV mapping. They can be used as profiles for the **Extrude**, **Sweep**, and **Lathe** modifiers to generate new geometry. **Closed** shapes can be the base for **Garments** used with the **Cloth** modifier, and **open** shapes can be used to define **Hair and Fur** geometry.

In this example, we'll generate shapes from existing geometry and use it to create a model connecting the Body and *Legs* of the vehicle constructed in the earlier sections.

1. Open the scene \Packt3dsMax\Chapter 04\ShapesStart.max.

2. Select Body by pressing *H* (**Select by Name**) and zoom and orbit so you can see the lower part (shown in the following screenshot). Press 2 to enter the **Edge** mode and select the loop shown on the end of the front protrusion.

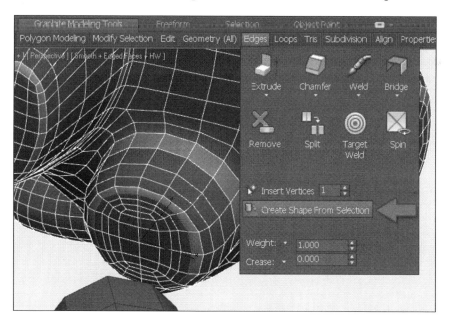

3. If you are using `PacktUI.ui`, you can right-click on it to access **Create Shape from Edges** in the **Quad** menu. If not, go to the **Edges** panel found in **Ribbon | Graphite Modeling Tools**, then click on **Create Shape From Selection**. In the pop-up dialog, for the **Shape Type** option, click on the **Linear** radio button. This means the generated Spline will look exactly the same as the edge loop it is derived from, without smoothing.

4. Name the object `LegRing`, then click on **OK**. You'll still be editing the `Body`, so right-click and choose the **Top-level**, then click on the new shape `LegRing`.

5. Press *Ctrl + T* (**Transform Toolbox**) and set the object pivot to **Center | Center**.

6. Repeat this for an edge loop on the end part of the `Leg03` object facing the region we're working.

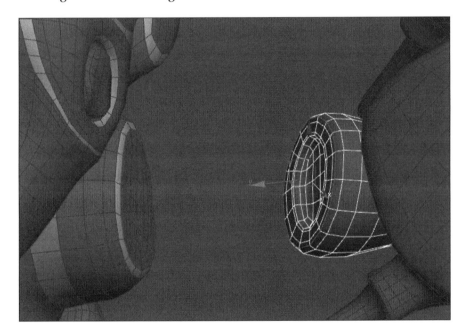

7. Right-click and choose **Create Shape from Edges**, making sure the **Shape Type** is set to **Linear**. After creating this object, at **Top-level**, select `LegRing`.

   We could use a **Loft** here, but it would be easier to just work with editable poly tools.

8. Convert both circles to editable poly, which will generate flat objects from the two rings. Select `LegRing`, right-click, and select **Attach** (`PacktUI.ui`), or in the **Modify** tab 🖉 of the Command Panel select **Attach** and then click on the other mesh you just generated to combine it into `LegRing`.

9. Right-click and choose **Hide Unselected**. In **Polygons** mode, ensure the two circular end faces are facing away from each other. You can use the **Flip** command to adjust them.

10. In **Borders** mode, select both sets of open edges and right-click and choose **BridgeSettings** (`PacktUI.ui`). Set the **Segments** value to 2, then in **Edge** mode, select the middle edge loop and transform it, as shown in the following screenshot:

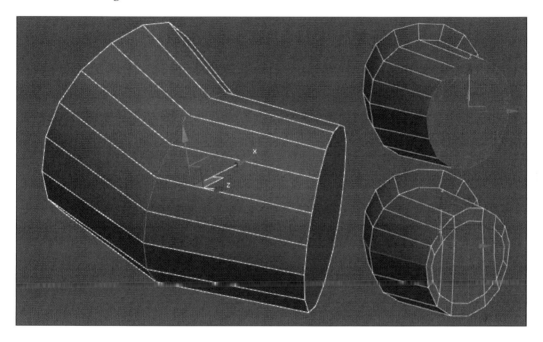

11. The ends of the object are single polygons with many points around the side. This can be fixed using the maxscript **Quad Cap Pro** by Marius Silaghi (`http://www.mariussilaghi.com/products/quad-cap-pro`), but unfortunately, this is not free. The long way around is to **Inset** the faces slightly, then use **Cut**, with **Vertex Snap** (*S*) active, to construct quads across, as shown in the previous screenshot.

Now that we have this bridging object, which touches the body on one end and the leg on the other, we need to construct a plausible fulcrum so that when the leg transforms (moves or rotates) it seems to be joined to the body. Being a creative challenge, there are many ways to achieve this. What we'll do is use the same **Create Shape from Edges** approach to create a profile curve. From that curve we'll generate the next part of the model. A profile is a single curve that represents the contour of geometry. We'll **Lathe** or spin the curve into a solid part.

The Lathe modifier process

This section details the most common usage of the **Lathe** modifier, starting from a shape extracted from an existing part of the model:

1. Select the Leg01 model, right-click, and choose **Hide Unselected**. In the **Edge** mode (2), use *Ctrl + LMB* to select the edge shown in the following screenshot. Make sure the edge selection goes to the center point indicated on the Leg01 model. Call the shape LatheShape.

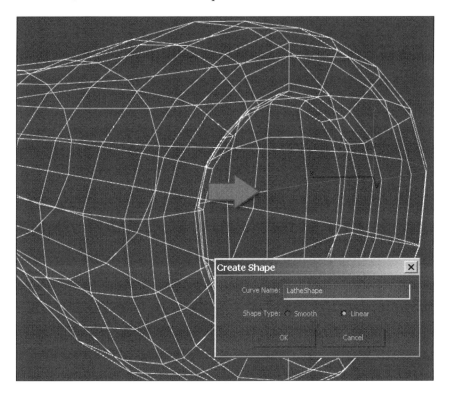

2. In the **Top-level** mode (6), select the newly created LatheShape. Press 2 to enter the **Segment** mode and orbit the view so you can see the Spline from the top, as seen in the following screenshot. Right-click and choose **Refine**, then click on the line to add a point where indicated. Be sure to work in the **Top** viewport.

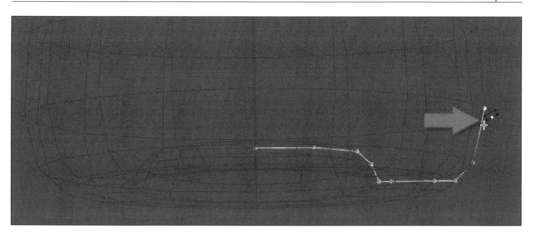

3. Drag the end point outward a small amount. At the **Top-level**, *Shift* + move a clone of the line, as shown in the following screenshot. Adjust the overlapping part so it lines up as in the lower part of the screenshot:

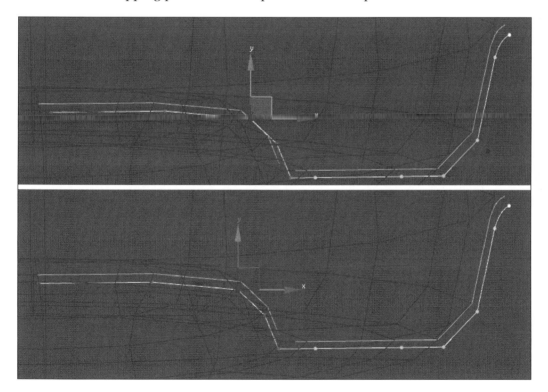

4. These two lines are unique objects, so attach them together and then close the gap. To do so, select one point, then right-click and choose **Connect**. A dotted pick line will be seen as you mouse over the target point, as shown in the following screenshot:

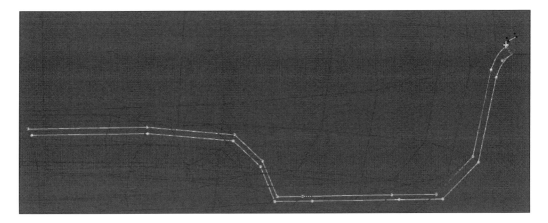

5. Having created the profile, make sure its pivot is aligned to the world. To do so, in the Command Panel, click on the **Hierarchy** tab ▦ and click on **Affect Pivot Only** in the **Adjust Pivot** tab, then click on **Align to World**.

6. To add the **Lathe** modifier, go to **Modifiers | Patch/Spline Editing** and select **Lathe**. Another way to expose the modifier's list rollout is in the Command Panel | **Modifier** tab ▨, and press *L* so the list jumps down to entries starting with L, of which **Lathe** is the first. The result you get will likely be in the wrong axis, so set the parameters of the modifier so that it works well, using the **Direction | X Y Z** buttons. You can also expand the [+] to show the **Axis** control of the **Lathe** and rotate it manually. If the model shows black, tick the **Flip Normals** tickbox. Also tick **Weld Core** so the center of the **Lathe** modifier doesn't have any small holes. If there are large holes, you can use **Cap Borders** to resolve them the same way we did in the previous section. In this case, if the **Segments** value is set to **16**, it matches with the radial segments in both the leg model and the bridging model. To avoid a hole in the first place, for the Spline the Loft is based on, ensure that its start and end points line up well.

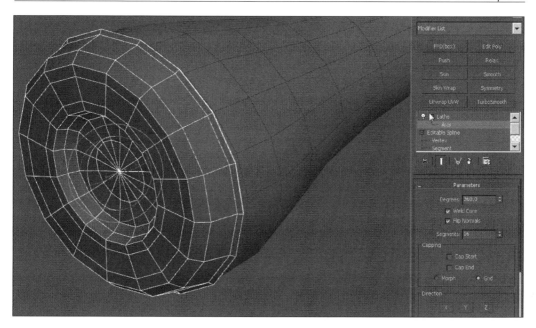

7. In the following screenshot, we are jumping ahead of the progression slightly, but still using the same tools we've already covered (mainly **Bridge**, **SwiftLoop**, and **Relax**). Some additional features have been added to the joint to complete the fulcrum. You can use **Attach** to combine the joint mesh with the **Lathe** result.

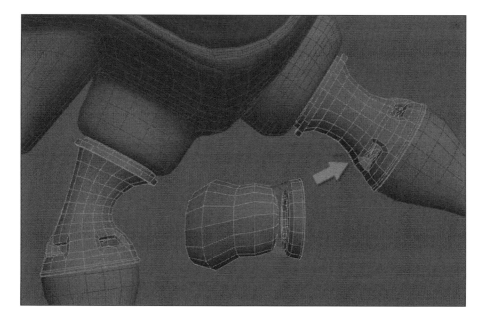

Shape construction and interpolation

An important aspect of generating geometry from shapes is the **Interpolation** value of the shape. **Interpolation** is similar to subdivision. In 3D, a curve is really a composite of straight segments, and the more you have the rounder your curve will look. A 16-sided cylinder, for example, looks quite chunky, but is still recognizably round. If you subdivide it once, you get a better idea of its roundness, yet the model is still only made of straight lines. Each Spline has an **Interpolation** parameter, which defaults to 6. In most cases the value is too high, especially if you are making a low-poly model that will be subdivided later. In the following example, we'll cover construction of shapes in more depth and also see how a change in interpolation affects the final model result. We'll use the **Sweep** modifier, which uses a path Spline and a profile Spline to generate a rail.

1. Open the scene `\Packt3dsMax\Chapter 04\SweepDemoStart.max`. The vehicle we've been working on so far is hidden, except for its one leg. Just as in the previous section, a Spline called `SweepShape` has been generated from edges of the model.

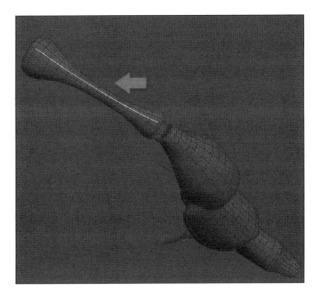

2. Let's make a profile to be swept along `SweepShape`. Go to the **Top** view (*T*) and then go to **Create** | **Shapes** and select **Arc**. An Arc is defined as a line from end to end, and then the curvature is added by dragging away from the line. Draw the Arc with any size and curve you like.

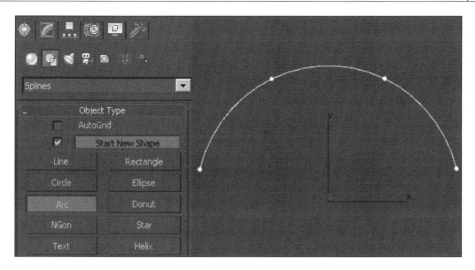

3. Turn off the **Start New Shape** tickbox, which is shown on in the previous screenshot. This means the next Spline you begin will be part of the current object. Drag in another **Arc** under it, facing the other way.

4. You may want to turn the **Start New Shape** tickbox back on after making the second arc under the first. For the lower arc, Marquee select its points and convert them to corners using **Corner** in the **Quad** menu.

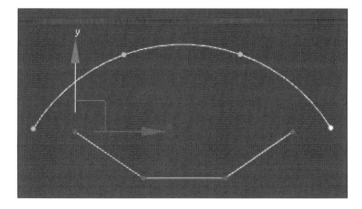

5. To join the gaps, right-click and choose **Connect**, as we did in the previous section. Let's add a V-shaped feature. To do this, right-click and choose **Refine** and click mid-way along the added segment to insert a new vertex. Move this new vertex down, as shown in the following screenshot:

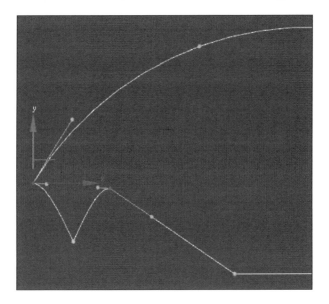

6. The initial points have handles that influence the curvature between the points. Using the XY plane of the transform gizmo (*W*), adjust the green handles so the V shape is straight. Sometimes the handle and the transform gizmo overlap, making it difficult to move in XY. To overcome this, shoot the handle out in one axis beyond the gizmo, then you can use the XY plane easily. Another way to deal with the problem is to mouse over a different point in the selection so the one whose handles you are trying to adjust isn't overlapped by the gizmo.

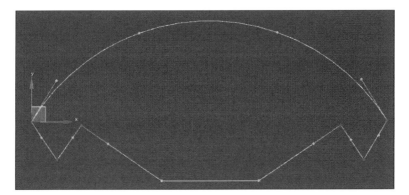

7. Suppose you want to combine or cut away a separate shape from the existing one. This can be done using the **Boolean** commands in the parameters of the Spline. First, we need to create a shape with which to affect the current one. Create a **Circle** shape and place it as shown in the following screenshot. Use the **X** option in the **Align** window to ensure the two shapes line up nicely.

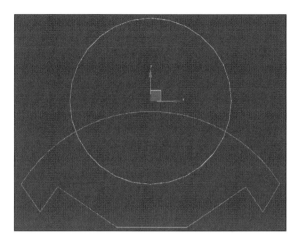

8. Select Arc001 and choose **Attach**. In order to subtract the circle, we have to first add it to the object. Then, in **Spline** mode (3), select **Subtract** 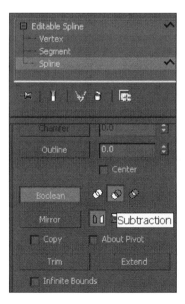 in **Boolean** and click on the added circle Spline as shown in the following screenshot.

The result you will get is shown below:

Now, we can sweep this profile along the SweepShape Spline on the leg.

1. Select SweepShape and add the **Sweep** modifier. It will automatically apply one of ten available preset profiles. We need to swap this with our own. Also, we need to set the scale and alignment of the swept geometry.

2. To set a custom shape, we first need to make sure the scale of the profile is agreeable. It will probably be much too large initially. To avoid that, select Arc001 and scale it down to about the scale shown in the following screenshot. Also press *Ctrl + T* to open the **Transform Toolbox** and click on **Center | Center** in the pivot options and then the **Reset Xform** button **R**. What this does is commit the scale amount you just set as the new 100 percent scale for the object.

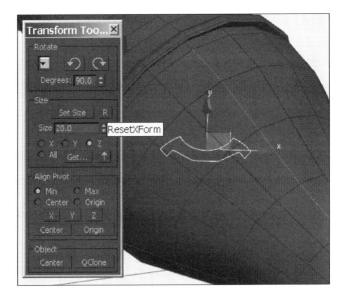

3. Select `SweepShape` again, and in the Command Panel, in the **Modifier** tab, 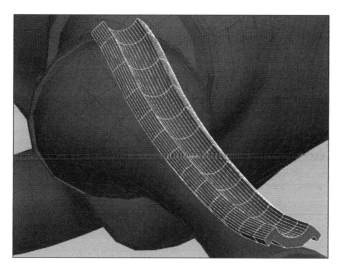 set the parameter for the **Sweep** so the radio button **Use Custom Shape** is ticked.

4. Click on **Pick** and then on the `Arc001` shape in the view, or use the **Select by Name** icon .

    The result you'll get should follow the path given by `SweepShape`. The nice thing is that you can still edit the profile shape and the path up to the point where you collapse the model to editable poly. What we'll look at now is reducing the polygon count of the generated model by reducing the **Interpolation** value of the profile Spline. It's good to see this as a comparison, which is why we haven't set it to the correct value already. Notice that the model has a nice curvature but too many lines. Also, the ends are **Ngons** (having more than four sides) because they are simply an open border that has been capped.

5. Select Arc001, and in its parameters, set **Interpolation Steps** to 1. This makes the swept model suddenly look very chunky, but we can always subdivide it later.

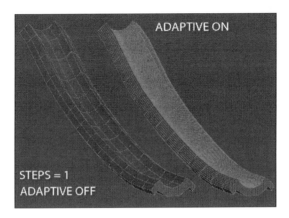

For an experiment, toggle on **Adaptive** and notice the mesh count of the swept model leaps skyward, but the curvature is now perfect. The problem is, it contains too many polygons. So make sure **Adaptive** is never ticked in this kind of situation. Where you might use **Adaptive** is when using Splines as camera paths.

6. Further down in the **Sweep** modifier parameters, set the **Align Pivot** location using the grid shown in the following screenshot. Using the bottom option (highlighted) means the profile will sit nicely on top of the SweepShape path and not penetrate the leg model.

7. Lastly, as we've done in the previous section, we can use **Connect** and **Cut** in vertex mode with **Snaps** (*S*) on to resolve the open endings into quads. The result is shown in the next screenshot.

If you add a **Turbosmooth** modifier with **Smoothing Groups** ticked on, you'll see how the geometry based on a low Spline **Interpolation** value of 1 subdivides iteratively to be much the same as the version with six interpolation steps. An example of the final part, using **Sweep**, is shown in `\Packt3dsMax\Chapter 04\SweepDemoFinish.max`. Since the legs are all instances, choosing `Leg03` and attaching `SweepShape` to it merges into all the other legs at the same time.

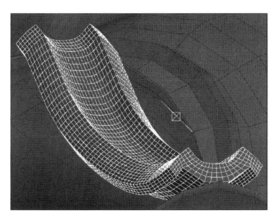

Comparing the Sweep modifier with the Loft object

The **Sweep** modifier is a simplification of the **Loft** compound object. What **Loft** offers is a way to project geometry between different profiles along the path Spline. So, you can have a square shape at one end of the form, for example, and a round shape at the other end. The **Sweep** modifier cannot do this. The **Loft** modifier—given it can blend between profiles—has topology controls, so the user can achieve both the look they are after and a good wireframe to work with. A tool related to the **Sweep** and **Loft** modifiers is the **Hose** primitive.

1. Open the scene `\Packt3dsMax\Chapter 04\LoftStart.max`. A new `LoftShape` Spline has been added along the underside of `Leg03`.

2. In the **Top** view, select `Profile01`, right-click on it, and choose **Hide Unselected**. Press *Shift* and move a clone off to the side. Set **Copy** not **Instance** in the **Clone Options**. Set the **Number of Copies** value to 2, which will give us three profiles to work with.

3. Marquee select all three shapes and right-click and press *P*; this opens the **Object Properties** dialog for the selection. When the dialog pops up, tick **Show Vertex Ticks**, then click on **OK**. This means that, in the view, you can see where the points are for the objects even when you aren't editing them.

4. Adjust the point distribution for the shapes as shown in the following screenshot. Don't add or remove any points. Since the topology of the **Loft** we'll create from these depends on the vertex structure of the Spline shape, differing vertex counts will make the **Loft** Skin slightly imperfect.

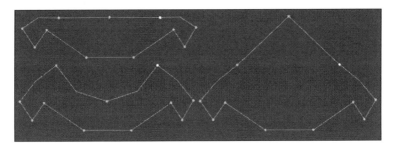

5. Using **Select by Name** (*H*), select the Spline called LoftShape, and in the **Command Panel | Create** tab ⬢ | **Geometry** ◉ section expand the roll-out currently showing **Standard Primitives**. There, choose **Compound objects**. Lofts fall in this category because they are made by combining more than one object.

6. Click on **Loft** and note that the **Creation Method** parameters appear below. Since you already have the **Path** component of the **Loft** selected, click on **Get Shape**. This will allow you to pick one of the profiles. Use **Select by Name** and choose Profile01.

7. Switch to **Command Panel**. Go to the **Modify** tab ✎, and in the **Loft** parameters, set the **Path** value to 25.0. This moves a marker along the path. Click on **Get Shape** again and this time choose Profile02. Turn off the **Get Shape** button.

8. Set the **Path** value to 75 and click on **Get Shape** again, and choose Profile03, then turn off **Get Shape** again. You should notice the geometry that's generated changes shape according to the profiles placed at each path step.

9. At present, your **Loft** will look fairly similar to the **Sweep** made in the previous topic, except the shapes of the profile are slightly different. Even this isn't too noticeable if their orientation is bottom-down. We can adjust each shape in the **Loft** at the Spline Sub-Object level (the source) but also within the **Loft** modifier itself. To do so, expand the [+] next to **Loft** and click on the **Shape** mode.

10. Once you are in the **Shape** mode, you can select, slide, rotate, and scale the profiles used by the **Loft**. Rotate each one 180 degrees and scale them to suit.

11. Slide the **Shape** to 25 percent along the path. Notice that, as it moves, the topology of the **Loft** adjusts. You can further adjust topology for the **Loft** modifier in the **Skin Parameters** section of the **Top-level Loft** parameters.

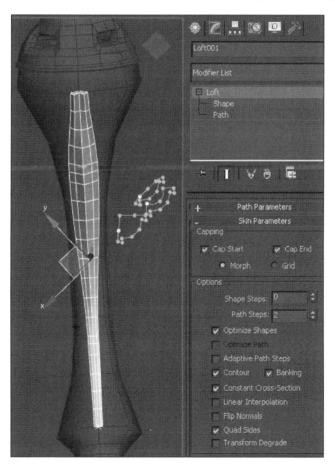

12. Drop the **Shape Steps** value to 0 and the **Path Steps** value to 2. Like the **Interpolation** value in Splines, these values regulate how dense the mesh will be.

Smoothing Groups

When you begin modeling from a primitive such as a Sphere or Cylinder, it has preset smoothing groups that make its surface look good. A smoothing group is easiest understood as a group of polygons that share the same smooth curvature. We'll look at some examples that show models with and without smoothing groups. Where you might notice smoothing groups for the first time is when you extrude from a round object and notice the extruded polygons look, by contrast, sharp and faceted. The other case is when you apply **TurboSmooth** to an object like a cube and it becomes very round. The **TurboSmooth** modifier includes an option to conserve any smooth groups demarcated within the editable poly object's **Smoothing Groups** settings.

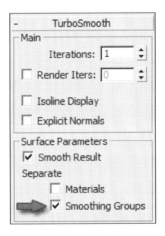

This example runs through the process of editing **Smoothing Groups** manually.

1. Reset 3ds Max and go to **Create | Standard Primitives | Tube**. Drag it out in the view, enter **Move** mode (*W*), and hold *Shift + LMB* and drag it to create a clone to one side. In the **Clone Options**, choose **Reference**. This means the copy will share changes with the original, but you can add additional modifiers to it that it won't share.

2. For the reference of Tube, go to the Command Panel and click on the **Modify** tab and add a **TurboSmooth** modifier. Select the original Tube and hold *Shift* + *LMB* to drag a further reference copy. Add a **TurboSmooth** modifier to it too, but this time, in its parameters, tick on **Surface Parameters | Smooth Result | Smoothing Groups**. An example is provided in the \Packt3dsMax\ Chapter 04\SmoothingGroupsStart.max.

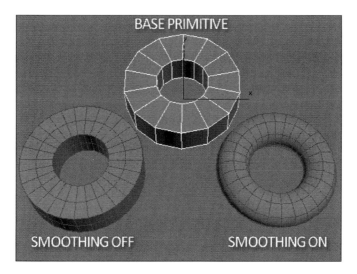

3. Make the **Height** of the original Tube 100, and set the **Height Segments** to 6.

4. Now we need to adjust the model at Sub-Object level, but we can't collapse the model to an **Editable Poly** because this will remove its relationship with the reference copies. Instead, add an **Edit Poly** modifier.

The **Edit Poly** modifier gives you access to Sub-Object level tools on a layer above the base primitive that you can still adjust. An alternative approach would be to collapse the primitive to editable poly immediately after creation and then produce clones from it.

5. For the original Tube, in the **Edit Poly** modifier, enter the **Polygon** mode (4) and select the polygons shown in the following screenshot:

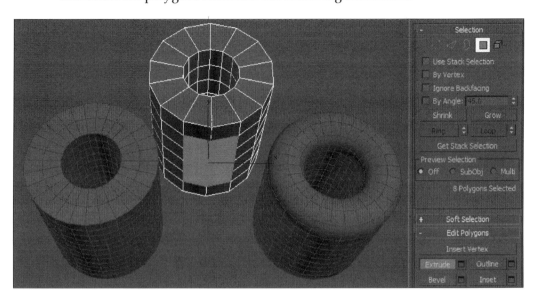

6. In the **Modify** tab, under the **Edit Poly** modifier's **Edit Polygons** section, click on **Extrude** (shown in the previous screenshot), and in the view, push out the Tube slightly. If you were to use **Extrude Settings**, a **Height** value of about 20 would be fine.

> Notice that for the **Smoothing Groups** on in the **TurboSmooth** settings, the end of the extruded part is sharp. Here's why: the polygons on the end of the extruded part originally belonged to the body of the Tube. They had a smoothing group already set. The polygons on the sides of the extruded part are new geometry, and they aren't assigned any smoothing value.

7. You can verify this by clicking a polygon on the side of the Tube and scrolling down the parameters of the **Edit Poly** modifier to find the **Smoothing Groups** section. You will see an array of numbers. Each one represents a smoothing group. The extruded faces and the side of the Tube both share the smoothing group **2**. This is why the number **2** in the array gets highlighted blue.

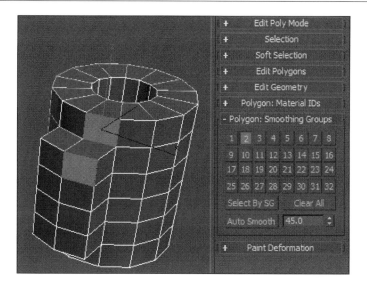

8. If you hold *Ctrl + LMB* on a polygon on the top of the Tube and add it to the current selection, the numbers **2** and **3** will go gray. This means that, from the current polygon selection, these two smoothing groups are being used, but aren't shared equally. The top uses **3** and the sides of the Tube use **2**.

9. Press *Ctrl + D* to deselect all, and then click on the sides of the extruded part. Notice that no smoothing groups highlight in the array. Where the extruded faces are new, they do not have a smoothing group at all. The edges bounding these polygons, therefore, are sharp in relation to the polygons adjacent to them. The following screenshot indicates how this works, where **0** equals no smoothing group:

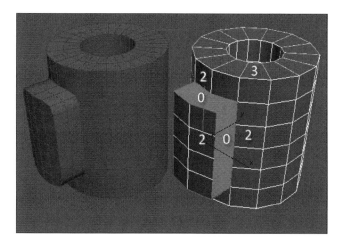

10. Assign number **2** to the sides of the extrusion. Notice that the extrusion becomes soft around its edges. Assign the sides of the extrusion the number **3**. It becomes sharp again. The **3** side is also used by the top of the Tube, but those polygons don't touch the current selection.

11. What if we wanted to assign a different smoothing group to the original sides of the Tube? There's a quick way to do this. First, press *Ctrl + LMB* on the polygons on the front of the extrusion. Once you've done this, select **4** in the **Polygon: Smoothing Groups** array to assign those a different value. Also, click on **2** to remove them from that group. Polygons can have more than one smoothing group assigned, but we don't want that now.

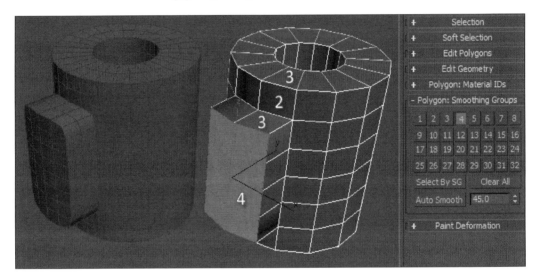

12. Having isolated the front-facing polygons by putting them in group **4** instead of group **2**, we can now press the **Select by SG** button (below the numbers in the array). This exposes a pop up with the available smoothing groups. Press **2** to select the outer and inner sides of the Tube.

    The ticked **Clear Selection** toggle will clear what you currently have selected, but if you want to add to a selection, you can untick it, which can be handy when you want to combine two selections into one group.

13. Assign the outer and inner walls to Smoothing Group **3**, and turn off **2**. Then press *Ctrl + D* to deselect all, click on one of the inner wall polygons, and hold *Shift + LMB* on another inner wall polygon to the side of it. This selects a poly loop. You can then assign the inner wall to Smoothing Group **1**, which is so far unused.

Each time you make changes, track the effect on the reference copy whose **TurboSmooth** has **Smoothing** on and **Smoothing Groups** on. The other reference copy, which doesn't, will not reflect these changes in any way.

14. Select the bottom polygons of the Tube and set their **Smoothing** to SG **2**.

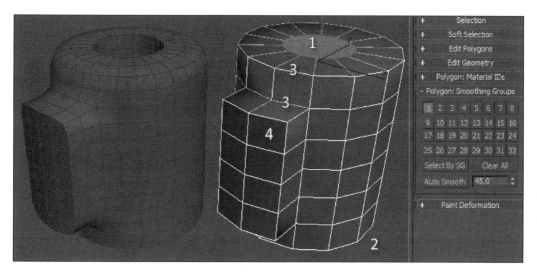

It is good to use as few **Smoothing Groups** as possible, as it gives the geometry calculations further down the line less to do. The state of the smoothed model above could be represented using just two smoothing groups. Try it out!

A further challenge would be to examine how adjusting **Smoothing Groups** could enhance the spidery vehicle model we've been building throughout the previous topics.

The main benefit of modeling with **Smoothing Groups** active in the **Turbosmooth** modifier above the **Editable Poly** is that you can selectively sharpen edges without adding geometry. A downside is that when you export a model, smoothing groups are not maintained from one software to another sometimes. The commonly used `.fbx` and `.obj` formats have the option to conserve smoothing groups.

In the following screenshot, the left-hand side has more smoothing groups, but the effect is overdone.

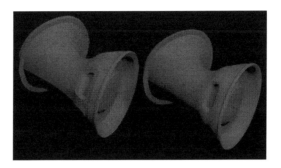

Generating model forms using Cloth

The **Cloth** modifier provides a powerful tool for simulating cloth deformation and animation. It can also be used to drape static sheets over other objects, such as a tarpaulin over a bike. In this section, we'll drape a cloth object over a `Spike` extending from the vehicle body, and in the end convert it to a net using the **Lattice** modifier.

1. Open the scene `\Packt3dsMax\Chapter 4\ClothStart.max`. A spike has been added to the front of the vehicle, using simple extrudes and insets.

2. In the Top view of the ground plane, add a Rectangle (**Create | Shapes | Rectangle**) with **Length** of 80 and **Height** of 80 and a **Corner Radius** of 10, as shown in the following screenshot:

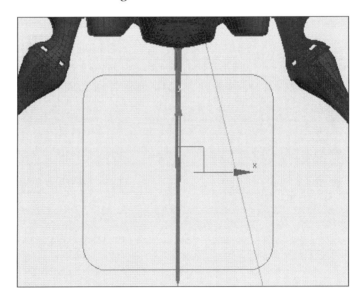

3. Add a **Garment Maker** modifier to the **Rectangle** object. What this does is generate a mesh from it that is constructed from evenly-sized polygons that are slightly irregular in distribution. For cloth simulation, this kind of mesh is better for folding than a grid-like polygon distribution (though that also works). Set the **Density** of the **Garment Maker** to 0.4, raising it a little, so the mesh is finer. Higher density meshes will calculate slowly, but should yield better curvature as they fold.

4. Expand the **+** of the **Garment Maker** modifier, and click on the **Panels** Sub-Object mode. Now click on the mesh in the view, which will go red like an element in an **Editable Poly**. You can raise it so that it sits just above the Spike sticking out from the body of the vehicle, as shown in the following screenshot:

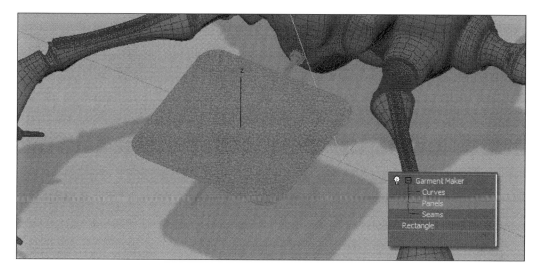

It is very important to construct the shape at **Position | Z** = 0, on the world plane, and then move the garment around the scene only in the **Panel** mode. Otherwise, the cloth simulation that comes next will not work.

A quick digression: work with an **Editable Spline** if you want to extend the garment to have several panels. To create this, right-click on a shape's label in the modifier stack and choose **Collapse To: Editable Spline**. Create some new shapes alongside and attach them together. To join them we use **Seams**. For these to work, first select all the vertices of the shape at **Editable Spline | Vertex** level, and right-click and choose **Break Vertices** so all the **Segments** are unique in regards to each other. Add **Garment Maker**, and set the **Density** parameter to suit. To make the pieces join, use the **Seams** Sub-Object mode in the **Garment Maker** modifier. In the **Seams** mode, there is a **Create Seam** button that lets you associate two selected edges that will bind together during a **Cloth** simulation. **Seams** that are too far apart in the scene may require a higher **Seam tolerance** value to be set in the **Garment Maker** modifier. **Seams** will pull together during simulation but won't actually join as one surface unless you turn off, prior to simulating, **Cloth modifier | Simulation Parameters | Use Sewing Springs**.

5. The **Garment Maker** modifier only surfaces the Spline into a mesh. To start actual cloth simulation, add a **Cloth** modifier. The following steps involve setting up the cloth, then simulating it to create a satisfactory drapery or "pose" for the cloth object or an animation, if required. The result is shown a bit further on, after the **Cloth** properties are set and the simulation has been performed locally.

Setting up the Cloth modifier parameters

Let's see how to set up the Cloth modifier's parameters:

1. The first thing to do is click on **Object Properties** in the **Cloth** modifier. This opens a window where you can set meshes as either **Cloth** or **Collision** participants. In our case, the Rectangle001 object is the **Cloth** and the Spike will be used for collision. In the **Object Properties** panel, click on Rectangle001 in the list, click on the **Cloth** radio button, and then select a preset from the **Cloth Properties | Presets** rollout, such as **Cotton**. The presets provide shortcuts to certain stretchiness and friction properties, but you can set your own using the values underneath the preset rollout.

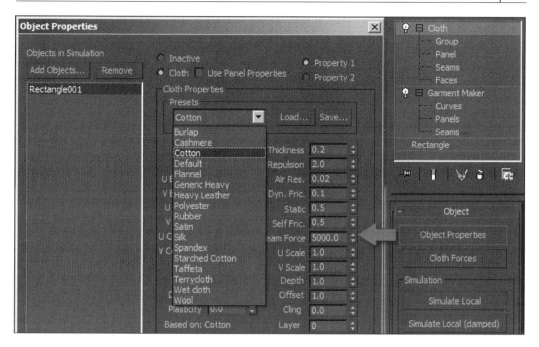

2. Next, click the **Add Objects...** button in the left-hand side of the window. This lets you include other objects in the simulation. Select `Spike` in the scene and assign it as a collision object, using the **Collision Object** radio button near the bottom of the window. You don't need to change any of the offset values in this case, but sometimes you may find there's a gap between cloth and collision, and adjusting the **Offset** or **Depth** values may help. Press **OK** to close the window.

> If you want the `Spike` to act like a knife, tick on the **Cuts Cloth** checkbox; then, if the garment contacts it, tearing will occur along the contacting surface. It'd probably then fall through the floor, which would need to be added to the Cloth simulation as a collision object too.

3. In the modifier parameters, expand **Simulation Parameters** and set the **Subsample** value to `10`. This forces the cloth measurement to calculate for changes 10 times per frame. Tick on **Self Collisions** and **Check Intersections** and set the **Self Collisions** value to `3`.

4. Next, click on **Simulate Local**. This is for initially draping or posing your cloth into a default state. Not many cloth animations begin with a perfectly flat panel. Wait until the panel drops down and interacts with the `Spike`, and then click on **Simulate Local** again to stop the process. This calculation can be undone with *Ctrl + Z*.

Note how that cloth is one-sided. To fix this, use a double-sided material for the cloth, or set a regular material to be two-sided in its properties, or apply a **Shell** modifier to it, which will give it thickness, therefore a back and front face.

If you want to record the animation of the cloth, especially if the `Spike` was already key-framed to move, you could use the **Simulate** button below **Simulate Local**. To remove an already simulated animation, click on **Erase Simulation** below **Simulate**. To remove everything after the current frame, press **Truncate**.

5. To get the state of this mesh, you can use **Convert to Editable Poly** or **Tools | Snapshot...** (which produces a copy of the mesh without destroying the original cloth object).

Vertex groups can be used to pin parts of the cloth together during animations. This is useful in the case above to stop the top surface from coming off the `Spike`. To set this up is a matter of assigning **Vertex Group** in the **Cloth** modifier's Sub-Object mode by selecting points in **Group** mode. Click on **Make Group** in the **Group** options list, and then tell the group to stick to a surface using the **Surface** option, for example.

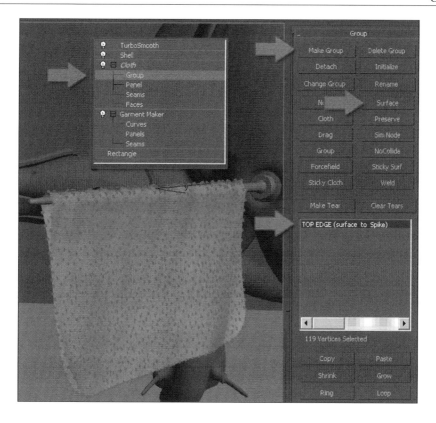

Summary

In this chapter we used modifiers for both modeling new objects and altering existing ones. We initially dealt with polygon loops and soft modeling, in contrast with the hard surface approach in the previous chapter, which gave us our base model.

In the first chapter, I raised the idea that what seemed tricky at first would quickly become second nature. By now, in terms of that idea, you should feel really at home in different Sub-Object modes, comfortable deriving geometry from Shapes, and understand the smoothing structure of polygons. Hopefully, you'll recognize that most modifiers, in terms of the stack and their parameters, use a very similar interface. You may notice that even in the **Help** contents the layout for UI information, procedures, and interface breakdown always follows a consistent format, making it easier to flip through newly discovered tools.

In the following chapters, we will focus more on enhanced working methods rather than, as has been the case so far, on essential modeling processes.

5

The Language of Machines: Designing and Building Model Components

This chapter demonstrates the usefulness of developing an internal library or vocabulary of visual memes for your tech, mech, and hard surface models. It is very difficult to make a fictional model of a man-made object without some familiarity with how real man-made objects get their look, especially in terms of fabricated or manufactured detail. In this chapter we'll analyze some prevalent ideas about depicting "sci-fi" tech along with time-saving methods for constructing parts to reference in models.

These are the topics covered in the chapter:

- A visual language for science fiction machinery
- Spare parts
- A Greeble factory
- From primitive origins...
- ...Into outer space
- A star ship construction walk through

A visual language for science fiction machinery

What design challenges do concept artists confront while planning game vehicles or machinery or technology art? It is practical to first consider the tropes and memes of art language, its symbols and icons, and its common threads across work.

In this case, what matters is to establish some of the givens, the things you always come up against when you try to make a vehicle or spaceship or robot for a game. The base idea is that there have already been a lot of these in games, films, comics, and books. Therefore, everyone can almost automatically identify certain design elements as being more or less appropriate. At least, it is easier to do this when you are viewing an artwork – it's not so easy when you have to make the artwork. It is possible to break from convention, but with caution. Usually doing so meets with the most success when you thoroughly understand the conventions and expectations people have.

Most non-specialists don't understand the engineering or manufacturing processes of a machine when they look at it, but seeing machines throughout their lives gives them a chance to build assumptions about how machines generally should look and how a machine should behave. Assumptions evolve too; a PC from the 1980s seems a lot more primitive than one from 2012, as shown in the following screenshot:

Processes and materials of manufacture change, and style follows along with that. For instance, in the movies most spaceships have massive rockets on the backend, since, from the 1960s, space launch has depended totally on rockets. This year, one of the surprising turn ups is teenager Aisha Mustafa from Egypt patenting a fuel-less space propulsion method using shaped silicon plates. Possibly what we can take from this is that, with regards to technology, while engineering trumps art, sufficient visual styling and familiar cues in the art are often enough to orient the viewer, but you have to be sensitive to the audience's increasingly savvy "genre kit".

By and large, artists (at least those who want to do vehicles and mech) should examine not only existing visual cues in examples from their favorite artists, but tropes from engineering and machinery design. Getting out with a camera to collect photographic reference of industrially manufactured components is a good start. Failing that, tailor your Internet image searches to trawl for tech references. The following screenshot is a spaceship orthographic. Along the bottom, I've isolated details that indicate some memes of the machine language one tends to see in a spaceship model, such as cut-lines, cavities, radial extrusions, mountings, exhaust vents, rails, trimmings, and arrays.

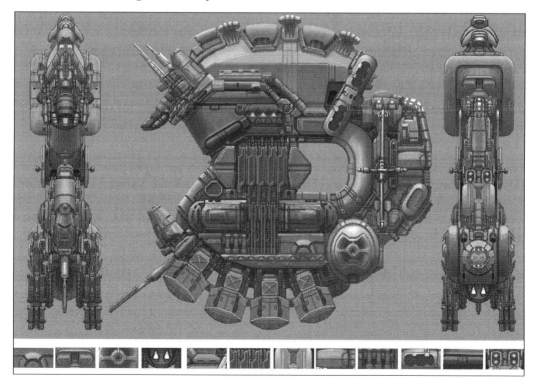

Machinery comes in different scales. For example, a panel useful on the side of a boat featuring rows of rivets and bolts would not be of much good use for the side of a massive orbital space station, as the rivets would be conspicuously out of scale.

In the next section we'll start to examine some of these memes in isolation, to start building a library of 'components' that could form the surface detail of some machinery.

Spare parts

This topic shows the progression from a 2D graphic component to a 3D component:

1. Open the scene \Packt3dsMax\Chapter 5\ShapeLibrary.max. This scene shows a set of simple radial forms that could be distributed as components on a large model. This kind of presentation imitates sculptors' studies of ears and noses presented in an array, as shown in the following screenshot:

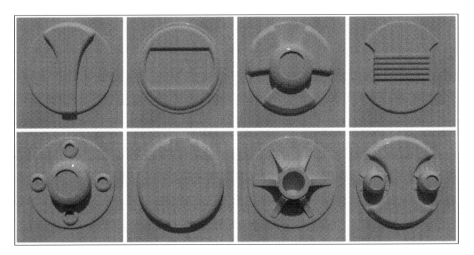

2. We'll make some additions using Photoshop's **Square Brush** in the **Default Brushes** as the motif. Let's start from the idea that most manufactured details could first be represented by black and white 2D graphic motifs, as shown in the following screenshot:

3. The first pass on the left-hand side establishes some base shapes. These could be interpreted many ways into volumes. Add finer lines over copies to give them an additional punch. Duplicate, flip, and overlap selections to generate more forms. While doing this kind of built-up you will very likely get some fresh alternative ideas. One reason to take this approach is its simplicity leads to speed, so you have the chance to try out the tangents you dream up as you go.

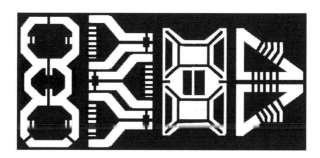

4. Key highlights and cast shadows would enhance the sense of volume for the motif. To add these, on a new layer, use **50%** transparent gray to reduce the whites. Then add another layer on top, and paint highlights with white and shadows with black. Gradients masked by selections that are faintly washed over the surface will intensify the effect, as indicated in the following screenshot, albeit loosely. Obviously it is possible to labor over such work endlessly, but we want to move on quickly to modeling the forms:

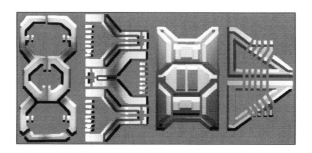

5. For the circular forms shown in the source file `\Packt3dsMax\Chapter 5\ ShapeLibrary.max` a Circle shape was the starting point for all the examples. This time, instead, let's use a ring-shaped cavity in a quarter cylinder, so we can wrap the detailing around it using **Symmetry** later.

6. In a new scene, create a quarter cylinder, first starting with a Cylinder primitive with 20 **Sides**, 1 **Height Segment**, and 1 **Cap Segment** as well. Probably the fastest way to get the quartered form, apart from using the parametric **Slice On** option built into the Cylinder primitive, is to delete polygons after converting to Editable Poly, then **Cap** and **Connect** the open edges, as shown in the following screenshot on the left-hand side:

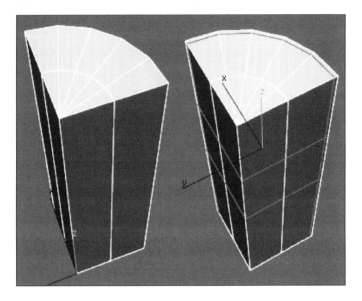

7. Also trim in some additional loops using **SwiftLoop**, as shown in the previous screenshot on the right-hand side.

8. Now we'll push the center polygon loop inwards, around the outside curve of the object. To do so, delete the polygons shown in the following screenshot:

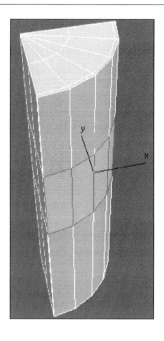

9. Select the top and bottom edges of the part bordering the opened hole, and *Shift* + Scale them inside (refer to left-hand side in the following screenshot), then click on **Bridge** polygons (right-hand side in the following screenshot):

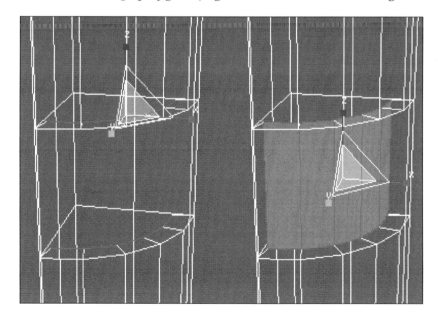

10. Don't cap the small holes on either side of the bridge. Instead, line them up in the top view with the straight sides of the Cylinder.

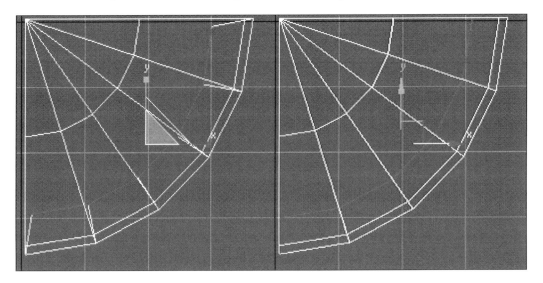

11. Delete the straight side of the Cylinder. This is so we can apply **Symmetry** to the object without having to worry about internally overlapping polygons, which sit along the mirror line.

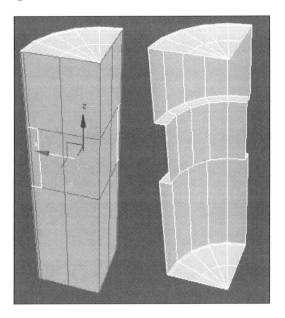

12. That may seem like a lot of steps to get a starting point, but it takes under a minute. If you want to start from here, load up from \Packt3dsMax\Chapter 5\ the scene SquareBrushShapes.max.

13. There are probably other ways to achieve the same result by doing the steps in another order, for instance, starting from a Cylinder primitive with its **Height Segments** set to 5. Then just move and scale the existing edge loops and delete the quarters after getting the extrusion inwards right. You could even start by making the object profile with a Spline shape and add a **Lathe** modifier on it, with an angle of 90 degrees to create the quarter pipe.

For the way that was shown here, note that the "delete faces and bridge" operation we performed makes nice **Smoothing Groups** (left-hand side in the following screenshot) compared to the same model made by just pushing edges inwards (right-hand side). It's a minor distinction, however. In any case, we now have a quarter pipe we can build our shapes on.

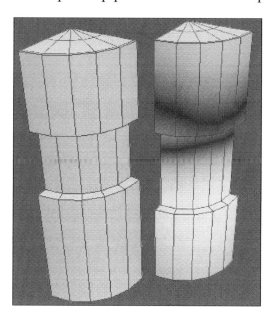

14. To start building the detail on the side of the Cylinder, we can apply the image guide as a texture on the surface. So it maps correctly, select the faces in the middle of the cylinder and apply an **UnwrapUVW** modifier, and then enter **Face** mode (3) and click on **Planar Map** (shown in the following screenshot) in the modifier's **Projection** parameters. This fits the selected polygons to the UV square.

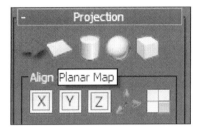

15. In the scene, open the **Material Editor** (*M*) and apply an **Autodesk Generic** material named Base to the entire Cylinder model. Create another **Autodesk Generic** material, this time with \Packt3dsMax\Chapter 5\SquareBrushRef_01.png as a bitmap in the material's **Generic_Image** channel.

16. Assign it to the selected faces as shown in the following screenshot. Right-click on the material and choose **Show Realistic Material in View**.

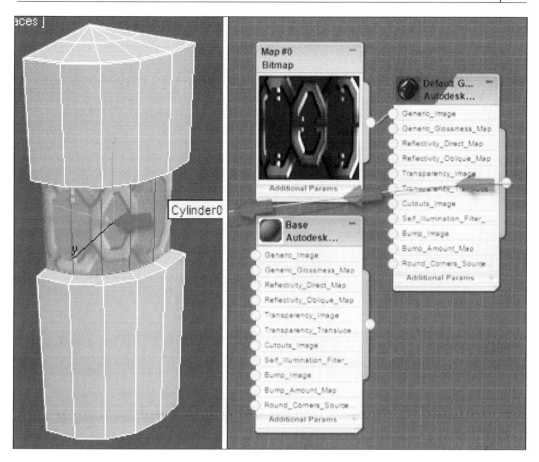

17. Close the **Material Editor**, and in the **Edit** menu click on **Hold** (*Ctrl + H*). This saves a temporary, holding version of your scene. If you need to recover it later, press *Alt + Ctrl + F* or go to **Edit | Fetch.**

18. Zoom into the imagery sitting on the middle of the Cylinder. To build this shape out from the model, we can save some time by splitting an edge sideways through the middle and just work on half of it. After adding the edge, just delete the bottom half of the model. Later, we can add back the content and the new detail using **Symmetry** in **Z**.

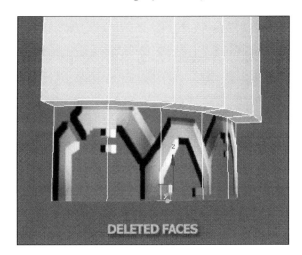

19. Start to use the **Cut** tool to create the outline of the reference image on the model. Take care to use as few cuts as possible to represent the contour. Watch out for cuts that are close to an existing edge. It may be better to move an existing edge than introduce a new edge too close to one that is already there. Be aware that as you cut, the added points are automatically mapped in UV space based on the current mapping, so moving them around will stretch the image. You can turn on **Preserve UVs** to allow vertices to be moved without distorting the texture. If you make a mistake, it's better to add new edges and remove old ones than wiggle the edges around.

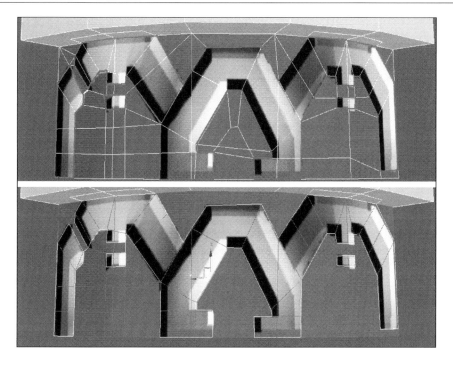

20. Make sure that on either side of the model the vertical points added are at the same **Z** position, as shown in the following screenshot. This is done to ensure they'll line up when the model is mirrored later.

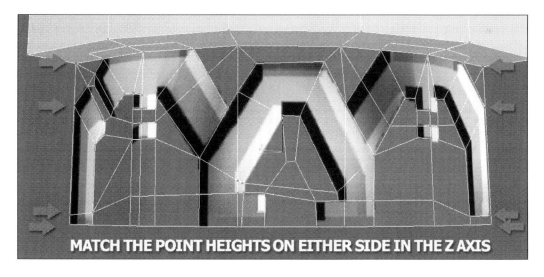

MATCH THE POINT HEIGHTS ON EITHER SIDE IN THE Z AXIS

21. At the top, add end corners in the **Vertex** mode (*1*) using **Cut** so the additional edges filter nicely into the main object body, as shown in the following screenshot:

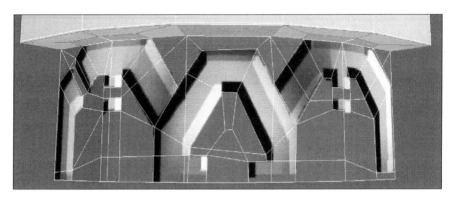

22. Select the polygons that make up the reference image's shape and right-click and choose **Extrude Settings**. In the settings, set **Local** as the method, and 2.5 as the **Height** amount, then press *Enter*.

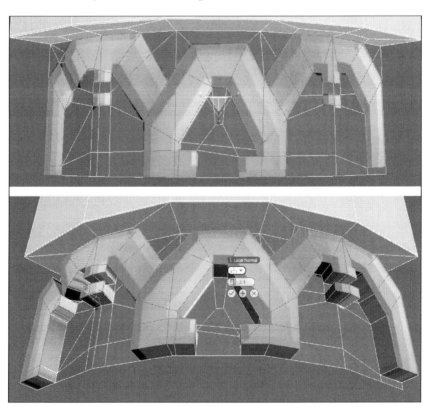

23. Here and there you may have to adjust corners on the extrude so they are neater. After this, you would delete the polygons along the bottom-most edge and on the outer sides. You'd also need to delete the four polygons which touch the top part, where they rub against other polygons. The corners, at the top, can be closed with **Target Weld**.

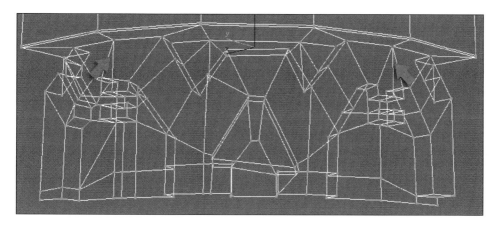

24. After the extrusion is tidied, you'll be less dependent on the reference image being on the model. You can apply the **Autodesk Generic Base** material to the entire model now from the **Material Editor** (*M*).

25. Keep the reference handy though, since we still need to chamfer the extruded edges and make sure the middle part extrudes out more than the sides.

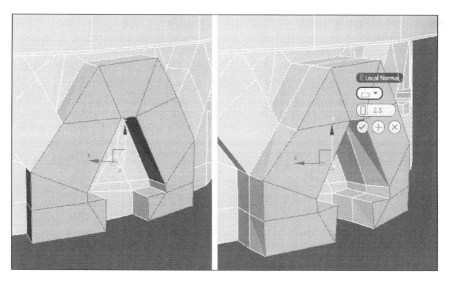

26. To chamfer the edges for longer middle extrusion is probably not as difficult as doing so along the two sides. When you use **Chamfer** on a corner it splits, and you will need to use **Target Weld** in many cases to rebuild the corner again. An alternative approach to using **Chamfer** would be to use **Inset** and then **Scale** the polygons. An **Inset** and **Scale** is shown in the following screenshot. The **Inset** amount that you can set will be limited by the angles of the polygon selection, particularly in the small corners. If you overdo it, they'll crunch together.

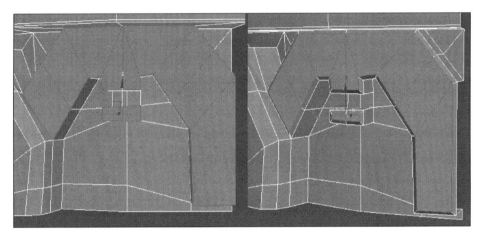

27. Where the beveled part of the sides touch the inner beveled part, you can cut edges to enable you to close the angular gap so they butte together nicely. After cutting in a support edge, delete the faces, then **Target Weld** to close the gap, as indicated in the following screenshot:

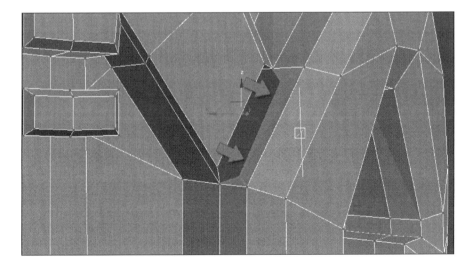

28. Do the same at the bottom of the mesh. After that, the rest of what's required would only involve slight clean-up transforms. Here and there you may notice square polygons with triangular shading. A fix for this is to select the polygons, right-click and choose **Make Planar** in the Quad Menu (\Packt3dsMax\UI Settings\PacktUI.ui) or in the modify panel under **Edit Geometry**. Also, you'll probably see ways to start removing edges from the form without changing its overall shape, to be more optimal.

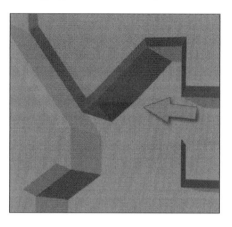

29. When you apply **Symmetry** to the result, remember the Mirror line will be at **Z = 0** and you can get the **Z** value of the bottom edge of the model and set the Mirror line there in **Symmetry | Mirror** sub-object mode. Then you can add additional **Symmetry** modifiers in **X** and **Y** to complete the cylinder.

An example of the finished modeling is provided in `\Packt3dsMax\Chapter 5\` `SquareBrushDetailCompleted.max`.

A Greeble factory

A lot of fictional technology modeling, particularly on a large scale, would take months to make if each detail was unique, followed an engineer's logic, and had some underlying function. Sometimes it's more satisfying to generate some random detail in the surface, using a script or scatter tool.

Greeble, a term which comes from physical prop modeling, is where various components, or *nurnies*, are jumbled on a surface to create an illusion of complexity from random aggregation of the parts. The Death Star in *Star Wars* is possibly the most well known example of an object almost entirely composed of Greeble. Often, physical modelers will use model kit parts such as tank treads, or wheels, and even the spars of kit plastic that form the scaffold holding the actual model. This is known as **kitbashing**. If you search for "Greeble" on Google images, you'll see many examples of complex surfaces made from simple but dense distributed components. A lot of city generation programs are based on the idea of targeted greeble, where the nurnies are derived from a library of buildings or architectural objects, with clever scattering parameters so they don't form strange effects. There is a free plugin for 3ds Max called *Ghost Town Lite* (`http://www.kilad.net/GTForum`) that works that way. A professional city generator with a plugin interface to 3ds Max is *City Engine* from `www.procedural.com`. If you are bothered to create an entire city at all it is probably worthwhile, given the time investment, to go for the commercial tools. However, for pure Greeble, on the lighter side, there is a satisfying script called *Greeble* from Klanky the Robot at `http://max.klanky.com/plugins.htm`.

Getting started with Greeble

In the following section we'll cover the basics of constructing surface Greeble:

1. Download the Greeble plugin for your 3ds Max version, and extract to any folder. There may be two variants (32-bit or 64-bit). Paste the one you need to your `C:\Program Files\Autodesk\3ds Max 2013\plugins` folder. Then launch 3ds Max.

2. Add a Tube primitive to the scene with the following parameters: **Radius 1 = 75**, **Radius 2 = 35**, **Height = 45**, **Height Segments = 1**. The rest can be left at their default values.

3. Add the newly added modifier **Greeble** to the Tube. You'll get some default Greeble, just like that, which can then be further adjusted. Let's step back and consider how we want the Greeble to work. Deactivate the modifier or ensure **Show End Result** is turned off in the **modify panel** options.

4. Add an **Edit Poly** modifier above the base Tube primitive, and at Edge level (2) add two **SwiftLoop** edge loops around the inner radius, just under the top and above the base.

5. Add a **PolySelect** modifier, and press *Ctrl + Shift* in polygon mode to loop select the inner ring, as shown in the following screenshot:

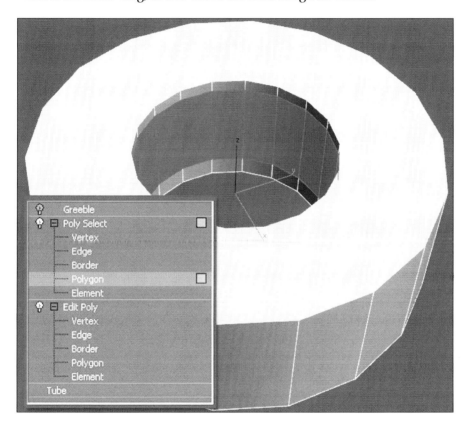

6. Now go back to the Greeble modifier, on top of all that. The first thing to understand is that there is a base per-polygon **Panels** extrusion going on in the modifier, and then its **Widgets** or nurnies are applied to the extrusion. Hopefully the next steps show why this matters – the details are applied to all new surfaces, even sideways.

7. In the modifier parameters, turn off **Widgets** via the **Generate** checkbox temporarily. Set the **Panels** values as shown in the following screenshot:

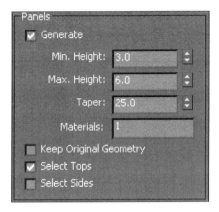

8. You should see something like the following screenshot, though the random **Seed** value will always produce different results:

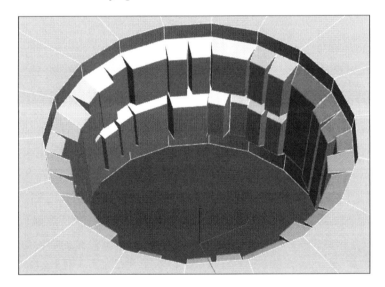

9. Set the **Widgets** section as shown in the following screenshot. Obviously, there is a lot of scope for settings to be done. This is up to you, however you prefer.

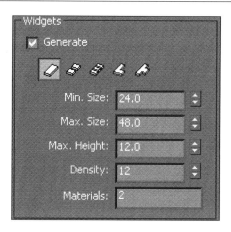

10. Added Greeble will only face inwards, but you can select the sides and the tops of the panels (and the sides and tops of the Greeble) in order to apply different materials to them easily when you apply an **Edit Poly** modifier on top of the **Greeble** modifier and assign the selected faces to **Material ID 3**. This will let you add a **Multi-SubObject Material** with, for instance, three materials within it for use by the **Material ID 1** (tube) and **Material ID 2** (sides) and **Material ID 3** (tops) polygon groups on the object. The 'tops' in this image face inwards and are blue tinted. The "sides" are tinted orange, as shown in the following screenshot:

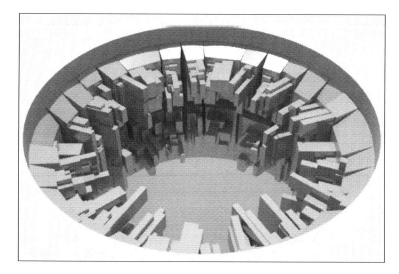

11. Add a **TurboSmooth** modifier and turn on **Smooth By | Smoothing Groups** to round off the Tube sides.

12. Finally, you can add another **Greeble** modifier to the mesh so far, and set it to have finer distribution, for a high frequency noise coating effect, as shown in the following screenshot:

The file \Packt3dsMax\Chapter 5\GreebleDemoExtension.max shows the previous screenshot. The image was rendered using **Octane Render** from Refractive Software (www.refractivesoftware.com). If you have this, the example scene is set up in GreebleDemoExtension_Octane.max.

From primitive origins...

When you design a ship it's normal to start with the overall shape or form, and then noodle down to details, perhaps dividing the work into sections or functions, according to the needs of the story. Think of the movie *District 9*, with its mothership floating in the air above Johannesburg. The overall form is a tube, but in the story there's a docking port where humans board to find out what's going on, and a drop-ship clamped under it that becomes the escape vehicle in the end, so these areas got a lot of extra attention from the designers. These are the notes from a concept artist who worked on the drop-ship in District 9: "Bevel all angles", "Many subdividing panels", "Body work is thin plates over thicker structure", "Far more mechanical structure [visible] in transitions and gaps", shown in *The Art of District 9*, a book by Daniel Falconer of Weta Workshop.

Artists who do a lot of 3D tend to get used to explaining the features of a design in terms of the tools that'll be used, like bevels, subdivision, layers, extrusions, loops, and cuts.

The following is a list of mechanical keywords that can help to pin down the features, and therefore, the look of a ship, which you might use as image search terms:

- Wire, Cabling, Pipes, Hosing
- Cladding, Coatings, and Solar panels
- Fans, Vents, Ducts, Intakes, Grilles, Radiators, Exhausts, Turbines, and Turrets
- Buttons, Drilled holes, Fulcrums, and Hinges
- Cut-lines, Rails, Scaffolds, Supports, and Corrugations
- Joints, Welds, Covers, Shells, and Flaps
- Sockets, Radiators, Connections, and Exposed infrastructure
- Roundings, Angles (chamfers), Nodes, and Nacelles
- Fins, Flaps, Struts, Beams, Gantries, and Conning towers
- Tanks, Valves, Interfaces, Anchor points, Clips, and Indicators
- Surface reductions, Form-fitting, Form-Breaking, Bearings, Cams, and Gears
- Radial (bushing), Concentricity (circles), and Seal
- Brackets, Housings, Connections, Fasteners, Tools, Magnet, and Coupling
- Heat sinks, Pistons, Aerial, Array, Spoiler, Pressure plate, and Landing gear
- Suspension, Hollow coils, Geospheres, Dishes, Airlocks, Portholes, and Blisters
- Landing pads, Docking bays, and Clamps

It also doesn't hurt to learn some metal shop processes, since the engineers who manufacture real machines have a terminology to accurately describe every single step of their work. A good starting point is `http://en.wikipedia.org/wiki/Machining`.

The next section deals with some approaches to establishing the major forms upon which you might design a ship, perhaps via a paint over to set the final look for a finishing artist.

Typically I will start from a primitive, such as a horizontal Cylinder, but with the goal of quickly building away from its extremely regular shape. To get underway, I selected the polygons at one end, as well as some strips of polygons down the sides. Then I deleted them and applied a **Shell** modifier to give the thin surface some thickness. I added a **Spherify** modifier to that with an **Amount** of **25** or so to give the straight edges some curvature.

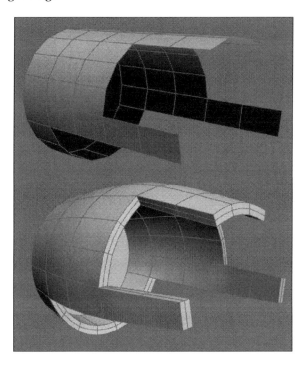

The result seems to have no apparent scale cue, so it could be built up into a massive vessel or a small component. Since we're chasing an entire ship, a paint over would provide a good guide at this point, bearing in mind that we already have some mesh fragments from earlier topics to play around with too.

As in the following screenshot, arrange in a painting program a few screen grabs of representative angles, as that will be a good start for the painting. In this case I chose the top, side, and the internal part of the object. I figured the front, being a big disk, could remain relatively flat. It can be good to render out the object with proper lighting, since the viewport lighting tends to give us very dark internal shading, which is hard to detail. A renderer would tend to fill the shadows with indirect light so we can see every part.

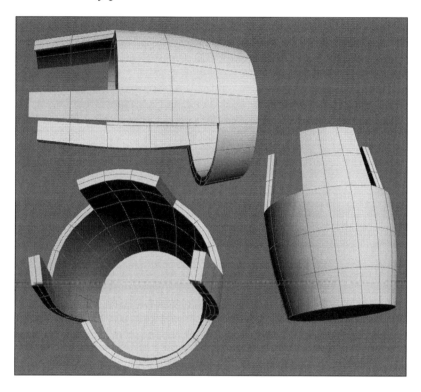

The next stage is to start layering in brush strokes in Photoshop. Most of the time it is a good idea to start from the larger surfaces, and think of adding only the forms that change the look of the object. Details can come in later. The other important starting consideration is to think of what kind of look you might be after, and what kind of purpose the ship might have. I really wanted to put engines on the internal disk, shielded by the body of the craft. I wanted to use existing loops to guide other edges, and have many panels or armor plates to vary the hull thickness. I also thought that perhaps the lower part might be dockable with another curved vessel, perhaps a habitat, and they'd fit snugly together. I recall Arthur C. Clarke's story *The Songs of Distant Earth*, where the ship requires a bore of ice fitted on the front to absorb cosmic dust, so I left the front flat. The key step when adding detail is to think a bit about how it might be modeled later on.

The provided content has the layered file \Packt3dsMax\Chapter 5\
ShipPaintOver.psd. It's included so you can see the build-up is really
straightforward. I just used one brush, working at first large size (marker pen), and
then fine (0.1mm pen) for outlines. I sampled most of the color from the tones that
came from the 3ds Max screen grab. While painting I was pretty sure that the side
view would inform most of the upcoming modeling. A lot of details are suggestive.
Even if the painting doesn't exactly capture the look of the ship, the familiarity with
the features that you'll get from doing a paint over will help get you close to that
goal. On a project when the model is constructed up to the level we're going to next,
an art director would likely do another paint over pass to refine the detail and cues
to any improvements.

…Into outer space

A particularly undetailed part of my painting is a band going around the top of the
ship's inside. I didn't detail it much as I already had that part made, from the topic
earlier in this chapter where we took a 2D shape and made some detailing with it
on a Cylinder. Duplicated to form a beam, and bent to fit the hull curve, this sits in
there nicely.

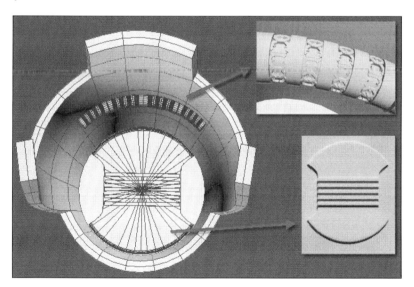

So we can already see an application of some of what's gone before. Similar steps could be used to generate a lot of the rest of the detail in the ship. Before getting into the details, we need to analyze additional pieces to add, and analyze the larger forms to establish those early. It'll involve processes we've already covered, such as adding edge loops, cutting, extruding and doing insets. The following screenshots show the major steps. You can track the file increments in the working files folder \Packt3dsMax\Chapter 5\3dsMax Scenes\Scene Increments.

Here's something we need to avoid doing! If you have your model sitting there with **TurboSmooth** turned on, and **Isoline Display** is on in its parameters, it looks pretty nice, right? So long as you don't collapse it to **Editable Poly** with **Isoline Display** active. If you do, you'll get every single edge segmented with a stray point, or more if you had the **TurboSmooth** subdivision iterations high. This makes it really difficult to edit the model, so best turn off **TurboSmooth** when you collapse down. If you want to keep the subdivisions when you collapse, be sure to turn off **Isoline Display** in the modifier parameters.

What follows is an illustrated breakdown of the modeling process for the ship. The essential steps that I followed during the modeling task included these notes:

Break the image into sections to work on in isolation before modeling; it may help if you identify the function or purpose of each section. Try to find a focal point in the design that you expect the viewer will be most likely to watch, and take extra care with that area.

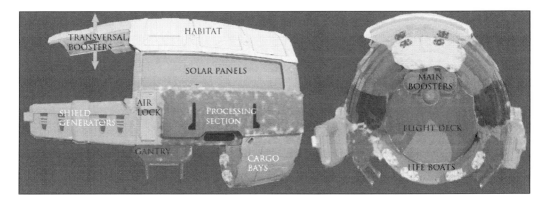

Set milestones for each section so you don't overwork one part at the expense of other parts; estimate if the first milestone has a day to complete, then how long the rest will take based on that.

When attaching parts made separately to the ship hull, build-in supporting edges on the hull that will make joining the part on tidy and easy. A circle fits in a square.

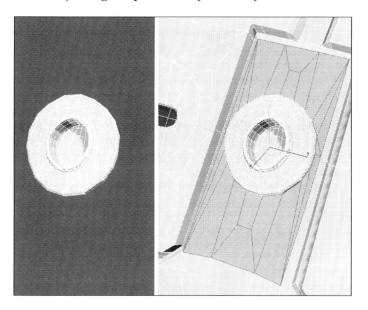

When building circles, create a frame of edges to confine it, and favor fewer polygons over perfect curves; the circle can always be refined later, as it is harder to edit high resolution curves. From the **Shape | Splines** object list, use a Circle as a guide to the polygon circle you want to build.

Look for sections that will be duplicated; manage the border so it is easy to clone off, translate, and rejoin elsewhere.

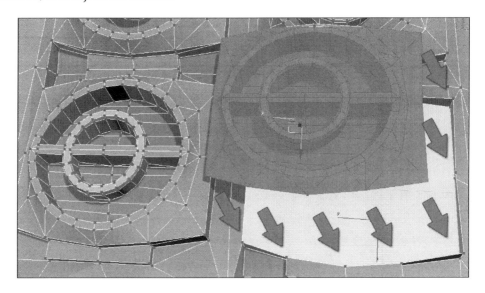

Mark key edge loops with a distinctly different material:

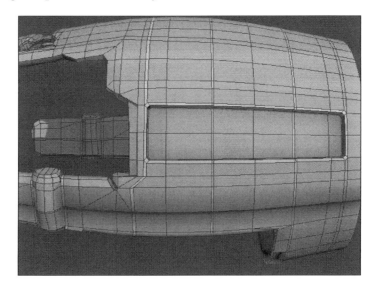

Work on large features first, and leave small details till the end, and decide what details could be painted or sculpted and then applied as a texture. In the following screenshot, there's still a lot of large, flat, empty space, which could be detailed via texture painting.

Do your utmost to keep to the design, but be ready to let it evolve if that's required or if it helps the end result – commercially, you'd only go for changes with proper approvals. In this case, with the front of the ship, the first idea was to keep it flat or cover it with ice, but instead I added a large "particle detector" array. Maybe it helps fuel the engines.

Keep turning the model and checking proportion; save view bookmarks for the area you are working on using the **Home** function. A nice, quick way to adjust proportions is to select points and apply an **FFD 3x3x3** modifier, and then tease the control points, as shown in the following screenshot:

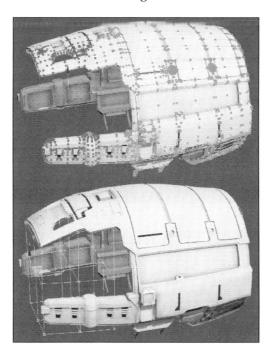

Leave asymmetrical detail to last if your basic model form can leverage symmetry. The following screenshot shows the tail detail and the row of blocks under the front boosters that have been deliberately left off the model. It can be added once the symmetrical part is done. They might even be added as additional models, detachable and modular.

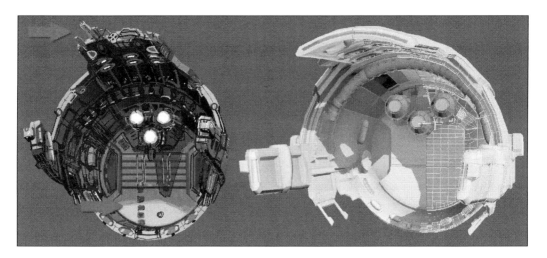

Work hard to keep the symmetrical border at 0 and absolutely straight. You can use **Align | Align X** in the **Graphite Modeling Tools** to do this. Make sure the Mirror line is placed at **X** = 0 as well. Take particular care with **Extrusion** operations on the symmetry line.

Save the scene incrementally so that if a file corrupts or a mistake is made you can revert back – this ship has 50 example files showing the workflow. You can set in the preferences to automatically save incrementally under **Customize | Preferences** in the **Files** tab by ticking on **Increment of Save**. Then each time you press *Ctrl + S*, a new file is created with a 01, 02, 03... enumeration.

Don't do overlong renders of the unfinished model, hoping the rendered lighting will improve the look of the viewport shading – it's a creature comfort to render, and wastes a lot of time.

You can view a turntable render of the completed untextured model at
`http://youtu.be/Jq9DOo1CMfY?hd=1`.

The notes we've just been through show the ship in a state near completion, at least the base, symmetrical part. Let's rewind to where we started, from a chopped-up Cylinder, the state at which the concept painting was done.

The following screenshot is the next step from there. It has a **Symmetry** applied, which will remain throughout. The holes through the top are added using **Bridge** on a polygon selection, and fortified with supporting loops using **SwiftLoop**.

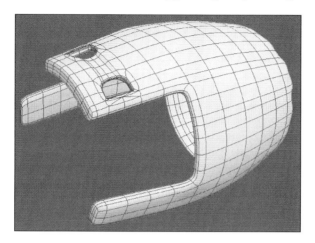

A **TurboSmooth** modifer has been added here temporarily. This gives a quick sense of direction, and it can also be used to look for problems with overlapping vertex problems (which sometimes occur when using the **Cut** tool to add edges, even with **Snap** turned on). It's really not common but given hundreds of operations are performed, a few slips can pass by that should be checked for.

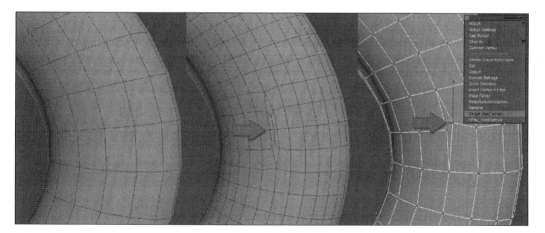

There are a lot of ways to expose point-over-point mistakes, and looking at the topology with **TurboSmooth** on is one since the points relax apart. Frequently, the problem is shown if you select a poly loop and it doesn't select around the loop as far as you'd think it would. At the end of modeling, I use the **Select By Numeric | >4** (polygons with greater than four vertices) in the Ribbon tool to look for point-over-point errors. This is found in the **Selection** tab of the Ribbon when in **Polygon Sub-Object** mode (4).

When cutting, if the operation doesn't work, there's a chance you're trying to snap to overlapping points. To perform a cut accurately, turn on **Vertex Snap** (*S*) or use **Connect** with two points instead of **Cut**. Generally, I fix overlapping points by wiggling one out of the way and using **Target Weld** to click from one to the other, which joins them visibly. You can also use the **Weld** tool with all the points selected, but there's less visual feedback.

Pressing *7* shows onscreen statistics, so you track polygon count. If you click on **[+] | Configure Views**, in the **Statistics** tab you can set either the **Total** for the entire scene or for the selected object, or both.

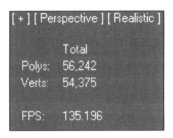

You can watch the statistics (*7*) for feedback when welding, or look at the stats in the modifier panel under **Selection**. The caddy also shows the before and after vertex count if you choose **Weld Settings**, as shown in the following screenshot:

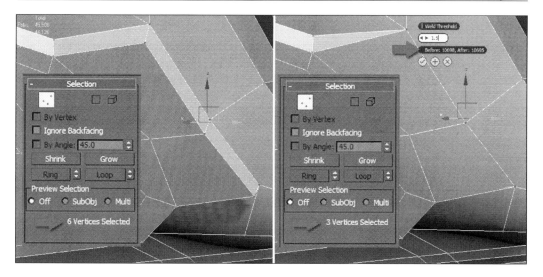

A very useful modifier to apply as a check for problems is the **STL Check** modifier, as shown in the following screenshot:

The **STL Check** modifier can check for four types of problems. The first is **Open Edge** cases. Looking for this is not necessary since you can just press *Ctrl + A* in **Borders** mode. The model's symmetry line is usually an open edge, and some models are meant to have open edges here and there, such as around the cuffs of clothes or around the back of eyeballs. The second problem **STL Check** finds is **Double Face** cases. **Double Face** is where two polygons coexist, facing the same way. It's hard to spot by eye. To use this mode, in the **STL Check** modifier click on the **Double Face** radio button in the **Errors** panel and the **Select Faces** radio button in the **Selections** panel, and then tick **Check**. You'll see a counter process to 100 percent and then a report in the **Status** area.

If there are errors, convert the model to **Editable Poly**, and those faces causing the problem will be automatically selected and you can troubleshoot them.

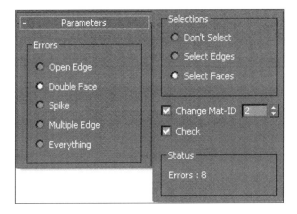

A **Double Face** problem can be fixed easiest by deleting the polygons in question, checking the border to fill, and choosing **Cap Borders** from the **Quad** menu, then **Connect Vertices** if you had to rebuild the quads on an N-gon. In the following screenshot, the left selection is actually a polygon, even though it looks like an edge. A polygon that is ultra-thin is as bad as an overlapping polygon. On the right-hand side of the following screenshot, notice that the two polygons selected do not have a nice red border all the way round, which is another sign of the problem:

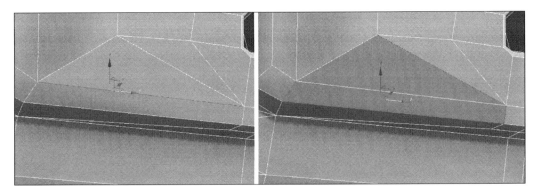

If those polygons are deleted, we're left with the ultra-thin polygon, shown selected in the following screenshot on the left-hand side. It's not too hard to select and delete, but it is hard to spot sometimes because of what may show behind it. After we delete the extra face, and cap the borders, and redo the connecting edge, the face selection shows a better-looking boundary, shown in the following screenshot on the right-hand side. By the way, if you're not seeing solid shaded polygons, you can set this in the **[+] | Viewport Configuration** dialog, by ticking **Shade Selected**.

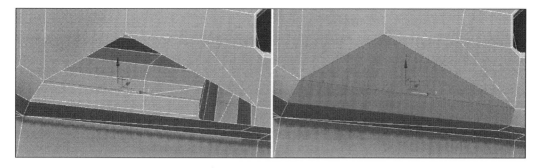

Going back to the **STL Check** modifier, the third error type we can check for is a **Spike**. Spikes are isolated faces that share only one edge with the rest of the object. The fourth error type to check for with **STL Check** is the **Multiple Edge** case, where you might have edges connected across each other, in parallel but not far apart enough to see. Once exposed by the modifier, wiggling the points in the edge selection will generally reveal the bad vertices you should dissolve out using **Target Weld**. You can also use the **Remove** command.

Why is it called **STL Check**? The term **STL** is an abbreviation for **Standard Tessellation Language**, a file format that describes only the surface of an object and is native to the stereolithography CAD tool by 3D Systems. It is an Autodesk partner company founded by Chuck Hall in 1986 that produced the first rapid prototyping system, which didn't require tooling (instead they used a slice-based 3D printing method). Some people refer to StL instead of STL, thinking of stereolithography. Solid modeling requires fairly tight specifications, in particular to be free of the errors the STL modifier detects. Check out the URL `http://www.3dsystems.com`.

Suppose you select a Border and the Border has edges extending from it into the surface of the object, as shown in the top frame of the following screenshot. There's a good chance you have an overlapping polygon or an unwelded edge. This is best fixed by deleting faces and rebuilding the surface. One way to rebuild the surface is to hold *Shift* and move an edge selection, which extrudes a new polygon, and then **Target Weld** its corners. This manual fallback is useful when a **Cap** operation would be tricky, such as when you have a polygon island enclosed by a circular hole.

In the following screenshot the problem face is shown selected in the middle frame – the thin red line by the arrow is a polygon without surface area:

We've spent some of our time raising potential problems and suggesting solutions. With that resolved, let's get back to the build-up of the spaceship.

A star ship construction walk-through

The following screenshot shows the addition of large form changes and chamfers on the tail and some cutting away of the initial primitive, marked by arrows. A drum on the side of the tail has been added and marked with yellow poly-loops.

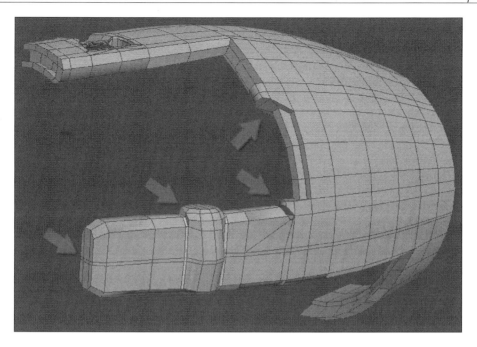

An **Extrude** outward and inward helps build the hull. Poly-loops help mark key areas.

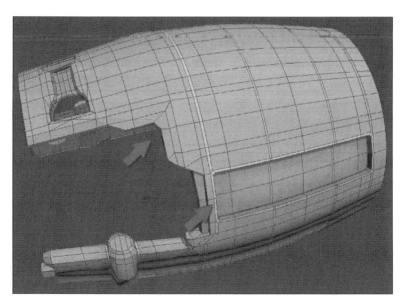

The selected polygons in the following screenshot are where the ship airlock will project out. It's good to shape the area where an **Extrude** will be added so it fits well into what surrounds it.

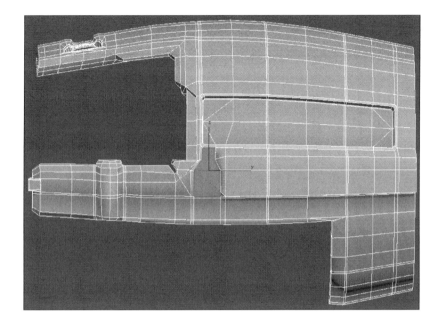

And here's the airlock, as shown in the following screenshot. Its shape is easy to make using **Extrude**, **Chamfer**, **Inset**, and **Cut**, the most common tools we've looked at so far.

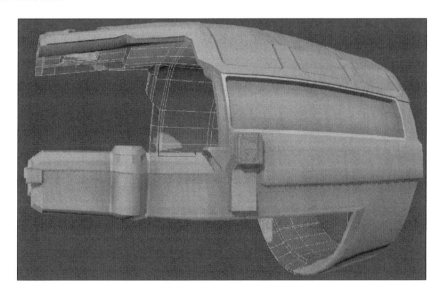

Similarly, it requires just a series of **Extrude** and **Inset** steps to add the panels on top of the hull. These are on the center line, so the new polygons facing the Mirror line should be removed and lined up to **X = 0.0**.

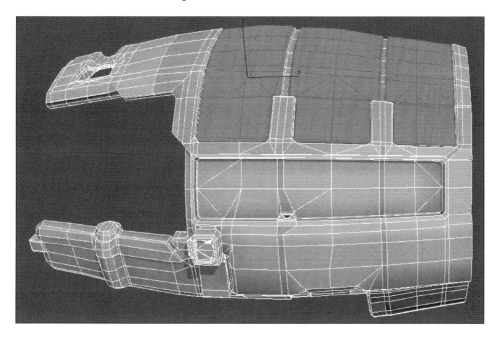

The following screenshot shows a close up of the lower edge of the hull, where the corner requires more detail:

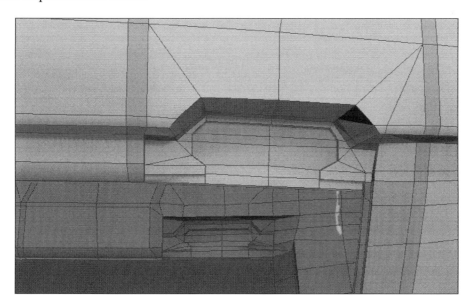

Below this we add a similar form change. About now you'll be noticing a lot of triangles in the structure. While worrying about the form build-up, I don't really pay that much attention to topology (at least not with big triangles – I'll avoid long, thin triangles, and N-gons at all times), preferring to check back over the model later in a separate "make quads" pass since it can waste time to fix up topology on the fly as it might need changing every step of the way as more features are added.

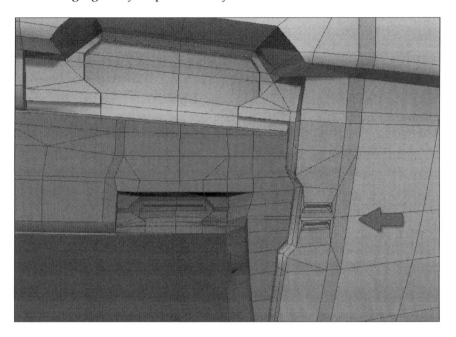

Next, the design requires an extrusion inwards at a 45 degree angle. Also, the panels on the lower part of the hull, being the same, are placed using **Detach to Element** and then welded back into the main element, which was touched upon earlier in the chapter.

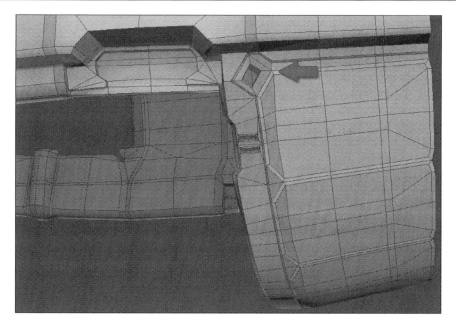

I mentioned avoiding triangles. Let's look at that more closely. Sometimes triangles help avoid polygons that have concave angles, like the one in the following screenshot:

The computer will add triangles automatically at render time, but it might add the middle triangle from the left corner to the top corner, which would cross the middle corner (the concave one) creating an apparent glitch, as shown in the following screenshot:

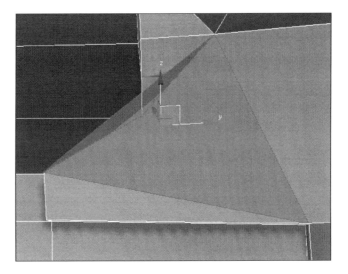

An edge from the middle to the bottom corner wouldn't be a problem at all, as shown in the following screenshot:

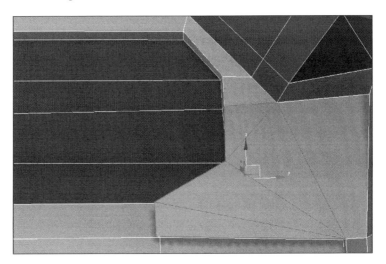

We could improve on things though by removing the middle edge, as shown in the following screenshot, then choose **ConnectEdgesOptions**:

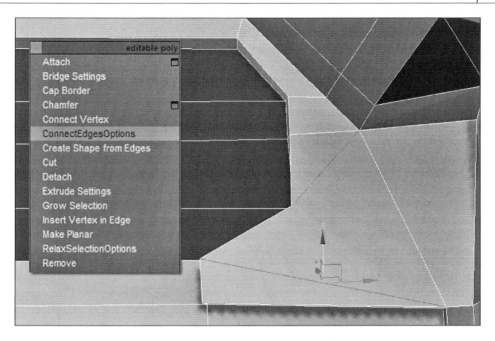

This lets us create quads, as shown in the following screenshot. Scaling the result, with the **Face** radio button turned on in the **Constraints** dialog will ensure the transformed edges don't affect the surface itself. They'll merely slide around on the surface:

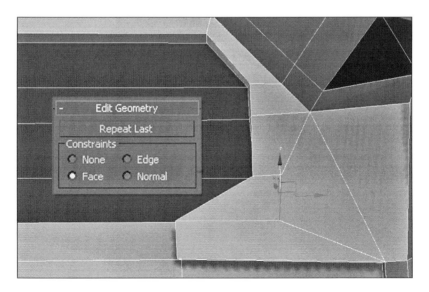

During the ship modeling run through we're constantly highlighting possible mistakes and fixes. If you model with a "model step, check step, and fix step" ethos, then you'll likely end up making fewer mistakes.

Moving on, the tail of the ship has a repeated "V" motif with horizontal lines across it, as shown in the following screenshot:

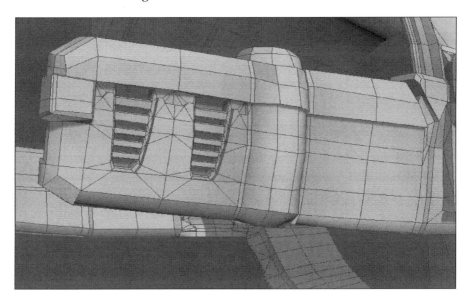

After noticing it has too many horizontal lines, I went back and matched the design, which only has three lines, and then repeated it. It's better to make sure a detail, which you'll clone is correct before reproducing it.

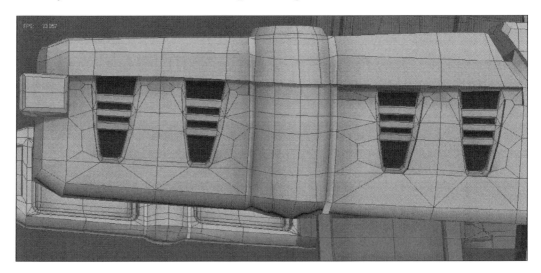

Here is the flip-side of the tail detail. The **Inset** and **Extrude** inwards is built within a 2 x 2 grid, as shown in the following screenshot:

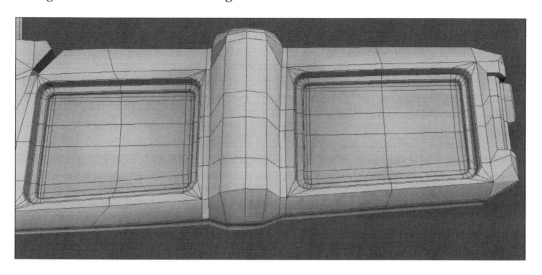

Around the curves of the inset are some bunches of triangles, which are redirected into quads in the following example. Bear in mind there's a trade off between keeping all quads and keeping the polygon count low.

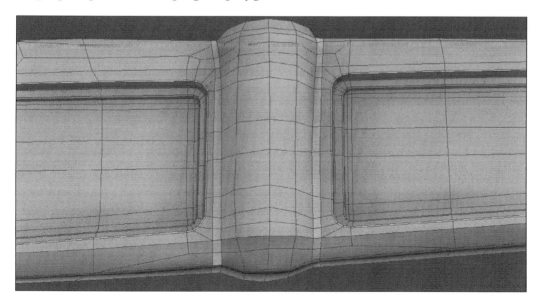

The next part of the ship to add is a large form at the bottom of the hull sides, which features spars, possibly gantry clamps that fix to another vessel.

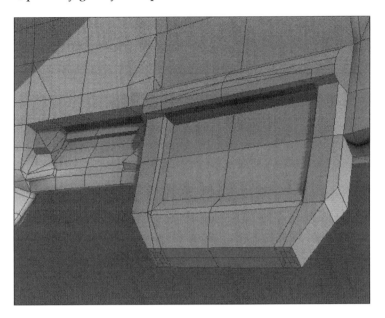

At the bottom, an inset is added where the spars will project down, as shown in the following screenshot:

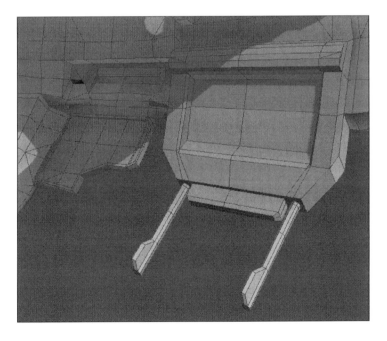

A separate floating panel is fixed in the corner of the bottom of the hull. Its outline fits into the other shapes, and its surface includes a curved cut-line at 45 degrees, and the flow of edges accordingly supports this, as shown in the following screenshot:

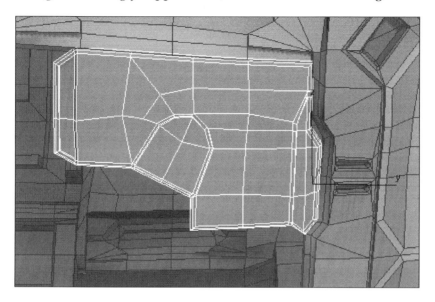

In the hull cavity, a cylindrical shape, made separately, is attached via bridging borders, as shown in the following screenshot:

An **Extrude** on the center line starts off the construction of the engine supports, slightly offset from the bulk of the hull, as shown in the following screenshot:

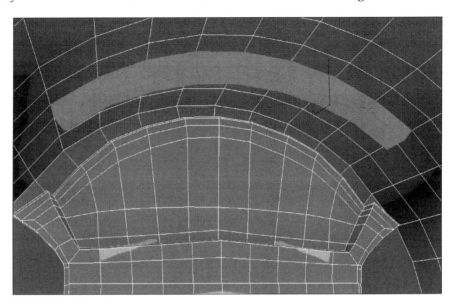

The engine support extends from the top of the hull to the backplate, all done with the **Extrude** and **Bridge** tools.

On top of this sit boosters (or possibly engine exhausts). These are separate objects, and not joined to the ship. They are symmetrical, so first a half cylinder was built, then mirrored, and this produced the side one for free.

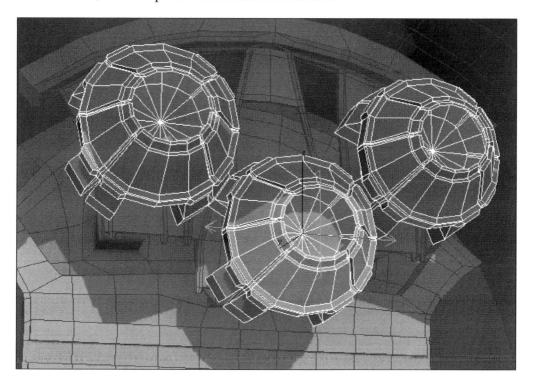

The following screenshot is the underside of the ship, showing most of the features. The second banded tube eventually was thrown out because it contains a lot of detail and this seemed to be an overload in such a small area:

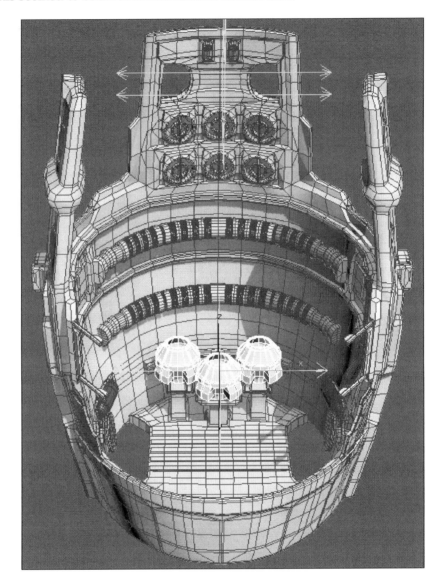

The following screenshot shows the bottom of the hull, where "escape pods" will be positioned along the curve. The arrows indicate where one piece, a kind of frame that the "escape pod" connects to, is defined and reproduced as a new element and then attached back on.

The "escape pods" are clones, but each one has to be attached back onto the model, so it is helpful that each point of joining is also a cloned part.

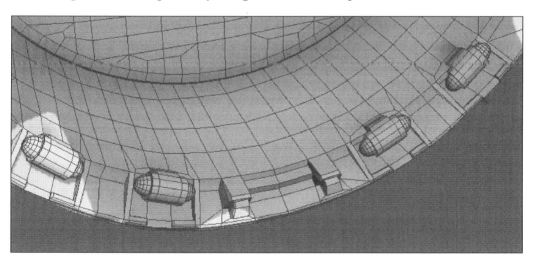

The top section of the ship, at the back, has a series of insets that form an interlocking pattern, as shown in the following screenshot. These needed repositioning and the **Edit Geometry | Constraints | Face** and **Constraints | Edge** options helped a lot with that, as the overall surface they sit on is curved.

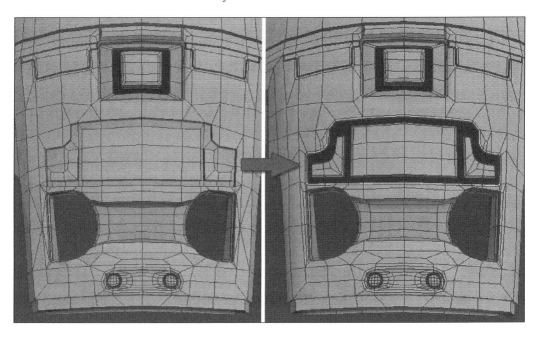

It can be hard to tell what constraint is active if the modifier panel for the **Editable Poly** isn't exposed, and also a little annoying to mouse over to the radio buttons to make changes time after time. It's possible to assign hotkeys like *Shift + N* = **None** for the Sub-Object transforms, as shown in the following screenshot according to the settings in `Packt3dsMax\UI Settings\PacktUi.ui`:

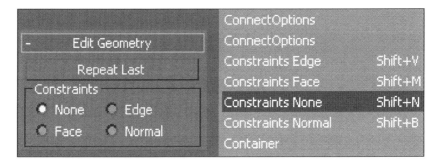

By now, the modeling methods used in the ship are visibly repetitive. The following screenshot shows a familiar cloning of an element, the production of a circle within a square, the framing of an extrusion using supporting edges, and the tightening of sharp edges with extra loops:

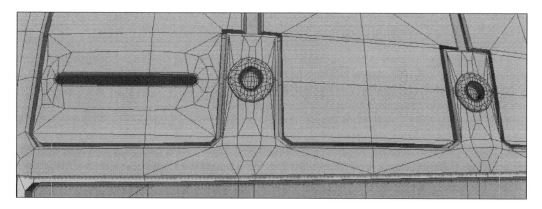

For the circle polygons, additional resolution was added by selecting them and then clicking on **Meshsmooth** in the **Editable Poly** menu (not the **Meshsmooth** modifier). This subdivides the selection and creates triangles around the border, but those could easily be cleared up into quads, as shown in the following screenshot:

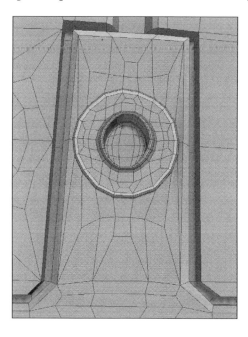

Again, we have a detail that is extracted to a cloned element, but this time it is flipped before it is attached again.

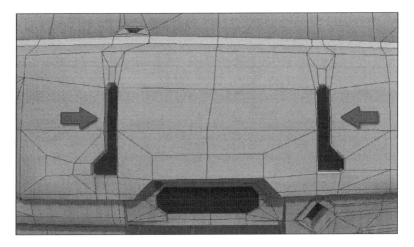

These last few screenshots show the concept art alongside angles on the finished base model, starting with the top. Remember, details can be painted or sculpted using a program such as Pixologic Zbrush or Autodesk Mudbox, and then reapplied as a texture.

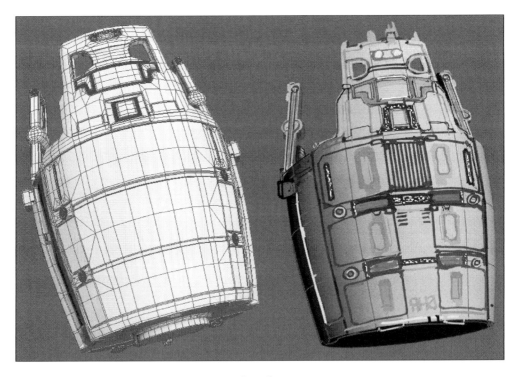

The following screenshot is the back view:

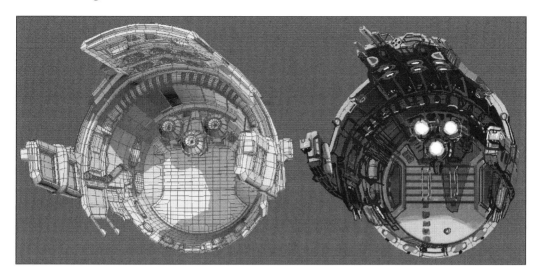

The side view is shown next, and that takes us through the modeling process based on the concept paint over, up to the point where further detailing could be added using textures to contain the polygon budget.

Before beginning that process and exporting to another application, it would be a good idea to go through the following checklist:

- Looking for redundant edge loops that could be removed
- Looking for N-gons and then triangles, and fixing the topology to be quads using **Select By Numeric | >4** and then **<4**
- UV Mapping (it is probably best to map the model as a half, and then separate the coinciding texture mapping afterwards rather than collapsing the model to an **Editable Poly** and then unwrap it as a whole)
- **STL Check** (also run this if you've dropped symmetry to check the mirror weld)
- Reset **Xform** (which I usually do through the menu **Edit | Transform Toolbox**)

You can view all the modeling steps in the provided content by opening /Packt3ds Max/Chapter 5/3dsMax Scenes/Scene Increments/ShipStart01-TheFront.max and so on. Compare this with the pass that is all quads Ship_Quads.max in the same folder.

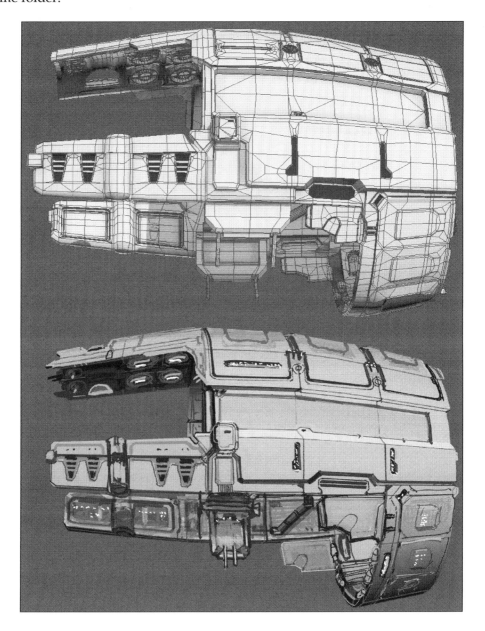

Summary

In this chapter we've covered a lot of polygon modeling procedures, common problems, and solutions. Now that we have a base model, in the next chapter we'll UV Map it for texturing. There are many avenues for texturing, including Photoshop, ZBrush and Mudbox, or even Viewport Canvas within 3ds Max.

UV Mapping and texturing can sometimes take longer than the modeling process. It's easy to underestimate the time texturing can take.

Probably for a game asset, you don't want a model that is really as complicated as this ship, unless it's a core asset or very large. In this case we needed to show some design approaches, diverse modeling procedures, and work out where to keep detail in the model, and where to hold it off for the texture painting process, which is covered in the future chapters.

6

The Cutting Edge:
A Closer Look at 3ds Max
Polygon Tools

This chapter examines newer features related to modeling in 3ds Max 2013 and some of the more peripheral modeling tools that are nevertheless really handy to know.

These are the topics covered in the chapter:

- New modeling and UI tools in 3ds Max 2013
  - Camera movement while a Cut operation is live
  - Customizable Workspaces
  - Tabbed Layouts
  - Interoperability with AutoCad

- Sub-Object level editing tools via the Ribbon
  - Edge loops selection and growth
  - Loop mode and live select mode
  - Dot selection, growth, and Step selection
  - Sub-Object editing in Manipulation mode

- Joining objects
  - Creating and cleaning Booleans
  - ProBooleans

- Ribbon tools

  - Paint Connect, Vertex, and Distance Connect
  - Freeform: Shift
  - Freeform: Optimize

If you are using 3ds Max 2012 throughout this book, you can follow references to `Packt3dsMax\UI Settings\PacktUI.ui`, which is a state of the 3ds Max UI that is saved (including hotkeys and Quad menu items). If you are using 3ds Max 2013, a different but identical version is used in `Packt2013_UI.ui`. As this chapter focuses on 3ds Max 2013 functionality, the provided scenes are built in the newer version and won't open in 3ds Max 2012. However, an `.fbx` model from the base scene and final scene can be imported into older versions. You can find this in the content folder of this chapter, at `\Packt3dsMax\Chapter 6\FBX\ScalpelStart.fbx`.

New modeling and UI features in 3ds Max 2013

Most of the new features in this version are either to do with continuing the effort to legitimate NVIDIA iray as a physically based GPU renderer or with its interoperability with other software (in particular, the CAD importing tools and After Effects connectivity). The availability of compositing operations in the Slate material editor is an interesting addition, especially given After Effects features and that there's already been a bundling of Composite with 3ds Max for a couple of versions. So for modeling, by contrast, the changes are fairly small, but they are in areas where you'll be using the tools very often. These features are supported by videos from Autodesk, coupled with brief descriptions, that can be found at `http://the-area.com/blogs/maxstation/n118_autodesk_3ds_max_2013_new_features`. What follows is my fairly short summation of what may be beneficial about those additions or changes.

To start with, a mention has to be made that in the 2013 release you can double-click on an edge to select the edge loop to which the edge belongs. You can still use *Shift + LMB* on an edge beside an edge, or the **Loop** icon in the Ribbon, or the **Loop** button in the Command Panel. In future it's likely Autodesk will do legacy UI clearance.

Camera movement while a Cut operation is live

Shifting (or not being able to shift) the camera while cutting is not something that ever caused me concern. One of the few times I worked in a studio exclusively working with Maya, one of the artists mocked 3ds Max for not including this feature, which to me seemed a trivial argument except perhaps that **Cut** is one of the most commonly used, and repeatedly used, modeling tools. Still, Maya didn't get **Soft Selection** until long after 3ds Max did, so the one-upmanship war still rages on, on both sides. Luckily, increased interoperability with Maya 2013 is part of what makes 3ds Max 2013 charming. You may not immediately notice the improved **Cut** feature, as it simply is built into the existing tool, and you can work with it as before, or try out moving the camera and notice that the **Cut** tool will wait for you to resume. It even stays live if you adjust the camera while the **Cut** tool's dotted **Pick Line** is active. This may float in empty space as you orbit or pan the view, but it repositions itself so its origin is where you cut from when you stop adjusting the camera. You can also move the cursor across two views (say you start in front and jump to left) and **Pick Line** will follow you accordingly.

Customizable Workspaces

In 3ds Max 2013, you have the option of setting up **Customizable Workspaces**, which are like saved states of the UI (such as the position of various toolbars and toggled conditions for the Ribbon, Trackbar, Command Panel, and so on). This is probably not a feature of immediate benefit to those starting out with 3ds Max, who may not yet know which toolbars are best to associate together. For instance, hiding the **Timeline** and **Trackbar** is great if you are a modeler, but it would quickly lead to an unproductive day if you are an animator. If your job has you wearing both hats, these Workspace states may become very handy indeed. The Workspaces are set and swapped between the top of the 3ds Max UI, within the **Quick Access Toolbar**, which itself is intended to be a way to customize the UI so you can rapidly access any tool that can be dragged to it (except it is restricted to Ribbon tools). To make a custom Workspace, you save the Workspace with a different name by clicking on **Save as New Workspace**, and then just change the state of the new Workspace (moving a panel here, or docking a floating toolbar there) and save it again by clicking on **Save Default State**.

The icon ▓ allows you to remove these saved states from the list, and you can double-click on existing states to swap between them. You may also tick the checkboxes in the **Manage Workspaces** dialog, according to what features you want the custom workspace to influence. For example, you can exclude changes to **Hotkeys** from your Workspace so you can keep a unified set of keys across all the different states you store. After loading a Workspace, it may still say **Loading...** even after it is ready to go, as shown in the following screenshot:

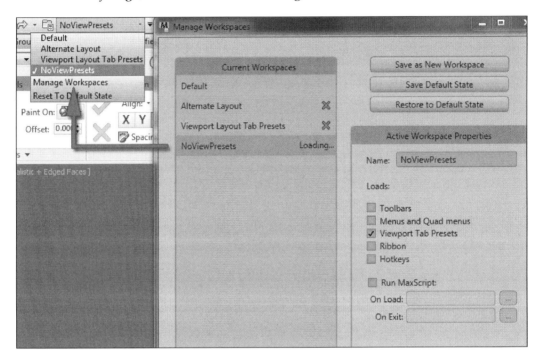

Tabbed Layouts

This lets users quickly swap between preconfigured View Layouts, but it seems a tax on viewport space. To effectively use presets, set a new Layout preset, then designate which particular views you want the Layout to involve (such as Left, Front, or Perspective). Those designated views are then stored for that Layout, which you can give a unique name. After that, you can create another Layout. Luckily, the panel, which takes up about 1 cm to the left of the screen, can be undocked, resized (while undocked), and turned off. One tip is to set up a series of similar presets so you can use this tool to quickly swap all views at once between shading modes. This is because each view preset remembers the settings for shading for each viewport involved. In the following screenshot, I set up an "Animation" Layout preset with two versions, one **Realistic** and one **Edged Faces**.

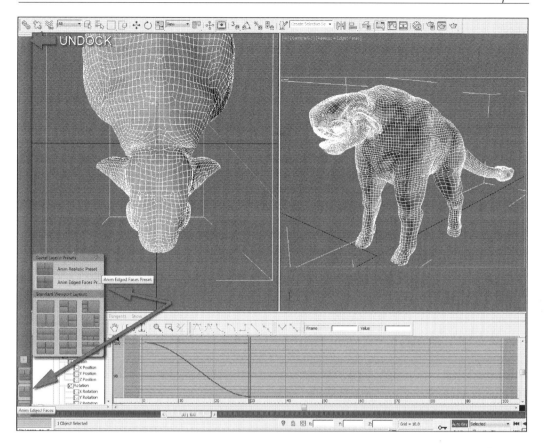

Once you've created some Layouts, you can delete them one at a time if you right-click on each and choose the **Delete** tab, or (if you have set at the top of the screen the toggle **Viewport Layout** tab) you can manage them by clicking on the icon , and then clicking on the pencil icon next to **Saved Layout Presets**. The interface seems to ape the iPad's method of removing unwanted entries from a list, with icons alongside the entries so you can delete them quicker in series.

A gradient for the viewport background

You may notice the Perspective viewport has been given a gradient, along the lines of Mudbox and other Autodesk software. If you don't like this, you can reset to a flat background by going to the **Views** menu and choosing **Viewport Configuration**, then clicking on the **Background** tab. Here, there are four options for the background color, shown in the following screenshot. They include **Gradient**, **Flat Color**, **Environment Background** (Color or Image), and an external file (which can be a frame sequence).

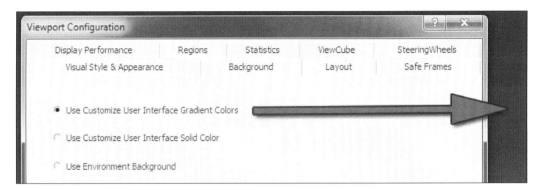

Interoperability with AutoCad

For modelers with an engineering bent, 3ds Max 2013 includes the Autodesk® DirectConnect family of translators, and users can use these to exchange industrial design data with other Autodesk CAD products and certain other applications. For the files you import or link (*Shift +]* opens the **File Link Manager**), the data is imported as native solids objects that can be interactively re-tessellated as needed. For a quick primer on native solids, take a look at `http://acad-atc.ic.polyu.edu.hk/native/design1.htm`.

Currently, users are required to have Autodesk DirectConnect installed before certain file formats can be imported using DirectConnect, such as Catia v4 or SolidWorks. DirectConnect comes with 3ds Max 2013, and with Maya, Alias, Showcase, and Opticore Studio. If you consult the Help menu for DirectConnect, you'll notice lists of supported OS cases for file types in various applications.

Once the installation is complete, the screen should look like the following screenshot:

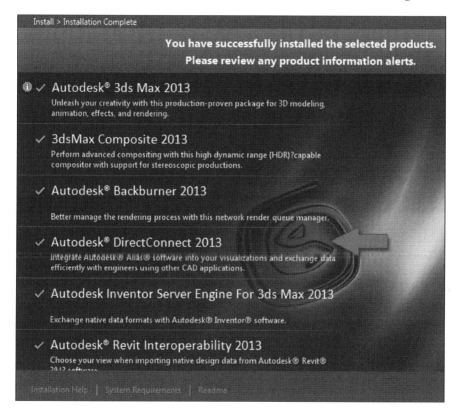

In the following screenshot, on the right-hand side, is an untessellated *3-way ball valve* with a **mental ray Arch & Design** Glossy Plastic material. On the left-hand side of the following screenshot is a DWG import of the same model with the same material, also untesselated. Note the higher quality of the native solid object, which looks visually a lot smoother with better-curved surfaces. The image was rendered using NVIDIA iray and the default Daylight system was used for lighting. The model, which is free, can be obtained at TraceParts (`www.tracepartsonline.net`) in various CAD formats.

Sub-Object level editing tools via the Ribbon

Getting back to regular modeling tools, in this chapter our project is to make a realistic scalpel, the kind used by graphic designers to cut out stencils and by psychotic surgeons to cut up patients. This project gives us a great chance to look in detail at some of the modeling tools we haven't fully covered, in particular the Freeform tools, joining objects, and the Snap tools. There is definitely more than one way to begin making an object like a scalpel in 3D, and since the tools we're going to look at are largely related to finishing the object, we'll start from an existing state of the model, assuming that you can find general Editable Poly process in the earlier chapters.

Getting started

You can find plenty of reference images in a Google image search; I chose to use a number-**10** blade and a number-**3** handle as these match in the real world. The reference images are included in this chapter's content, at `\Packt3dsMax\Chapter 6\Scalpel Reference`. As the metal includes lots of extracted form, you can see that there is plenty of scope for creating the shape using Booleans, and we'll also be looking at edge loop control using **Snaps** and the **Ribbon Freeform** tools. So, our starting model is the bulky, unextracted form.

Open the file `\Packt3dsMax\Chapter 6\ScalpelStart.max` or import the FBX `ScalpelStart.fbx`. If you import the model, you will need to apply to the *Plane* object a material with the bitmap `\Packt3dsMax\Content\Textures\Scalpel_ Complex.png`. Then, set **Show Realistic Material in Viewport**.

Perform the following steps as set up in the sequence shown in the following screenshot.

1. In **A**, the polygons on the facing side of a Cylinder at the base of the handle are extruded up the handle neck.

2. In **B**, another smaller Cylinder forms the top of the handle and is extruded back towards the tapered neck. These end parts are joined using **Attach** and **Bridge**.

3. In **C**, because the top Cylinder has a curved edge, added edge loops in the neck will curve, as shown in the following screenshot. Instead, use **QuickSlice** to chop a straight edge loop through and use *Ctrl* + **Remove** to remove the curved ones.

4. In **D**, the negative space of the blade will be created via a Boolean subtract, so we need to create an object there that is made in the same way as the handle, extruding polygons off the side of a Cylinder and fitting them to the image.

5. In **E**, for the blade, a **Spline** with points that pair off on either side is a good starting point. I set the **Interpolation** value of **Spline** to **3**.

6. In **F**, after applying an **Extrude** modifier with a value of **0.5** to the **Spline**, I used **Connect Edges** to add more vertical segments so the straighter top edge of the blade would match the curvier cutting edge of the blade.

7. In **G**, the paired-off points on either side of the blade are connected. At the tip and base of the blade there are four unconnected points. This is our starting point. You can load the file `\Packt3dsMax\Chapter 6\Scalpel_DistanceConnect_Start.max` or import `\Packt3dsMax\Chapter 6\FBX\Scalpel_DistanceConnect_Start.fbx` to follow on from here.

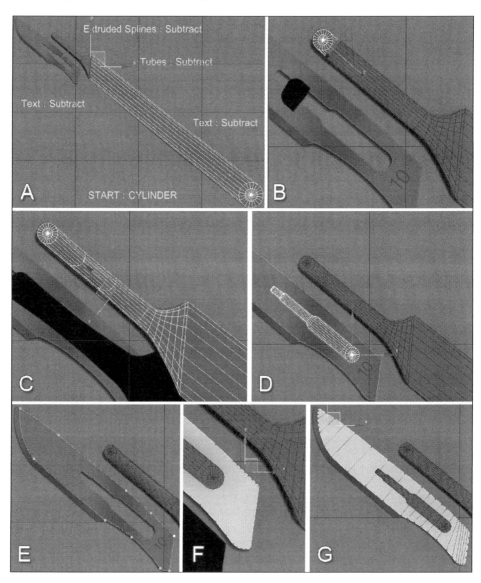

Edge loop selection and growth

As shown in the following screenshot, the object can be analyzed into a few simple operations. The handle can be begun as a Cylinder. The image has been saved with a gray backdrop, so that in the 3ds Max viewport it is easier to work over when applied as a texture on a plane.

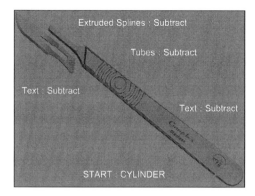

Let's start by beveling the sides of the handle. This is a bevel that is much wider at the neck of the handle than at the bottom end. Grow the edge loop using the **Grow Loop** icon ⊹ under **Modify Selection** in the Ribbon, and then pull in the sides. The loop next to it doesn't need to be pulled in, because later that area will be subtracted out.

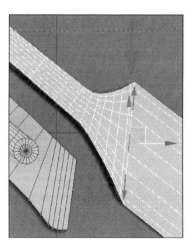

Loop mode and live select mode

It's important to arrange loops prior to doing a Boolean operation so that joined or subtracted sections don't overlap existing edges unnecessarily. In the Ribbon, you can find a **Loop Mode** toggle that allows you to directly select loops, rather than double-click (2013) or use *Shift + LMB* (2012). **Loop Mode** will stay active until toggled off, and in the viewport there will be a HUD notice when it is on.

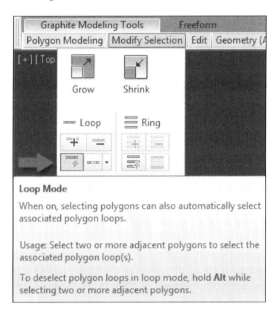

With the scalpel, we'll be cutting objects out of both the handle and blade, so take care arranging the existing edge loops where the changes need to be made. As you are matching it to the back plate image, press *Alt + X* to view the model in **See-Through** mode, a kind of X-ray shading. If that isn't transparent enough, go to **Object Properties | Visibility** and set the value to 0.2 or 0.3, enough that you can read the writing on the scalpel handle.

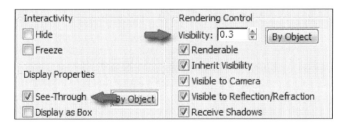

Rather than using **SwiftLoop** ⚊ as we've done so far to add segments, in the Ribbon, under the **Edit** tools, use **Quickslice** ⚊ to add edge loops to ensure they are straight. This matters because the end of the handle has a curved loop, which would affect other loops if you used **Connect Edges** or **SwiftLoop**.

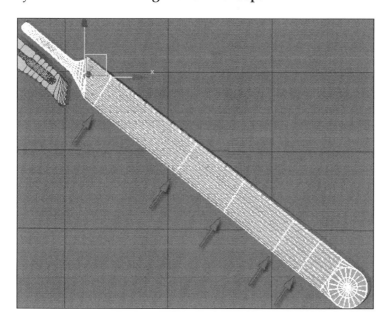

Use **SwiftLoop** while holding *Alt* to slide currently selected loops along the handle. This is not that convenient if you want to shift multiple edges. In that case, it's easier to turn on **Constraints | Edge** in the Editable Poly parameters in the Command Panel so that the loops slide when you move it.

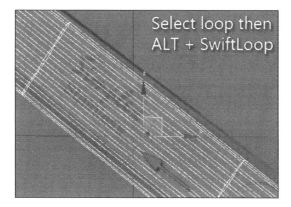

You may want to use the **Loop Spacing** tools to adjust the distribution of segments in the loops for the handle. The **Center** button will place one loop directly between two on either side of it.

You can also use live selection to allow you to dynamically step between **Vertex** selection, **Edge** selection, and **Polygon** selection, depending on where you place the mouse over the object. In the parameters of the model in the Command Panel, you'll find the **Preview Selection** panel, which features **SubObj** + **Multi** modes. We might use these modes here to quickly swap between edge loop selection and manual vertex cutting. **Multi** selection is the default in some modeling programs, such as Blender and Maya, so you may prefer it to be set on all of the time.

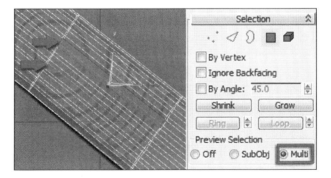

Dot selection, growth, and Step selection

Ring selection is used to select edges that flow perpendicularly between two edge loops.

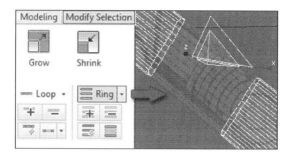

Just as edge loops have a **Loop** Mode toggle ⚞, edge rings have a **Ring** Mode toggle ⚟. You can also **Grow** ⚎ and **Shrink** ⚍ a **Ring**, just as you can grow ⚎ and shrink ⚍ a **Loop**.

There are matching tools — **Ring + Loop, Dot Ring + Dot Loop, Ring Mode + Loop Mode** — but there is no Step Ring. **StepLoop** and **Step Mode** help you to select edges in a loop between two selected edges. While **StepLoop** defaults to the shortest distance, you can specify the longest distance instead by pressing *Alt* when you click on **StepLoop** ⚎. For loops, there is also a **Fill Hole** option ⚎, where you click within a closed loop to select the enclosed area. This works well when you are turning a Polygon selection into its edge outline (hold *Shift* and click on **Outline** ⚎ in the **Modify Selection** tab of the Ribbon). The Ribbon provides pop-up guides to these tools. I learned to model before some of these tools were introduced, via the merged-in Polyboost scripts that preceded the Ribbon, so I don't habitually use all of them. I have noticed, however, that students introduced early to these tools will adopt them much more readily, and becoming accustomed to them means they get the benefit of the added speed and efficiency that these tools were designed to enable.

Sub-Object editing in Manipulation mode

These two shift commands don't shift selected Sub-Objects (like **Freeform: Shift Brush** does), but cycle the selection one way or another, basically stepping. If you turn on the **Manipulation** mode ✛ while in **Edge** Sub-Object level (2) for Editable Poly, you will see the caddy for these tools; you will also see the **Weight** and **Crease** tools for edges. Clicking on the icon for Ring Shift ◉ turns it to two arrows ◉▶, and you can tap either side to move the selection one step over. If you hold *Ctrl* while pressing the same icon, you'll cumulatively step round the ring. The same goes for **Loop Shift** ◉. If **Soft Selection** ▣ is enabled, the **Manipulation** caddy lets you adjust **Falloff** ◉, **Pinch** ◢, and **Bubble** ▣ in the view.

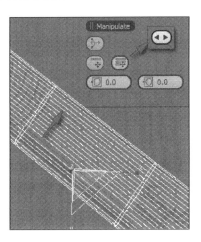

For the next step, the text **Stainless** and numbers are made with **Create | Shapes | Text**, and their Spline Interpolation is reduced to 2, with the **Font** choice being **Arial**. The larger text **Complex** was created using a font called **Magneto**. The real scalpel is branded as **Simplex**, but the font is a bit curvy, and I wasn't sure if I'd be allowed to recreate an actual branded product. I chose a font that is still script-like but has some straight edges. As shown in the following screenshot, some of the letters overlap, which needs to be fixed manually (center image). Then, **Refine** lets us add extra points so that the quads can easily be made when the **Extrude** modifier is added to the text (sketched in the bottom image), generating a polygon mesh that is used to **Subtract** as a Boolean from the scalpel blade. It's true that if you are going to extrude text and don't plan to do anything else to it, you don't need to clean it up into quads, but as a matter of good habit, the clean up allows you to do so much more after you've generated the extruded model, such as chamfer edges, sculpt the surface, subdivide and relax it, and and so on.

Once the **Complex** text is extruded and converted to Editable Poly, the top face will need to be subdivided into quads by hand. It's more accurate to join two points using **Connect Vertex** rather than **Cut**. If you try to **Connect** across an existing line, it doesn't do anything. In the illustration we encounter, the first case is the upright of the letter M. There are a few ways to approach this. As we'll see later, **Distance Connect** is an option. Another way to insert a vertex is using **Insert Vertex** on the middle edge in **Edge** Sub-Object mode, and then **Connect** through it. Another, shown in the following screenshot, is to **Quickslice** through the object and then **Target Weld** the new points at the ends to the original points, preserving the shape but getting the required internal edge quickly. **Quickslice** is similar to **SwiftLoop** , but lets you place the edge using a pick line in the viewport.

Distance Connect is easiest to use when the unconnected points you are trying to join, where they cross intervening segments, are enclosed within quads. This situation doesn't always arise, so it's best to know a few different ways to skin a cat!

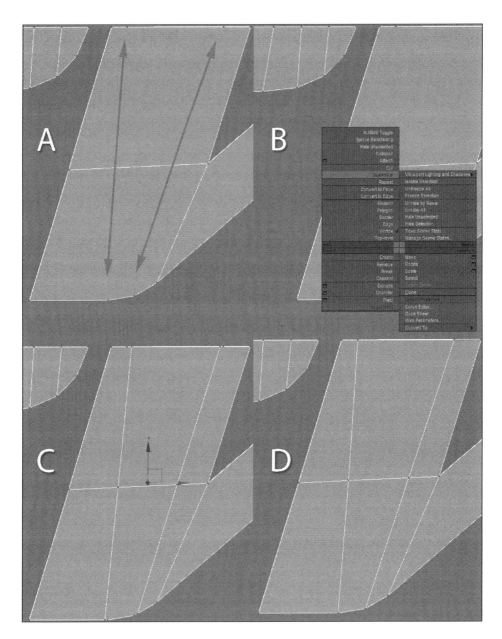

Use the following method to add an edge:

1. In **A**, the problem is that edges can't be added using **Connect** across the middle segment.

2. In **B**, right-click and choose **Quickslice** ✄ or access it in the **Edit** section of the Ribbon.

3. In **C**, drag-and-release to add an edge, using **Quickslice**.

4. In **D**, right-click and choose **Target Weld** to join the added points to the original points.

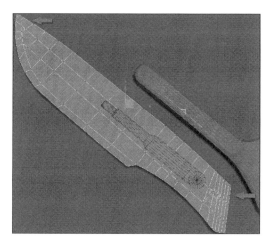

From point to point the previous example would be suitable for **Distance Connect** ⊞ to add edges. For the following screenshot, because there are N-gons in between, it wouldn't work:

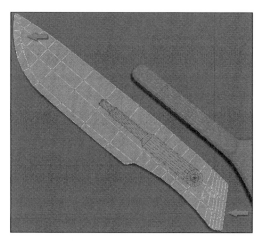

Joining objects

Concentric tubes will allow us to cut away from the handle the distinctive curves in the middle. The distance between the **Inner Radius** and **Outer Radius** is 4 in each case, but as they get larger, they have more sides segments. Be sure to drop the default value of **Height Segments** from **5** to **1**, as fewer segments is better when the height of the tube doesn't feature any curvature. A **Height** value of **5** is enough.

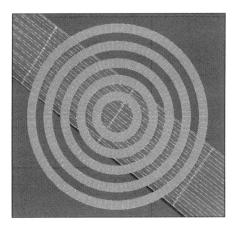

Creating and cleaning Booleans

Once the text objects are extruded and cleaned, we can Boolean them where they overlap the scalpel model and then clean up the result.

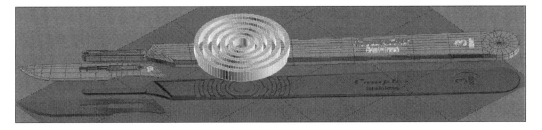

Usually, Boolean operations triangulate participating edges, and sometimes the result is not very tidy. To reduce complications it really helps to frame the part that will be joined or subtracted so that connecting edges are contained close to that area.

The previous object is an extruded Spline. Extruding it gives us the basis for the first subtract operation. Select the handle and choose **Create | Compound Objects | Boolean.**

In the **Boolean** dialog , you will notice the options to create a **Union, Intersection,** or **Subtraction** (A-B or B-A). As we're removing the extruded object from the handle and the handle is selected, we want **Subtraction** (A-B). When the Boolean gets calculated, you can choose to leave the original source via a copy, show only the result (**Move + Result**), or show only the operands. In this case, the defaults will work best.

After you perform the Boolean, the surface will change and you'll probably see serious N-gons around the affected surface, as shown below on the right-hand side of the following screenshot. N-gons are multi-sided polygons that, generally, you should sort into quads, or at least quads and tris. If you again click on **Create Boolean**, the mesh will triangulate automatically, as shown in the following screenshot on the left-hand side. You can then convert the model to editable poly for clean up. A good step in this process is to remove triangles from the area so you can determine for yourself a better edge distribution. Remember to let the loops flowing into the area connect as much as possible.

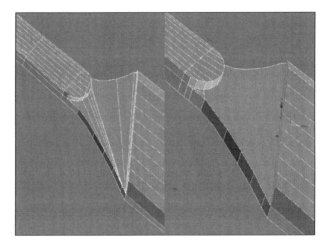

In the following screenshot, the clean up for the previous Boolean is done primarily using **Cut** and **Connect**.

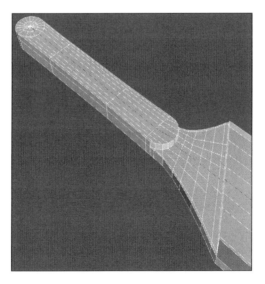

Around a negative space, such as in the blade, it is good to add a framing loop so that when the points in the subtracted space are connected, they don't wind up being overlong, stretched polygons.

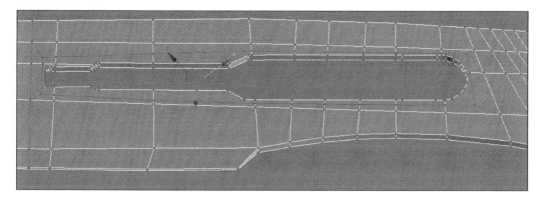

The following screenshot is the result of tidying up the blade, again using **Cut** and **Connect**. Notice that the clean up is contained mostly within the framing edge that was just mentioned.

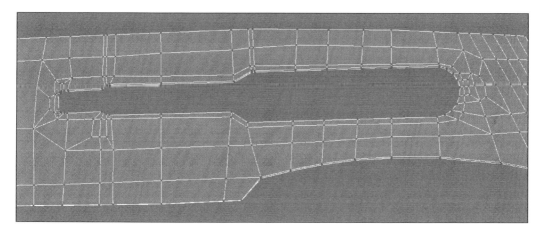

It's useful to bear in mind that a lot of the work involves going from a cluster of tight vertices to a broader section with fewer vertices, adding as few edges as possible.

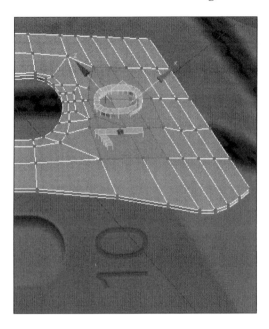

In the case of the number **10**, which also began from a well-framed area of the blade, an unusual scenario arises, where the number **0** gets capped during the operation, as shown in the following screenshot. The reason the capping occurs is because there's a closed curve in a closed curve.

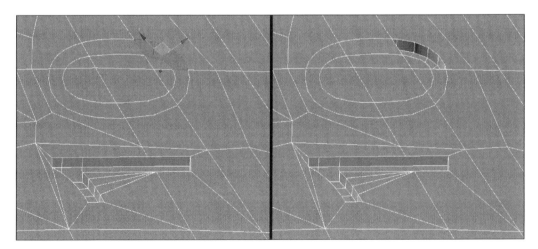

Actually, in this case, rather than using **Subtract** when creating the Boolean, you could opt to use the **Cut** option in the Boolean object parameters. You could also try **ProCutter**. Both of these take the contact edge where the two surfaces overlap and create edges on the source object's surface. Then, you could select the polygons and **Extrude** inwards.

In the following screenshot, to handle the inner surface of the number **0**, you could delete the faces, select the border edge, and hold *Shift*, then **Scale** inwards to inset the surface, and then use **Cap** and **Connect** to finish it up (or the Quad Chamfer script discussed in *Chapter 9, Go with the Flow Retopology in 3ds Max*).

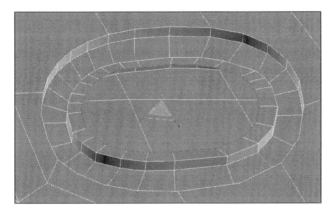

In the following screenshot, the clean up around the number **10** is contained within a small area, all quads:

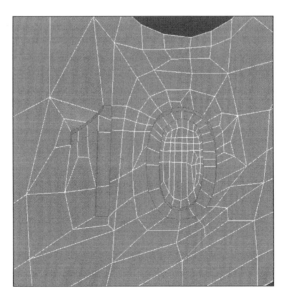

ProBooleans

With Booleans and ProBooleans you can translate operands (before you convert to editable poly), and with ProBooleans you can reorder a series of operands, which can change the look of the resulting mesh. The biggest difference between Booleans and ProBooleans is their post-tesselation approach and the decimation options available after the operation. ProBooleans are given a neat, quick demonstration at `www.mrbluesummers.com/1307/blog/introduction-to-3dsmax-probooleans` and at `http://goo.gl/xeUgn`. ProBoolean operations are designed for cases where you want to repeatedly drill a series of holes in an object, or append objects, or both, all in one go, adding the operands sequentially and then creating the surface in one step (whereas Boolean results are calculated incrementally).

In our case, the rings on the handle could easily be done using ProBooleans. As the entire surface of the model gets recalculated after picking the operands, a nifty trick is to break off the area that will be affected, to preserve the mesh for the area that isn't affected. Imagine, on a head, you spend a lot of time on the topology of the nose, and then you add ears to the head, and to join them the nose is also recalculated, risking a change to your topology.

After this, you can start with the file `\Packt3dsMax\Chapter 6\BooleanStart.max`.

Select the polygons on the blade where the rings are, and **Detach** them to a new object, and with the detached piece selected choose **Create | Compound Objects | ProBoolean**.

In the **ProBoolean** dialog, **Subtraction** is default, and that's what needed here, so just click on **Start Picking**. It doesn't really matter in what order you choose the tubes. You'll immediately see an intermediate stage result that is not tessellated but shows the subtraction for each piece as you pick it. After this, you could convert to editable poly and manually **Cut** and **Connect** vertices to make the model all quads. Or, you could open the **Advanced Options** parameters of the **ProBoolean** dialog and use the tools there to take you further down that road with less work. To get an effective result, tick the **Make Quadrilaterals** button and then enter a **Quad Size** of 30 percent. Too small a value will create more polygons than are needed. Experiment with the three radio button settings: **Remove All**, **Remove Only Invisible**, and **No Edge Removal**. In this case, **Remove Only Invisible** gave the best result, that which was easiest to tidy up.

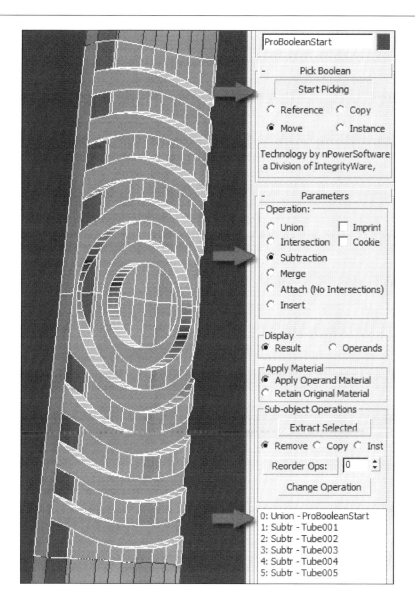

Once the ProBoolean is performed, some of the quads have a concave area, which is not a good thing. This is shown in the top part of the following screenshot. Flowing the edges in from the left- and right-hand sides, where the detached piece meets the rest of the handle, is the easiest way to tidy up the subtracted result into tidy quads, shown in the bottom of the following screenshot:

For the text **Complex Stainless** you could subtract it or use the **Cookie Cutter** function, which leaves only the outline (as an open edge) where the two surfaces contact. You can then extrude inwards, giving you more control over the edge flow. The **Cookie** checkbox has a corresponding **Imprint** checkbox, and you can toggle these to see their effects. In the following screenshot, the subtracted model has been removed and an open border for each letter is left:

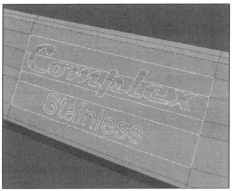
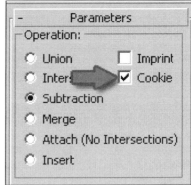

After the Booleans are performed and cleaned up, the model should be UV-mapped. Even if it will have a procedural metal texture which looks fairly uniform. For reflections to calculate properly the mapping of the surface should be coherent. In this case, so long as the upper surface and bottom surface are peeled separately, the result will allow the reflections to not present artifacts.

Once the model is cleaned up, you will probably find plenty of loops to reduce, shift, and arrange more tidily. For this, I generally use **Move**, **Relax**, **Target Weld**, **Remove**, and **Swift Loop**. **Swift Loop** will allow you to tighten some of the sharp edges, for instance around the top and bottom of each letter and around the circular curves of the handles. In the next topic, we'll look at some additional Ribbon tools that can help with final editing.

The following screenshot shows the model after mapping, rendered in the scene that comes with 3ds Max called `C:\Users\~\Documents\3dsMax\scenes\Studio_Scene_ Share.max`. The scalpel has **Material Autodesk Arch + Design** with the preset **Metal** set to **Stainless Steel**, and the renderer is set to NVIDIA iray. The light comes from the three **Sky Portal** lights already in the studio scene, slightly color-adjusted.

You can open the content for this project in the `\Packt3dsMax\Chapter 6\` folder and use `Scalpel_StudioFinish2.max`. No doubt a scalpel is not typically a major model in a game, as opposed to a highly detailed machine gun, but I chose a deliberately simple object to focus on the Boolean techniques and also to show how even simple forms are often surprisingly detailed.

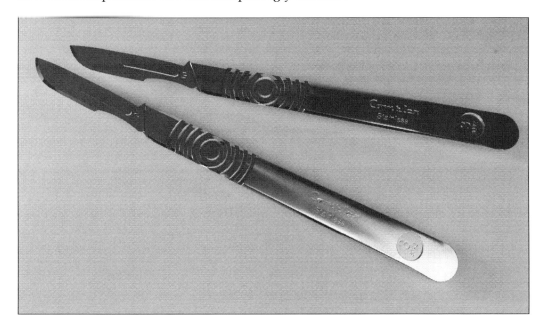

Ribbon tools

To make it easier to obtain detail in a model, new tools such as **Paint Connect** enable you to speed up editing the mesh. Some newer tools are not found in the command panel editable poly tools and only appear in the ribbon. Open the scene `\Packt3dsMax\Chapter 6\Creature_RibbonEditingStart.max`. This shows a creature that needs some detail refined around its feet, and we're going to use a few tools we haven't looked at yet in the Ribbon, in particular **Paint Connect**, **Shift**, and **Optimize**. The creature is also used as the asset to explore retopology in *Chapter 9, Go with the Flow, Retopology in 3ds Max.*

Paint Connect, Vertex, and Distance Connect

Zoom until you are looking at the front of the foreleg, open the **Graphite Modeling Tools** part of the Ribbon, and look in the tab labeled **Edit**. Here, you'll see shortcuts for tools we're fairly familiar with, that you can access in the **Quad menu** while working in the viewport—**Quickslice (Qslice)**, **SwiftLoop**, **Cut**—and you'll also notice **Paint Connect (P Connect)** , which has a pull-down option **Set Flow**. Turning this on from the start makes new edges position themselves in respect of the existing edges. Leaving it off makes the edges insert more like they would if using the **Cut** tool. **Set Flow** works similarly to turning on the **Snap** option **Midpoint** (right-click on the **3D Snap** icon and set this in the options). What it does is it snaps the newly added points to the center of an edge, as you brush over it.

What we're after is a better split around the hoof of the creature.

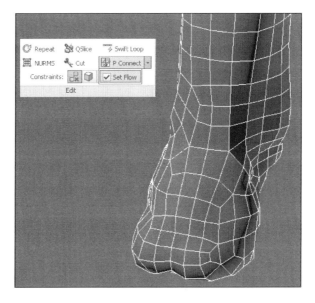

To start with, turn on **Set Flow** and use **Paint Connect** to add two lines up the middle of the hoof, on either side of the center. Note, in the following screenshot, that **Paint Connect** highlights the vertices added where they cross an edge:

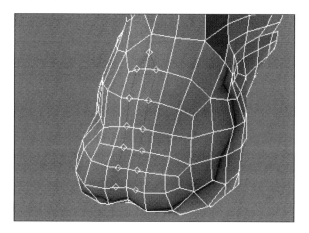

If you are in the **Vertex** mode, switch to **Edge** mode and you'll notice the new edges are added to the current selection. **Undo** will step back one added segment at a time, so if you want to get rid of the entire added loop, use *Ctrl* + **Remove**. Make sure though, that there aren't other edges already selected. It's probably a good habit to use *Ctrl* + *D* before using **Paint Connect** so your selection is clear when you start.

Use **Cut** to add the corner edges for the added loop, as shown in the following screenshot:

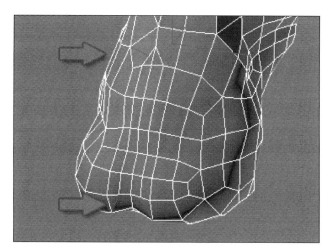

This introduces two triangles at the bottom, so select those edges and use **Paint Connect** to cross through them. If you hold *Ctrl* while brushing with **Paint Connect**, you can select and connect vertices too. This is equivalent to using the **ConnectVertex** tool, except you brush through the points, so if you are carrying out many operations, it is faster. It helps if you zoom in close to where you are working, so you don't miss.

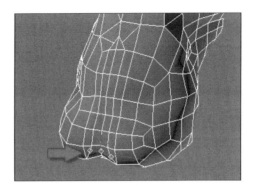

Where the loop turns, the vertices could be placed better. Currently, there are quads with four vertices, but a triangular shape. One of the vertices lies directly between two others. There are a lot of ways to fix this that we've already looked in previous chapters, but lets use a tool from the Ribbon, within the **Freeform** tab, called **Relax/Soften**, which is brush-based. When you click it, a brush floater shows the **Size** and **Strength** of the brush. Set the **Size** to **0.25** so it's much smaller. Then, hold *Alt* and brush on the surface where the loop we added turns (at the top and bottom). Holding *Alt* preserves the shape of the mesh. In this case, it isn't a big deal, but it's worth knowing.

Once you have set up your preferred radius, to speed up your workflow add the tool **DeformRelax** to a hotkey. In `Packt3dsMax\UI Settings\PacktUI.ui`, it is set to *Shift* + *R*. This alleviates the need to swap back and forth between the **Freeform** and **Graphite Modeling Tools** tabs.

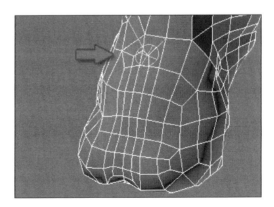

You may also want to try the **Freeform: Pinch/Spread** brush to pull together the crease added to the hoof.

Going back to **Paint Connect**, hold the mouse over the icon 🖉, and note that if you press *Y*, the tool tip plays a short demo video. You'll see in particular that you can remove points using this tool in combination with *Alt*, but you'll want to make sure the **Set Flow** checkbox is not ticked for this to be effective. **Set Flow** is actually not needed; instead, use *Shift* + **Paint Connect** to make sure the added edges follow the midpoints of the edges you brush across. So, with *Alt* you can remove points while brushing, and with *Shift* you can "flow" them better. Besides removing points, you can remove edges or loops, through the combination *Ctrl + Shift* (removes edge loop) or *Ctrl + Alt* (removes edge). A good case for trying this out would be to go round the base of the hoof to make the edge sharper.

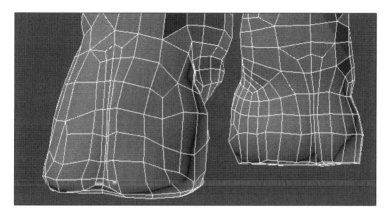

Freeform: Shift

The **Shift** brush 🖱 is the big brother of the **Relax/Soften** brush we already looked at. It is a screen space aligned transform based on the brush radius. For instance, if you set the **Full Strength** and **Falloff** values to be very tight, so you can move only one point, it is the same as the **Move** function using the **Screen co-ordinates system**. Along with **Relax/Soften** and **Pinch/Spread**, which I mentioned earlier, I suggest adding this tool to the **Quick Access Toolbar**. To do this, open the **Freeform** tab of the Ribbon, right-click on *Shift* 🖱, and choose **Add to Quick Access Toolbar**. This places it at the top of the screen, available no matter what state of the Ribbon you have showing.

The **Shift** brush, unlike the others, has a hotkey to control the brush. Drag vertically while holding *Ctrl* to change the **Falloff** radius, and drag vertically while holding *Shift* to change the **Full Strength** radius (the inner white circle in the following screenshot).

With the creature, a good use for the **Shift** brush would be to paint inward from the ankles, a bit above the hooves.

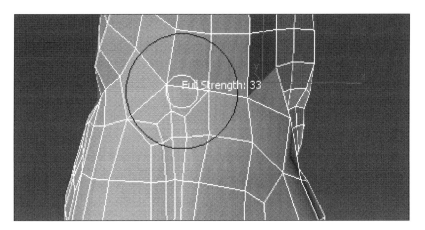

Freeform: Optimize

If you are familiar with the program Sculptris, which features a brush-based triangle reduction tool, you'll be happy to find that 3ds Max has a brush-based reduction tool, too. As with other brush tools in the Ribbon, there are a lot of hotkey combinations with which to control its effect. You may want to practice on the bottom of the creature's hoof—where the surface is relatively flat—to reduce detail there, using **Freeform: Optimize** . Note that this shouldn't be confused with the modifier **Optimize**, which reduces the polygon count of an entire mesh (or polygon selection) parametrically.

If you hold *Shift* + **Optimize**, you're effectively carrying out the same operation as a **Target Weld**, from vertex to vertex. Unlike **Target Weld**, however, if you continue dragging from vertex to vertex in a brush-like manner, from one to another and so on, you'll continue dissolving out detail.

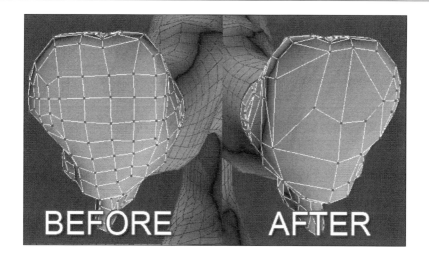

Like the **Extend** brush (just above **Optimize**), if you hold *Ctrl + Shift + Alt* while brushing, you can move existing points around. The **Extend** tool is covered in more detail in *Chapter 9, Go with the Flow Retopology in 3ds Max*, which is about retopology. You can also use the **Optimize** brush to remove edges, edge loops, and edge rings through the following keyboard shortcut combos:

Optimize keyboard combinations:	Description
None	Click edges to collapse them, combining two vertices into one.
Shift	Drag from one vertex to the next, to target weld the two, combining the first with the second. If you continue dragging to further vertices, you can weld several with a single stroke.
Ctrl	Drag between vertices to connect them with edges.
Alt	Remove a vertex by clicking it.
Shift + Ctrl	Remove an edge loop by clicking an edge belonging to the loop.
Shift + Alt	Remove an edge ring by clicking an edge belonging to the ring.
Ctrl + Alt	Remove an edge by clicking it.
Shift + Ctrl + Alt	Move a vertex by dragging it.

In the Ribbon, there is an icon **Constraint to Spline** , which allows you to use the brush-based **Paint Deform** tools constrained to a Spline shape in the scene. It's similar to the Curve tool in Mudbox. You can set a custom Spline or generate one in **Edge** mode using **Create Shape from Selection** off the existing mesh. Either way, to specify the Spline to use, click on **Pick** under the icon . Click on **Pick** again to clear the current Spline. This tool works with any mesh, but is more responsive on high-density surfaces. It works particularly well with the **Push/Pull** brush type, which moves vertices outward based on the surface normal, or inward if you hold *Alt* while brushing. If you don't like the result of the painting, you can click on **Cancel** or **Revert** . You can also **Commit** changes at any point to update the point that **Revert** will jump you back to.

Summary

In this chapter, we've looked at new tools for modeling in 3ds Max 2013 and methods of modeling using the Ribbon, in particular the fine control selection tools and the Freeform tools: **Shift**, **Optimize**, and **Paint Connect**. Getting used to these tools takes time but is well worth the extra effort.

In the next chapter, we move on from modeling to model preparation for texturing.

7

The Mystery of the Unfolding Polygons: Mapping Models for Texturing

This chapter demonstrates methods of UV Mapping and emphasizes the importance of becoming fluent in the process of preparing a model for texturing, a stage which bridges modeling and texture painting while calling on somewhat different skills. The challenge is simply to put a 3D surface onto a 2D image plane. 3ds Max's mapping tool set ensures the user is well-armed to meet the challenge.

The following topics are covered in the chapter:

- The goal of UV mapping
- Gaining familiarity with the UV editor
- Combining texture islands to save draw calls
- Just getting on with it
- Additional UV layout tools
- Soft Selection
- Setting UVW editor hotkeys
- Aligning points
- A handy script for fixing up UVs
- Mirror and Flip commands
- Packing the layout
- Finalizing the layout
- Making a Photoshop texture template
- Send to Mudbox
- 2D View in Viewport Canvas

The goal of UV mapping

Turbosquid, a commercial online model repository, recently established guidelines that asset contributors should follow so their work meets a common standard of production readiness. They call it **CheckMate Certification**. Having good UVs is a key feature of it. It's not nice to buy a great looking model, and then open up the UV editor and see a pancake view, where all the polygons are projected from only one angle. This is a big risk for anyone who downloads models, because models can take a lot of time to map and the whole point of the purchase is that you may not have the time for it in your project. For more on the subject, look up http://support.turbosquid.com/entries/20210308.

Now that we've made the spaceship mesh we face a similar and daunting problem. The following is what we face when we add an **Unwrap UVW** modifier to the model and click on the **Open UV Editor** button:

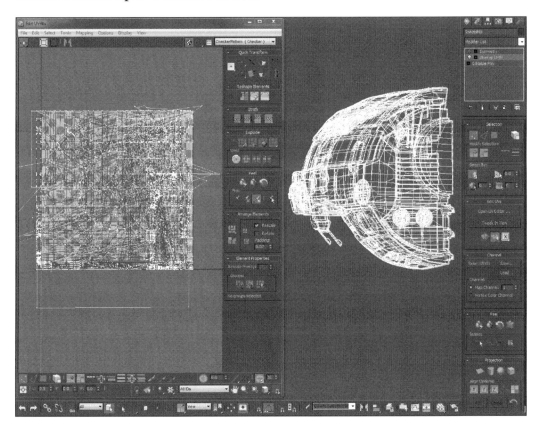

By and large the concept of mapping is to neatly pack into the UV mapping square all the object's polygons in suitable clusters. A cluster (or texture island) is good if it is composed of adjacent polygons that more or less face the same direction and therefore can be easily flattened. The green lines drawn on the model represent the boundaries of texture islands in the UV editor. At the moment there are far too many and they are disorganized and overlapping. Let's show what we're aiming for with the model now, to give a sense of direction. The model actually has two mapping tasks since it uses two painted textures.

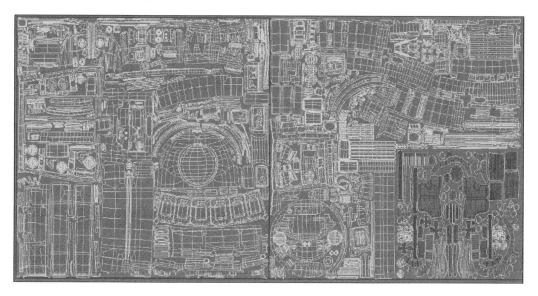

The light edges and, on the right, the dark edges represent two different models that share the same texture space. Two textures are required for this combined UV mapping.

In the previous example, it looks like there is almost no space between the UV islands. This is because of the reduced image size. It is good to keep a little space between the islands to allow for image filtering, especially when Normal maps will be extracted or MipMaps (texture complexity reductions based on camera distance from the object) are calculated.

It is worth noting that there are some mapping tools like **Unwrella** and **UV-Packer** (`http://www.3d-io.com`) that automate the steps of mapping; however, for a complex model the parts to auto-unwrap still need to be assigned by the artist. ZBrush provides a method of deriving UVs from every face of the model, mapped to a grid with precise, fragmented packing, but not every model suits this. It also can unwrap wholesale via its plugin UVMaster. The Pixar technology **PTex** provides a way to assign a texture per polygon, which is good when working on film content, but not so useful (yet) for real-time situations. Having pointed out some additional options, the 3ds Max **UVW Unwrap** editor is robust and, if you know how to use it, lets you get the job done quickly enough.

To get started with this topic, you can open the file `\Packt3dsMax\Chapter 7\ Ship_Quads_UnwrapUVW_Start.max` saved out from the end of *Chapter 5, The Language of Machines: Designing and Building Model Components*. The model is shown without symmetry, as that'll reduce the initial workload.

Gaining familiarity with the Unwrap UVW editor

In this topic we'll walk through the basics of everyday mapping using a section of the spaceship model. This simple example sets the scene for mapping the entire ship.

1. When you want to add a modifier, you can click on the **Modifier List** rollout and press the first letter of the modifier's name, such as *U* for **Unwrap UVW**. This jumps you down the list. You can also right-click with the model selected to add **Unwrap UVW** from the upper-right Quad menu if you are using the provided `Packt3dsMax\UI Settings\PacktUI.ui` customized interface.

Make sure you are in **Top-level** mode when you apply **Unwrap UVW**. If you are in Sub-Object mode, particularly if you haven't actually selected any polygons, you will only unwrap the current selection. Sometimes mapping just a part of an object is useful, but if nothing is selected, you'll be mapping nothing, which is very difficult since you won't see anything in the UV Editor. I've noticed students frequently make this mistake, and at first they find it totally baffling.

2. In the modifier panel, in the **Unwrap UVW | Selection** category, you'll see three Sub-Object modes: **Vertex**, **Edge**, and **Polygon**, as well as a **Select by Element XY** toggle , which is off by default. Don't mix up these modes with the similar modes at the base level of an **Editable Poly**. You can't model with the modifier highlighted, only adjust the UVs.

3. Moving down the **Selection** category to **Modify Selection**, you'll notice **Grow** and **Shrink** commands, and **Loop** and **Ring** commands, designed to make it easier to select parts of the model surface.

4. Moving down the **Selection** category to **Select By**, you'll see there's another toggle called **Ignore Backfacing** . While on this, it prevents you from selecting polygons that face away from the current view when you do a Marquee selection. This is on by default whenever you apply the modifier, and that can be a little annoying given that most of the time you'll find it easier to work with this off.

5. To open the **Edit UVWs** window, click on the **Open UV Editor ...** button in the Unwrap UVW modifier's **Edit UVs** panel, shown at the bottom of the following screenshot. You can also press *Ctrl + E* with the model selected. One of the first things to do is size the window to fit the screen so you have sufficient screen real estate for viewing both the model and the UVs. Having two screens makes unwrapping more pleasant.

6. In the **Edit UVWs** window, press *Ctrl + A* to select all, and then click on the icon ⊡, which is a **Freeform Mode** widget designed to combine the transform tools, shown in the following screenshot:

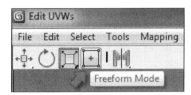

The **Freeform Mode** widget places a border around the selection with square handles you can drag to manipulate. If you drag on the corner handles, it will scale in the direction you move the mouse. If you drag on the side handles, the mode changes to rotate, and you can turn the selection around. If you move the cursor inside of the **Freeform** widget border, you enter **Move** mode and you can shift the selection in UV space.

7. Move the selection upwards, so it sits above the main mapping square. Also, scale it down a bit. By the time we're done, this cluster of faces will be pulled apart, rearranged, and nicely fitted to the main mapping square. Click the icon 🌐 at the top-right of the editor. This is a toggle that shows the active map in the dialog. At the moment we don't want to see the checkerboard, but later we'll replace that with our texture and toggle it back on again.

8. If you were in a hurry, and your model was simple, you could use **Mapping | Flatten** to set the UVs. In our case, the model has many polygons, a complex form, and would not flatten well at all. I find that even with simple models I rarely use this tool.

9. So instead we need to determine sections of the model to work on. We can select polygons in the usual way in the viewport, or select them in the **Edit UVWs** window. You can click on polygons, use *Ctrl* to add to a selection, and use *Alt* to remove from a selection. You can click-and-drag in the empty space to begin a Marquee selection. Right now, we'll have to select in the viewport, since the UVs are currently really scrambled up.

10. Orbit (*Alt + MMB*) the **Perspective** view so you can see the front of the ship, make sure the **Unwrap UVW** modifier is in polygon Sub-Object mode. Marquee select the line of polygons shown in the following screenshot:

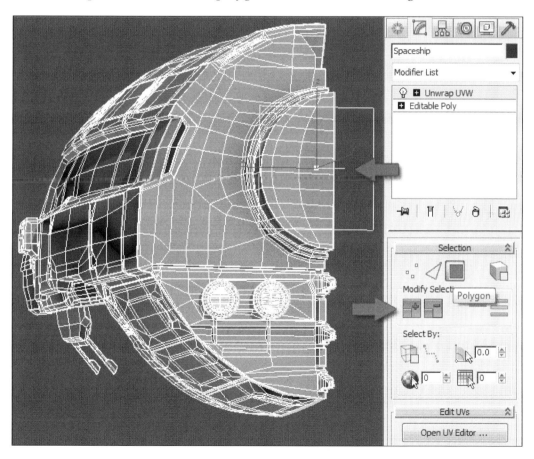

11. Then click on the **Grow** selection icon three times 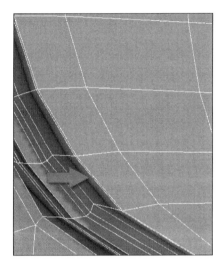. This should expand the selection to the edge of the front circle.

You'll also see there's a **Grow** tool with the same icon in the lower icon area of the **Edit UVWs** window. They do the same thing, but this one will only grow up to a green **UV Map Seam**, while the one in the modifier panel will grow across the entire mesh.

Note there is a very fine poly loop around the edge of the circle. This helps to keep the circle's edge tight should the model be subdivided during a detailed sculpt. The loop is shown in the following screenshot:

12. To UV map this selection is pretty easy, because it is flat. Notice there is a yellow square in the view surrounding the selection. This equates to the main mapping square which the polygons are being fitted to.

13. If you were to click on **Mapping | Flatten** now, and go with the default values you'd get a reasonable result, but the thin poly loop trim would be detached to a different texture island, not kept with the rest. This is because it has a slightly different surface angle to the flat part, and the **Flatten** calculation notices this. Instead, we can use a different projection preset by going to the **Unwrap UVW** modifier's **Projection** panel and clicking on the **Planar Map** icon, which produces a planar mapping. It helps to first click on **Best Align** , below that, so the shape we end up with doesn't happen to project sideways as a line. The align axis in this case is **Y**, if you don't trust **Best Align**. You can also press *Enter* to rapidly apply the **Planar Map** projection to selected faces.

14. After using a projection preset like **Planar Map**, its icon remains toggled on (blue). You have to remember to click on it again to turn it off (not blue).

15. In the **Edit UVWs** window, the front circle now fills the whole main mapping square. This is because the shape of the selection is not square, and it has stretched to fill it. You could scale it sideways so that it closely resembles the way it looks in the viewport.

16. Instead, we can try out another tool, which will have given us a better result anyway, called **Reset Peel** . You'll find this in the **Peel** panel of the **Edit UVWs** window. This creates a projection equivalent to the **Planar** method, but it keeps the proportional scale of the polygons as best it can, as shown in the following screenshot:

17. The only downside is it may rotate the selection to a funny angle to fit into the main mapping square. This is easy to adjust, using the rotate handle of the **Freeform Mode** transform widget.

18. You can avoid the problem in the first place by using the **Axis Align** tool in the **Edit UVs** panel of the **Unwrap UVW** modifier, changing the fly-out showing **X** to **Y** or to Normal , and then clicking on the **Quick Planar Map** next to that. Follow this up by clicking on the **Relax Until Flat** icon in the **Edit UVWs** window, in the **Reshape Elements** panel. You will notice a slight spreading of the thin poly loop around the edge of the selection, giving it a slightly larger area to receive texture.

> Because you'll be looking at the spread out polygons quite closely while mapping, sometimes you may see errors in the modeling that you didn't spot before. There's no need to panic. Just select the polygons around the problem area and collapse to editable poly. Your mapping is retained; you can fix the issue and then add a new modifier. Be aware that small changes like a Target Weld or adding an edge loop won't break the UV mapping work you've done, but newly created polygons via an Extrude or Bridge will need to be mapped freshly.

19. If you click on **Quick Peel**, it does the same thing as **Reset Peel**, but doesn't place the result to the mapping square, leaving the polygons where they were. It also doesn't automatically break a selection off of any adjacent polygons connected to the current selection. We can try this by selecting the next set of polygons, a loop, as shown in the following screenshot:

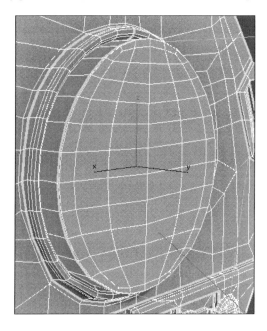

20. Those polygons are contiguous with the first selection, so just click on **Grow** and they'll be added to the current selection. To select only the added polygons, in the **Edit UWWs** window, hold *Alt* while dragging a Marquee selection around the polygons we already mapped before, which is easy to do because we placed them off to the side. This deselects what we don't need, leaving us only with a strip of polygons. To map these, click on **Quick Peel** and notice they line up in a straight row but don't move from where they were. Also they are still attached to other polygons. To detach them, right-click and choose **Break**. Now when you move them, they don't drag the unmapped polygons with them.

Another way to map a strip of polygons, like the single row we just did, is to use the **Mapping | Unfold** command, with its default option **Walk to closest face**. This will place the result into the main mapping square, lined up either vertically or horizontally. You can rotate a selection by clicking on the icons and .

An important strategy for UV mapping is to decide if you will use just one mapping square and one texture, or use several overlapping Material ID channels that split up the UV information and can be separately assigned to specific textures, or use several mapping squares and multiple textures (supported by Mudbox and Mari, for example).

Real-time game engines tend not to support multiple mapping squares, so that method should be avoided unless you want to adopt a texture atlas approach, something like the one shown at `http://www.scriptspot.com/3ds-max/scripts/texture-atlas-generator`.

Combining texture islands to save draw calls

The first time I worked on a game doing environments, a programmer came up to me one day and gave me, very gravely, some instructions on how a game engine renders to the screen. The point of the discussion was that, since I was unwrapping models for texturing, I should use fewer UV islands. Every UV island, at least in a game engine, tends to represent a draw call, so the more of those you have then the more costly assets using the texture becomes. For a tree, for instance, if you have two textures (one for the wood and one for the leaves), that's two draw calls. On top of that, if your UV mapping has two islands for the front and back side of the tree trunk, for example, you're adding more draw calls. Games often have lots of trees, so efficiency is the key.

In the following steps we'll look at how to join two texture islands together, continuing from where we left off:

1. We have a strip of polygons and a flat circle. They are contiguous on the model, but at the moment they are separate in the **Edit UVWs** window.

2. There will be a trade-off between having few UV islands and being able to pack all of them closely together. Compare the two shapes in the following screenshot. On the left-hand side, there is nice use of space, but there are two pieces or two UV islands. On the right-hand side, there is one piece, but the use of space isn't as nice. Notice that if you select some polygons, contiguous polygons on the model show with a blue edge. This will help you navigate what Sub-Object components belong together.

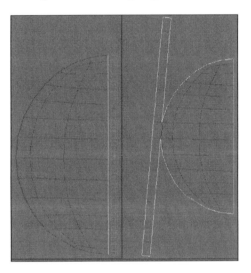

3. It is entirely optional, but I prefer to set the color for contiguous edges to light blue, because the unselected edges in the editor are also dark blue and the change makes it easier to see. To change this, in the **Edit UVWs** window click on *Ctrl + O* (or **Options** | **Preferences**) and then click on the color swatch under **Show Shared Subs**.

4. In this case, however much the ardent instructions of former colleagues echo in my mind, I'd probably keep the two pieces apart. Efficient use of space is also very important as it lets you expose more surface area to paint in the texture.

5. Let's move on to another case, where joining would make more sense, and look at some methods on how to join UV islands together. The tools to use are **Target Weld**, **Weld** (in the **Vertex** mode), and **Stitch**, usually used to fill small holes.

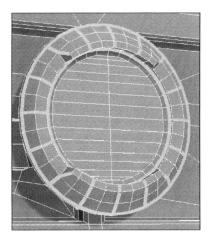

6. Find, on the front part of the ship, the circular form shown previously. In the
Edge mode, select an edge on the circular green map seam. You can change
the thickness of seams in the **Configure** panel using the **Thick** and **Thin**
radio buttons. You can also toggle **Map Seams** if you don't want them to
display on the model. Having selected an edge, click on **Loop: XY Edges**
in the **Selection** panel, as shown in the following screenshot. The hotkey
to toggle the display of seams is *Alt + E*.

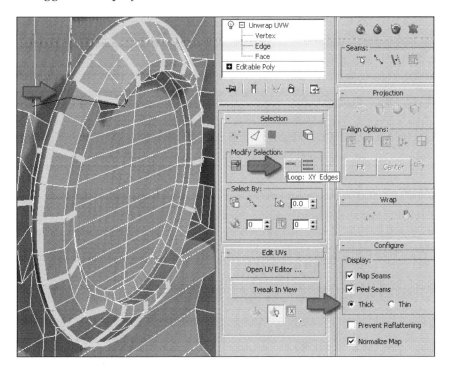

7. Once the loop surrounds a set of polygons you can mark it as a **Peel Seams**. Go to the **Peel** panel and click on **Convert Edge Selection to Seams** .

8. In the **Configure** panel, tick off **Map Seams**. Leave **Peel Seams** ticked. Now press *3* to switch to **Face** mode, and in the viewport select a face within the blue circular seam. As before, look in the **Peel** panel, and this time click on the **Expand Face Selection to Seams** icon, as shown in the following screenshot:

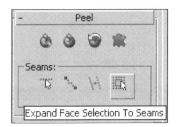

9. This fills out the selection to the confines of the blue seam. We can now unwrap the selection. Click on **Open UV Editor** and scroll the mouse to zoom out and show the current selection, then click on **Reset Peel**.

10. Like the first piece we mapped, this flat circle has an extra loop of polygons, which we can easily select. Click on the **Grow** icon  in the modifier panel. Then click on **Reset Peel** again. Notice that the first part we mapped and the added part are treated separately. This is because we added the blue map seam, which acts like a separator. Right-click in the **Edit UVWs** window and choose **Stitch** or click on the icon **Stitch: Custom**, which will join them together, but with some distortion. Then click on **Relax till Flat**, which will sort out the distortion nicely.

11. This is quick and easy because the added selection was conducive to joining on the first part. Let's look at a situation which will require joining by hand.

12. With the same selection active, click on **Grow** again in the modifier **Select** panel. This adds an additional polygon loop. Click on **Reset Peel**, and notice the first piece and the new piece again break off. Clicking on **Stitch: Custom** will not produce a nice result, even if you add **Relax Until Flat**. So instead, move the two pieces until they overlap, as shown in the following screenshot:

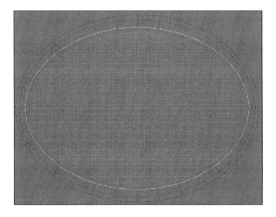

13. We're going to join the edge of the inner part with the corresponding edges of the outer part. First, notice the blue line in the last image. This means the edges contiguous with the selection are on the outer border, not the inner one. Also, though the shape of it looks like things will match up, the outer piece is actually rotated 90 degrees.

14. To show this, press *1* to enter **Vertex** mode and then click on one of the points on the blue line. Its buddy, a blue dot on the inner piece, will be 90 degrees offset. To fix this, click on the **Select By Element UV Toggle** icon and then click on the outer piece. The whole piece will be selected and you can use **Rotate** mode or **Rotate 90 degrees around Pivot** to turn it and scale to refit it so it matches up well. You may also have to use the menu command **Tools | Flip Vertical** to ensure that the correct **Vertex** points line up, as shown in the following screenshot:

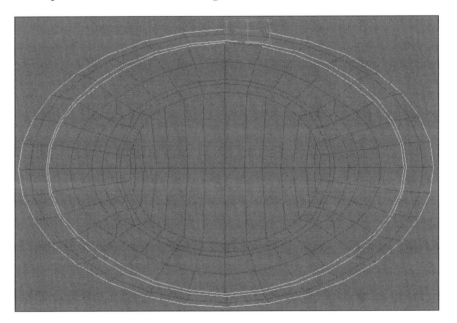

15. To solve the problem that the outer edge should be the inner edge, we can select loops and scale them accordingly. Enter **Edge** mode (2) and select an edge on the outer piece, on its outer edge, then click on **Loop** at the bottom of the **Edit UVWs** window. Use **Freeform Mode** to scale the selection outwards. Then deselect, select the outer loop, and scale it inwards.

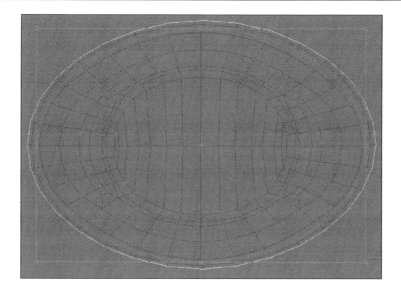

16. In the **Vertex** mode (*1*), right-click and choose **Target Weld** or press *Ctrl + T* to begin joining outer points to inner points. Left-click and drag a vertex to its corresponding vertex on the other island. It will take a while to pick your way around the gap we need to close up. When you're done, scale the entire piece sideways until it has more of a circular shape. The following screenshot shows the points that need welding:

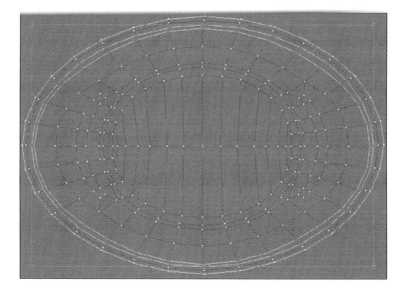

Before the **Peel** tool was introduced to 3ds Max, the **Pelt** tool ▓ was the next best method to quickly unwrapping a complex selection. It works like this: imagine a bear pelt stretched on a wood frame, so it is flat. It's not good for the bear, but for our UV mapping needs, this concept of flattening is perfect. That's what we want with polygon selections. The downside is that the pelt can sometimes be a over-stretched, but the upside is that it is very fast to use and offers some controls of the stretched shape. It works from the same blue **Map Seams** we used to isolate the circular shape in the last example. A great way to assign Map Seams is to use the **Point-to-Point Seams** tool ▓, which lets you begin and end a seam by clicking on the model in the viewport, and it is fast and accurate.

You can check the scene so far in the provided content, in the scene: `\Packt3dsMax\ Chapter 7\Ship_Quads_UnwrapUVW_Steps01.max`, and subsequent steps in the file iterations.

Just getting on with it...

Although only a couple of pieces of the model have been mapped so far, for the most part the rest would involve only repetition, up to the time where every part is chunked out, each one a non-overlapping UV island. After that, packing will be required and there's a new topic coming up on that.

One quick warning is that although you can copy and paste UV selections, quite often the polygon matching when pasting is not correct. For the circular shape we just mapped and the one next to it, the topology is the same, but copying and pasting the UV data is only partially successful (which means not at all in a sense) as some parts don't match, as shown in the following screenshot. For this reason, it is best to map every part as a unique step. If you have mapped geometry which matches geometry in another area of the model, instead of mapping the identical geometry again, you can clone an Element from the mapped part at Editable Poly level, delete the unmapped target polygons, and *Shift* + **Move** a copy of the mapped Element where the target part was.

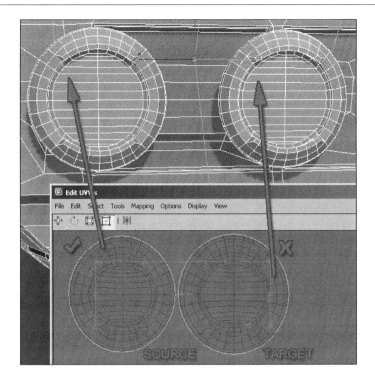

Some artists like to apply a custom mapping texture, usually a checkerboard, sometimes numbered and color coded, to help ensure that mapped sections are scaled correctly and to spot areas that may be stretched. You can download some and read about this concern at `http://blog.duber.cz/misc/custom-uv-and-tracking-maps-for-vfx-professionals`. You may also find these easy on the eye: `http://www.pixelcg.com/blog/?p=146`. The arrows and letters in these grids identify areas where the texture is mirrored. Also, the desaturated colors in the later ones are very easy on the eye while mapping a model. Personally, I like a grayscale grid texture. You can add it to the **Generic_Image** channel of an **Autodesk Generic material** or the **Diffuse** channel of a **Standard** material, in the **Material Editor** (*M*). Don't forget to right-click and choose **Show Realistic Material** in viewport.

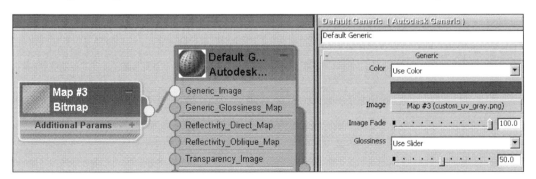

You will need to display the texture on the object as shown in the previous screenshot, and also in the **Edit UVWs** window, so click on the icon ⬡ that we turned off earlier, and choose **Pick Texture**, and then choose from the list the texture assigned to the material the ship model is using.

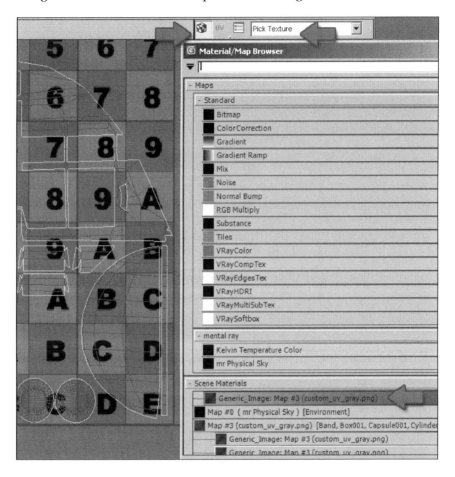

Having decided on several discrete chunks or groups of polygons that will either unwrap easily or all face more or less the same way and are contiguous, the repetitive side of using **Reset Peel** and occasionally **Mapping | Unfold** becomes apparent. To avoid this repetition from slowing you down, it is best not to try and start packing or organizing the UV islands using **Scale** and **Move**, but just shift them out of the way.

For this model, once I'd done the entire front of the ship, I started to arrange the results, but mostly just as housekeeping before moving on to the sides of the ship. In the following screenshot, you'll notice on the left-hand side that the front part has nice-looking checkers; some scaling of the bottom and top halves so their size ratio matches is needed, but it looks a lot better than the default mapping on the rest of the ship.

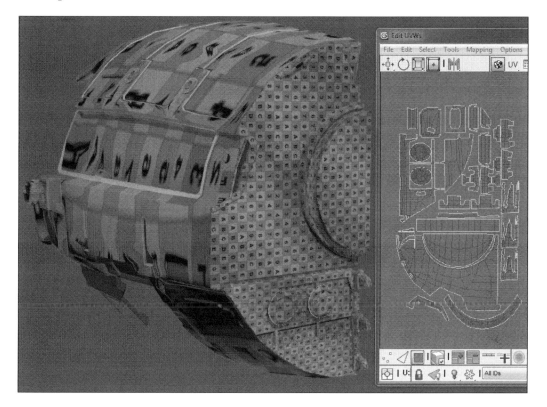

Moving on to the ship's sides, a piece like the one in the following screenshot is best selected using *Ctrl + LMB* and is fairly easy to map as it is planar:

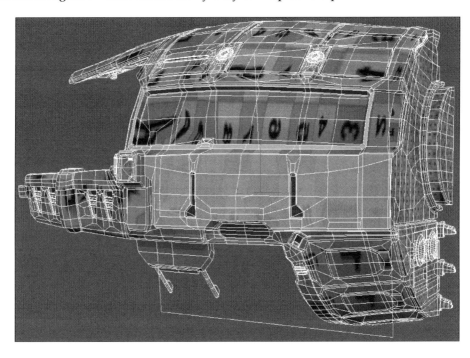

You could either use the **Planar Map** method or **Reset Peel** or even **Mapping | Normal Mapping | Left/Right Mapping**.

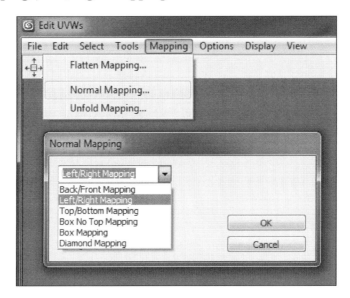

So now we have mapped this key piece, some of the surrounding pieces that we map after it could be joined on to its boundary using **Target Weld** in the **Vertex** mode.

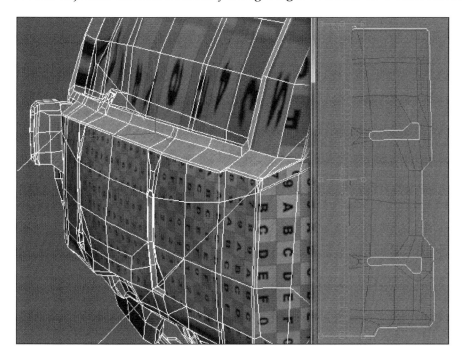

When you **Target Weld** one piece to another there will be some parts that stretch slightly, and we can use the checkerboard texture on the model to spot this, and wiggle each UV vertex as required to set the mapping straight. If you can, use **Relax** to achieve this as it will save time, however, with some layout situations the **Relax** tool can be too aggressive.

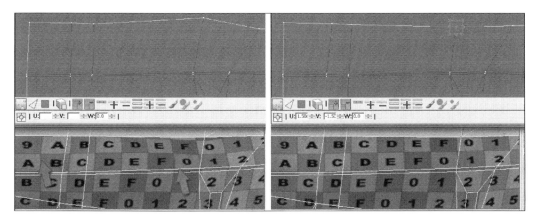

Another way to adjust kinked UV mapping like this is to use the **Tweak In View** tool, in the **Vertex** mode, and you can then click on points in the model and adjust them using the cursor in the viewport.

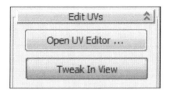

You may want to split part of a UV island with a custom mapping seam to help it lay out well. A handy trick for this is to first select the area you want to map, and then click on **Pelt**, and straight away **Commit** it. This generates a **Map Seam** around the border of the selection. Then you can use the **Edit Seams** tool or **Point-to-Point** tool to add additional seams within its boundary. The following screenshot shows an example where this works well, around the corners so they are split apart to remove stretching there:

When you have a mainly cylindrical form to map, in the **Projection** panel use the preset **Cylindrical Map**. This lines up a cylinder gizmo to the current selection, and you can roll it in local space until its seam is positioned optimally. You may want to start by clicking on **Best Align**. The green seam along the length of the gizmo represents the split from which the polygons will peel away. Remember that the **Projection** preset modes need to be toggled off once you're happy with the result before you can resume editing.

The cylindrical projection will map to the main mapping square, so if your polygons form a thin cylinder you may need to scale the UVs after unwrapping to better represent the form. Something to watch out for when using the **Cylindrical Map** method is that sometimes the vertices along the green edge don't weld, even though they are in the right place. You just have to select them all and right-click and choose **Weld** in the **Edit UVWs** window.

Additional UV layout tools

Like modeling, the majority of the mapping process lies in using the same tools frequently and fast. There are some additional tools that are worth covering, in particular the spacing tools, transforms, and tools to display and hide UVs.

Soft Selection

For more organic models, where you can allow some stretch and may have fewer UV islands to handle, there is a **Soft Selection** tool, which drags with a falloff, a lot like the modeling mode with the same name, but in this case it affects selected UV points. To use it, click on the **Soft Selection** toggle ◉ at the bottom-right of the **Edit UVWs** window. A colored falloff will be visible around selected points. The falloff is based on XY distance, not contiguous points, and you can control the degree of the effect using the spinner next to the icon ◉. Note the default is **0.0** (which means you have to set a value before you'll see any result). There is a **Falloff Type** fly-out, shown in the following screenshot, that lets you set the shape of the falloff. There is also a **Falloff Space** fly-out, switching between XY or UV space, where UV affects only the active element.

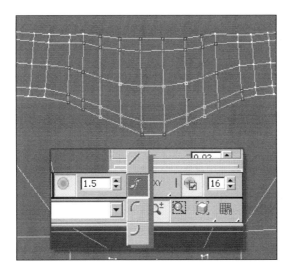

Setting UVW editor hotkeys

If you open the menu **Customize | Customize User Interface**, you will see the **Keyboard** tab, and it defaults to the **Group: Main UI**. If you click this rollout and choose **Unwrap UVW** instead, you'll see there are many commands for the **Edit UVWs** window and mapping processes that can be assigned hotkeys. For example, I usually map polygons first, and then use *Shift + 2* to swap the selection to the **Vertex** mode (**Face to Vertex Select**) or *Alt + 2* to swap to **Edge** mode (**Face to Edge Select**). Alternatively, you can swap to the **Quads** tab, and set up a unique **Unwrap UVW Quad** menu. In the following screenshot, the same subobject conversion shortcuts are added to the **Quad** menu:

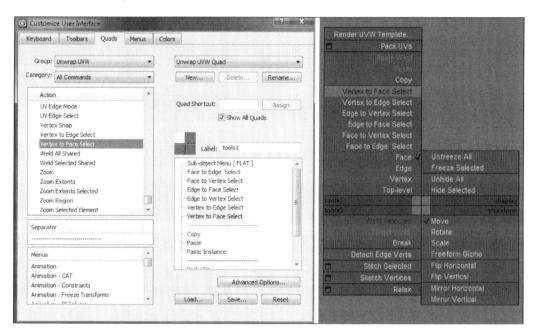

Aligning points

For fine-tuning, there are several tools that allow us to make sure rows of vertices are lined up. In the following example, to map the polygons, each UV island was laid out using **Reset Peel**, with **Map Seams** added to the corners so they'd spread out nicely. But although they are the same shape, there are slight differences of vertex position we can easily fix using align. Assuming the pieces are the same, it may prove quicker to map one of them then clone it to create the others with identical mapping. If you plan to have the same texture artwork on all the strips, then you could overlap the UVs. If you need to have unique artwork on each one, you have to lay them out as shown in the following screenshot:

After selecting a row of points, even if they are not contiguous, click on the **Align Horizontal** icon , or **Align Vertical** icon if the selection is vertical. Depending on the requirements of the model, you can also click on **Linear Align** which was added in 3ds Max 2012, which spaces the points along a line at even distances. In the case shown earlier that wouldn't be useful, because the side parts of the selection are thinner than the top parts.

In the following screenshot, the rotated parts are aligned straight, and also the three segments to the left are spaced equally apart. Such accuracy may be helpful if you plan to texture in Photoshop using rectangular Marquee selections and a lot of pasted content.

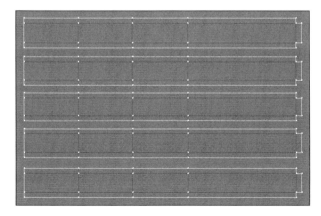

A handy script for fixing up UVs

While spacing UVs using the tools mentioned earlier is fairly easy, you may want to try the free Maxscript by GARP called **UV Strip Straightener**. It is available at `http://www.scriptspot.com/3ds-max/scripts/uv-strip-straightener`, which also shows an example. In its options it includes a checkbox for spacing evenly, or averaging, the segments in X, Y axis or both.

Setting up the script requires the following steps, after download:

1. From the download folder, drag-and-drop the `.mzp` on the viewport. This copies files to their required locations within the 3ds Max installation folders.

2. In 3ds Max, from the drop-down menu Maxscript, select **Run** and browse folders to find the `UVW Unwrap-straightenUVstrip.MCR` file in `C:\Users\Username\AppData\Local\Autodesk\3dsMax\~\enu\UI\usermacros` (where the ~ symbol represents the version of 3ds Max you are using), and select it to run it.

3. Restart 3ds Max.

4. Go to **Customize | Customize User Interface**. Select the **Keyboard** or **Quads** tab and check that **Group: Main UI** is showing, and set the **Category: UVW Unwrap** using the rolldown list. There you'll find the link **Straighten UV Strip** to launch the script, and you can assign it a shortcut or to a quad.

5. You can also launch it within the **Edit UVWs** window interface. Look under the menu **Mapping | Straighten UV Strips**.

Users have contributed many scripts to `Scriptspot.com`; here is a free plugin for 3ds Max by Francis O'Brien that can unwrap UVs available at `http://www.pullin-shapes.co.uk/page8.htm`.

Mirror and Flip commands

You can set hotkeys, such as: *Shift + H* = **Flip Horizontal**, and *Shift + V* = **Flip Vertical**.

There are several ways to flip a selection of UVs besides assigning hotkeys. You can use the menu **Tools | Flip Horizontal**, or the **Mirror** icon , which is a fly-out containing variations. You can also access **Flip Horizontal** and **Flip Vertical** in the Quad menu in the **Edit UVWs** window.

Packing the layout

When you have picked out and unwrapped all the parts of a complex model, you may feel like you have completed a marathon; except a final lap remains, which is to fit all the pieces as efficiently as possible into the main mapping square. While 3ds Max has an autopacker built into the **Unwrap UVW** modifier, it is not really useful. A human is needed to puzzle out the most compact, optimal arrangement. It's best to think of it as a sort of puzzle game. You can quickly get an adequate result, but it takes real skill to achieve an optimal result. In terms of method, all you'll need to do is turn on **Face** mode (3), tick **Select By Element** in the **Edit UVWs** window and use **Freeform Mode** to start transforming the UV islands. Here and there, you might nudge a vertex over a little or break a piece in two (or join two pieces), but there's no trick involved.

This is what I ended up with after unwrapping the pieces. At this stage, I wasn't too worried about welding together every possible matching pair of UV islands, nor was I overly concerned with their relative scale and packing.

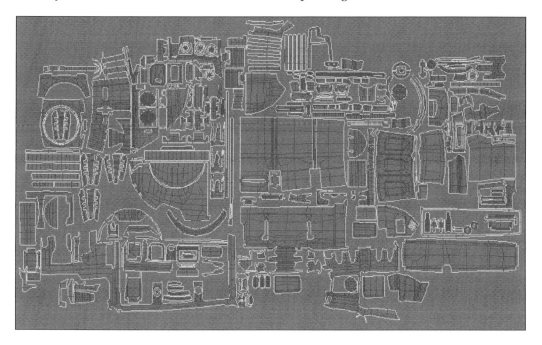

There is a handy tool in the **Arrange Elements** panel of the **Edit UVWs** window called **Rescale Elements** 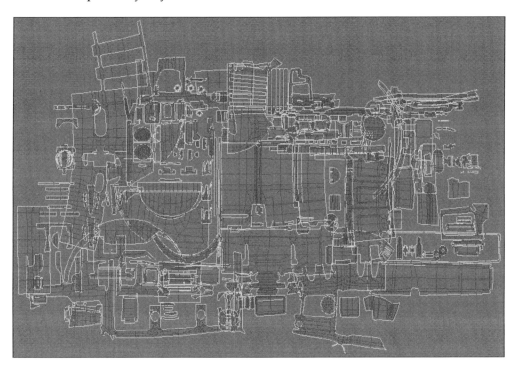 that does a good job of proportionally balancing the scale of all the pieces, though it doesn't notice overlap when autoadjusting, as shown in the following screenshot. This isn't a big deal as we have to pack everything we have so far into a square anyway.

I haven't found an automatic UV packer I like; you may want to check the commercial option UV-Packer 1.11 from 3D IO: `http://packer.3d-plugin.com`. The 3ds Max packer puts a bit too much space around UV islands and tends to fit them to a grid, but if you need to batch through a huge number of models, you could try it, using this maxscript to fire it up:

```
FOR batch in selection DO
(
local newUVW = Unwrap_UVW()
addmodifier batch newUVW
newUVW.pack 0 5.0 true false false
)
```

The batch will apply the packing settings to a number of models. The settings `0 5.0 true false false` are applied to the settings in the packing dialog in the **Edit UVWs** window, shown in the following screenshot:

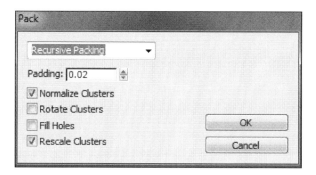

For this particular model, it is important to remember it has been mapped as a half model, expecting Symmetry to be added. There are also additional meshes which could be attached and mapped together with the main hull. Given the model is large, it might be beneficial to map to two or three mapping squares (to the right of the first). It depends on the goal software for the texturing. To understand this concept, check out Mari or Mudbox painting methods; a good source for that is Digital Tutors (`http://www.digitaltutors.com`).

For this example, we'll use two separate 4096 x 4096 textures and the outer surface and inner surface will be split. Most of the supplemental meshes are within the interior, so those will be added to the inner surface mapping. The process to perform that split will be to collapse the model to Editable Poly (which retains the texture co-ordinates from the collapsed modifier), and then select the polygons to **Detach**, add a **Symmetry** modifier to each half, reapply **Unwrap UVW** and then do the packing by hand.

In *Chapter 3, The Base Model – A Solid Foundation in Polygon Modeling,* we glossed over one of the selecting methods, **Stored Selections**; the commands in the **Selection** tab of the **Ribbon** are convenient for joining Sub-Object polygon selections together. This is especially helpful in this case because the outer and inner surfaces are close together, so there's a high risk of selecting the wrong polygons and it would be annoying to lose the selection for any reason. So we can store it as we go by selecting a set of polygons and clicking on 🔲, and then selecting some more and clicking on 🔲, and then joining these 🔲, and storing them with 🔲 and starting over. There is a **Recall Selection** command 🔲 to paste in the previous selection and a **Clear** command 🔲.

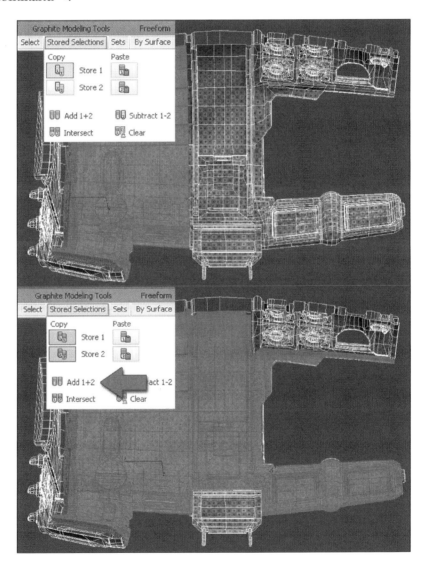

After packing the outer shell of the ship, this is what I arrived at:

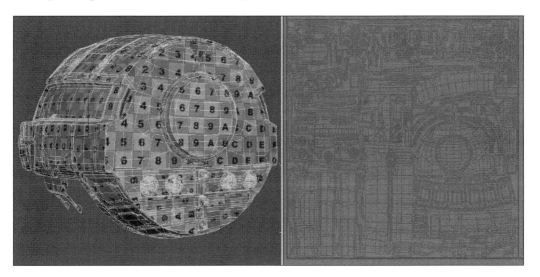

There's still some room for tweaking but essentially all the pieces are at the right scale, arranged to fit the main square, and there's not a lot of empty space. I didn't work out how many of the UV islands could be welded together, so there are more small pieces than would be ideal. It is important to have a slight gap around each island for Normal Mapping padding. To evaluate whether the result is okay, I apply a Material on the model, add a 4096 x 4096 .png, and start painting in **Viewport Canvas** to check that the resolution around the smaller details will hold up. If it isn't up to scratch, I weigh up splitting the UV islands to more texture sheets, to increase the available surface area. Our goal is to create a game asset, not a film production asset, so it's better to have fewer textures rather than more. The provided checkerboard texture loaded during UV mapping is 1024 x 1024, so an estimate can be made from that. If it is clear in the viewport, then a 4096 x 4096 texture should be too. To begin to paint using Viewport Canvas, refer to *Chapter 8, Custom Body Job: Painting using Viewport Canvas*, which covers this topic.

For comparison (and this really holds true the more you try to do a complex model in one hit), here is the result of using the plugin **UV-Packer** set to have a **Gutter Padding** threshold of **1**. So it's clear that if you want a fast, workable result it could be used, especially on low poly count models, but human care and attention will often get a better result, although it takes a while longer. The only glaring problem with the plugin is that it doesn't successfully detect and fill holes in the UV islands. It's important to point out that the UV-Packer takes only seconds to give a result, but it will only offer one solution. Some artists use it as a starting point for their own packing.

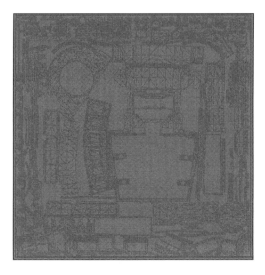

When mapping two objects together at once, they'll share the modifier as an instance. You can work on one model at a time, or select both and see their texture coordinates in the same view, which is what you need to pack both together into one texture space. At any time, you can hit the **Make Unique** icon under the stack, and break the instancing.

Finalizing the layout

A few times I've pointed out the need to determine a mapping strategy according to your end goal, be it a self-contained, single game texture or a series of texture sheets for high-resolution model painting. In this case, we've wound up with the outer and inner parts on two different textures, and the additional meshes mapped with the interior. The ship hull has been split into two pieces, so we have to assign a unique material to each, to preserve their mapping, before the halves are welded back together.

Then we need to prepare the asset for painting, and there are a few different options for this. One option is to render a texture template from the **Edit UVWs** window, which is good if you plan to work in Photoshop (for a model that suits this, like a low poly prop). Another option is to paint directly on the surface. In this topic we'll look at how to prep for Mudbox painting, and at how we can view the UVs while painting in Viewport Canvas as well.

To map the supplemental meshes and the larger inner surface, I set a grid in the **Edit UVWs** window using *Ctrl + O* and then set the **Grid Size** value to **0.5**.

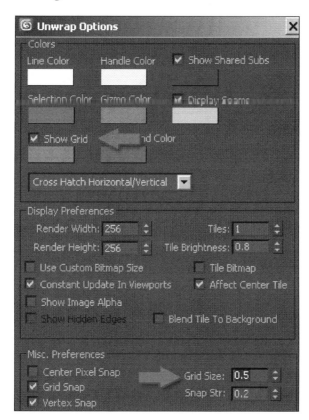

After that, having mapped the small pieces into a square, I used the **2 x 2** grid to scale them down to a quarter size, as shown in the following screenshot, and then pressed *Ctrl + H* to hide the selected polygons. You can also do this from the **Edit UVWs** menu **Display | Hide Selected**, and you'll also find the **Unhide All** command here.

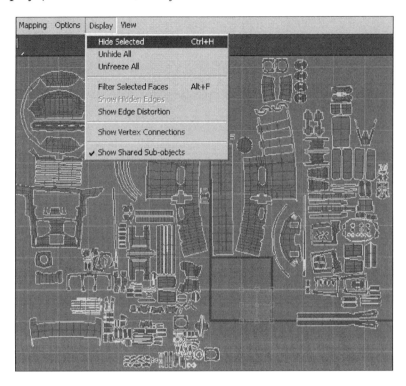

When using **Attach** to recombine the two ship halves, the UV layouts from each will overlap. Before welding the pieces, add a new **Unwrap UVW** modifier and in Face mode (3), in the modifier panel, click on **Select By Element** and then click in the scene on the outer part. You can then assign it a distinct material, which also gives it a **Material ID 1**, and invert the polygon selection (*Ctrl + I*) and apply a distinct material to that, which gives it another **Material ID 2** too, as shown in the following screenshot.

If you click on the **Pick Material from Object** icon in the **Slate Material editor** (*M*) and click on the model with it active, you'll thereby expose a **Multi/Sub-Object** material with two ID channels automatically. Name the material components as Outer and Inner, and the material name as Spaceship.

A final check to run on your UV layout is to enter **Face** mode (*3*) in the **Edit UVWs** window and choose **Select | Select Overlapped Faces**. This exposes any overlap cases so you can manually fix it.

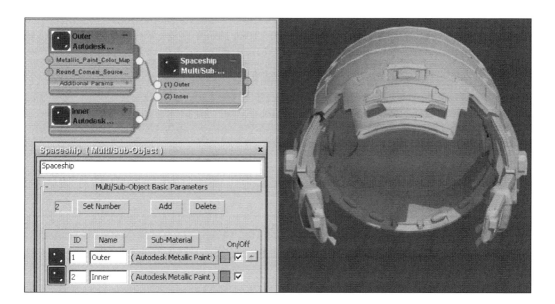

A good way to quickly join two large and complex parts of a mesh that were detached earlier is to go to the **Editable Poly** level of the model's modifier stack and enter **Border** mode (*3*) and then select the unwelded borders (which should coincide) and choose **Convert to Vertex**. Then you can choose **Weld Settings**, making sure to set the **Weld Threshold** to its lowest value, **0.0**. This would ensure that the weld isn't joining points on the border that are close to each other but not exactly touching.

After welding you'll no longer be able to use **Select By Element** to isolate the polygons used by each material. Luckily there's another way, which is to select the polygons by their Material ID. This is found in a rollout inside the **Edit UVWs** window, at the bottom, as shown in the following screenshot:

Clicking on **All IDs** will restore everything, which currently you'll notice is overlapping.

We can now shift the UV selection for **Material ID 2** one square to the right, using the command line, as detailed next.

In the main 3ds Max scene, right-click on the pink **Listener** panel and choose **Open Listener Window**.

This exposes a running log of what you've been doing. Make sure that only **Material ID 2** is showing (via the UV Editor rollout just mentioned) and then select all the polygons. Switch the **Move** mode so it is constrained to **X** using the fly-out shown here:

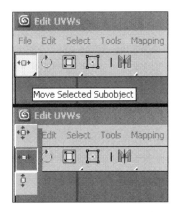

Then nudge the selection to the right a bit. Notice in the **Listener** you will see feedback on this, which includes an XYZ value. Given this, you can copy the line, undo the movement, and then paste the line into the command line (under the pink **Listener** feedback):

```
$.modifiers#unwrap_uvw.unwrap2.MoveSelected 1,0,0
```

Before you execute the command, be sure to set the **X** value to **1**. What this does is offset the polygons to the next mapping tile along. Relatively the texture space is the same. The supplemental meshes, which share the same material as the inner ship hull, don't need to be offset.

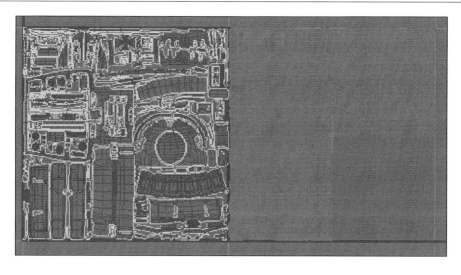

Making a Photoshop texture template

You can render the texture coordinates and save the result to file as an image, which is useful for importing into Photoshop for indirect texturing (as opposed to painting on the model itself). In the **Edit UVWs** window go to **Tools | Render UVW Template....**

A dialog will then pop up letting you specify the size of the rendered frame, and it also helps to turn off the display checkbox for **Seam Edges**. After that, click on **Render UV Template**, and save the resulting frame to .png using the **Save Image** icon 🖫. Note that if you chose a large render size, such as 4096 x 4096 the rendered frame will display at **1:8** scale and you can scroll using *MMB* to zoom in and out if you wish.

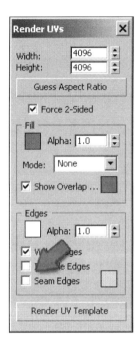

In Photoshop, conventionally, you would prepare the image for painting by highlighting the UV layer and proceeding with the following steps:

1. Right-click and choose **Duplicate** in the **Layers** dialog (*F7*). Name the new layer as **UV**.

2. On the **UV** layer, press *Ctrl + A* to select all, and press *Ctrl + I* to invert it.

3. Set the UV layer's composite mode to **Multiply**.

Click on the icon 🔒 to lock the layer content. You shouldn't try and paint on this layer. Select the bottom layer and press *Ctrl + A* and then choose **Edit | Clear**. This leaves you with a paint layer. Some artists fill the base layer with black and insert a new layer above to begin painting on. Using black means that if there are any painting holes, especially around edges, the area will simply look dark on the model, which is, if nothing else, better than a spot of white, given white tends to catch the eye. When the texture is ready to display on the model, click on the icon 👁 to hide the UV layer.

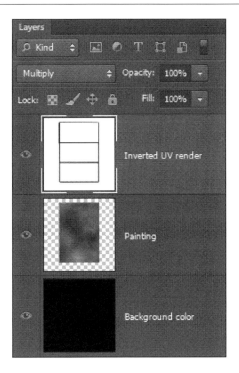

Send to Mudbox

Mudbox is able to paint on multiple texture sheets at once. So long as they are ordered to the right of the main mapping square. To transfer the model to Mudbox, go to the **File** menu and choose **Send To | Send to Mudbox | Send as New Scene**. There are also options to update or replace the content in the current scene, as you cross back and forth. Formerly, you would need to choose **File | Export | Export Selected** and save an .fbx file, and then open that in Mudbox. To save memory, Mudbox allows the different texture sheets to be exposed individually, although more than likely you won't notice this and just paint them all at once. *Ctrl* + Up Arrow is the default hotkey for **Load All Texture Tiles**, and *Ctrl* + Down Arrow is the hotkey for **Unload All Texture Tiles**. In the preferences, under **Windows | Preferences**, you can expand the section **Paint** to find a checkbox for **Color Unloaded Tiles**. Note that when you use **Send To** or **Export** it is possible that your .fbx model will be triangulated during the transfer. In Mudbox, if you used **Send To**, a connection to your scene will remain in place, with a signal at the bottom-right of the screen **Connected to 3ds Max**, and a button called **Update**. When you update in 3ds Max, any painting you've done in **Paint** mode will be applied to the model. You may have to press *Ctrl* + *Z* immediately after the update to clear the triangulation back to how your editable poly was before sending (the mesh and material are handled separately in the update).

To view the texture coordinates for the imported model in Mudbox, click on the **UV View** tab. You can't paint here, but the view will reassure you that your UV mapping carried across okay. To resume painting, click on the **3D View** tab.

Besides being able to paint on multiple texture sheets or tiles at once, an advantage of painting in Mudbox over Viewport Canvas (within 3ds Max itself) is that you can view multiple material channels at the same time while painting, such as **Diffuse…**, and **Specular…**, and **Bump…**. In **Viewport Canvas**, you can only see the channel currently active while painting. Mudbox uses the suffix u1_v1, u2_v1, and so on to label texture tiles in the updated material in 3ds Max.

Bear in mind that when sending from 3ds Max to Mudbox and back, the material type on the model that Mudbox understands is a **Standard** material, so if you are using, for example, an **Autodesk Generic** material, that'll get wiped off and replaced.

2D View in Viewport Canvas

In the next chapter, the spaceship painting process is explained in detail. Because we are dealing with UV mapping, the foremost concern is to discuss how the UVs can be displayed and painted on directly when in the **Viewport Canvas** painting mode. To open **Viewport Canvas** select the model and choose **Tools | Viewport Canvas**. In the **Options** panel, about halfway down, you can select the channel you want to paint on by clicking on **Pick Map**. If you simply click on the big paintbrush icon ✐ at the top, it will either use the active channel or prompt you to choose one if you haven't already.

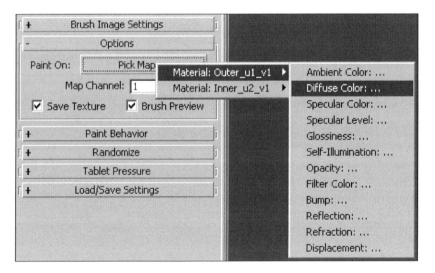

If you haven't already painted on the texture, you'll need to assign an image to paint on, in the following dialog:

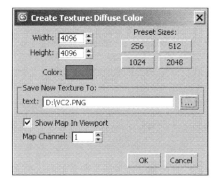

This texture is more or less a placeholder, as later it will almost certainly be replaced by a multi-layered `.psd` image. But the dialog won't accept `.psd`, so we have to add a flat format like `.jpg` or `.png`. When you add layers in Viewport Canvas, you can either flatten on save, or save to a `.psd` and replace the texture in the active material.

Click on **Paint** and notice that under the **Color** swatches both the **2D View** and **Layers Dialog** buttons activate. Click on both. 2D View exposes the UV layout and you can paint in here directly, unlike in the **UV View** in Mudbox. In the **Layers Dialog**, you can set a new layer and in the **File** menu, save your texture as `.psd`. Actual painting will be discussed in the next chapter, but you can try it out by stroking on the model to see how the 2D View updates. Take note of the three icons along the top of the 2D View (**Toggle UV Wireframe**, **Fit Texture to View**, and **Full Size** or **1:1**). You can also manually zoom by scrolling the *MMB*.

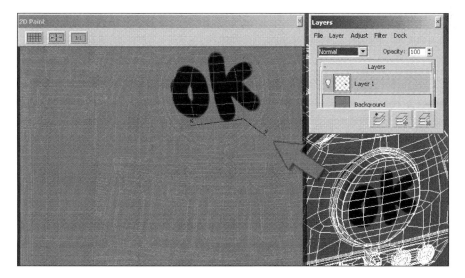

Summary

In the first few chapters, the goal was to gain familiarity with handling models and building them. This time we've looked at preparing a model for texturing. In the next chapter, we look at texturing using the same content. You will probably have noticed that modeling is an involved process, and so is UV mapping. Also it should be no surprise that so is texturing, and the amount of time for each can grow, stage to stage, if you are really shooting for high quality.

Actually, UV mapping is not difficult, but there is a lot of repetition and you have to be willing to handle the puzzle of UV packing with a light heart and think of it as a game. It's not much fun to try it under intense deadline pressure, for example, though increasingly there is a move towards automation along the lines of PTex or UV-Packer. For instance, both Mudbox and ZBrush include UV mapper tools that can do a lot of this work for you. At the end of the day, as a modeler you should appreciate how UV mapping works and be able to isolate and fix problems in the mapping, be able to transfer models from application to application without losing or reverting mapping, and know what method of mapping will work best for your intended outcomes.

8

Custom Body Job: Painting using Viewport Canvas

This chapter is about a method of texturing that lets you harness the tool inside 3ds Max called **Viewport Canvas**, and also builds upon processes discussed in earlier chapters regarding the Slate Material editor, and introduces Substance Procedural textures. We'll use highlights from the rather massive task of painting the ship constructed and mapped in previous chapters to describe Viewport Canvas functionality, and after that show a more progressive view of texturing a character.

These are the topics covered in the chapter:

- Direct painting versus indirect painting
- Starting a paint session
- Channel selection
- Shortcuts and 2D View painting
- Brush Images and Custom Maps
- Using the Clone brush
- Direct painting using spherical and depth brush settings
- Layers
- Loading maps into other channels
- Tablet settings
- Swapping material type using Slate
- Substance procedural textures
- Asset texturing walk-through

A lot of recently improved functionality in 3ds Max, and many other 3D products, involve asset interoperability (think GoZ and Send To Mudbox), so there's no reason to stick with 3ds Max for texturing.

However, Viewport Canvas does sit on a powerful engine for real-time interaction, has good brushes, layers, and is great for touching up details or marking the model for various purposes (such as where you might want to add hair).

Direct painting versus indirect painting

You can import a 3D model into Photoshop (CS4 or better) and paint on it, which is very interesting to try out but is not featured in this book. You can view information about 3D in Photoshop CS5 Extended in the following documentation from Adobe: `http://goo.gl/mz0tO`. The actual link has been shortened as it contains a very long number.

Some kind of models suit being painted in Photoshop, particularly objects with largely flat surfaces and straight edges, such as low-poly models of logs, tables, shields, or architectural content. A benefit of painting in Photoshop is you can copy and paste imagery into a rendered UV mapping template and very easily control quality or resolution. In the versions of Photoshop available until now, it was a big disadvantage, besides not seeing the update on the model in real time, that for a complex model, reading a UV template in 2D was pretty tricky so it could be hard to know where to paint. Newer versions allow you to paint with UV and model side by side, with instant updating. A few commercial tools exist that connect Photoshop 2D paint changes to the 3ds Max display, such as Marius Silaghi's Projection Painter (`http://www.mariussilaghi.com/projection_painter.htm`), which is rather similar to the discontinued GhostPainter 2.5.1 by Cebas.

In Viewport Canvas it is possible to paint in the 2D View as though in Photoshop, which is what we'll explore before looking at the 3D painting process.

Starting a paint session

In this topic, we will be preparing texture folders, checking whether our base textures for the paint session are okay, and launching Viewport Canvas' working windows, including **2D View**, the **Layers Dialog**, and the **Brush Images** window.

In the provided scene, `\Packt3dsMax\Content\Chapter 8\Ship_Quads_VP_Start.max` two 4096 x 4096 blank textures `VP.png` and `VP2.png` have already been applied to the two Standard materials used by the ship hull. This can be viewed in the Material Editor by pressing *M* and exposing the Slate canvas. You may have to re-path the textures from the provided content by double-clicking on them and browsing to locate the texture files.

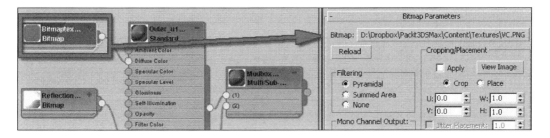

When working with materials that may have been assigned on a different machine or by a different user, it is good to set a texture repository and set an external path to it so that loading scenes will search there if any texture assets are missing. To do that, go to **Customize | Configure User Paths** and in the dialog, click on the **External Files** tab. There, click on **Add...** and browse to your desired texture folder, and click on **Add Subpaths** use subfolders too if you arrange your textures in subfolders. Now, this folder will be checked whenever a model uses a texture that has a location which can't be found, to see if there is a copy of the texture there. If you develop the habit of only having textures in a dedicated Textures folder, then it will avoid file path problems. If you use a server folder or a cloud service such as Dropbox (provided there's enough space in your subscription), it's easy to manage work across multiple computers. An example is shown in the following screenshot:

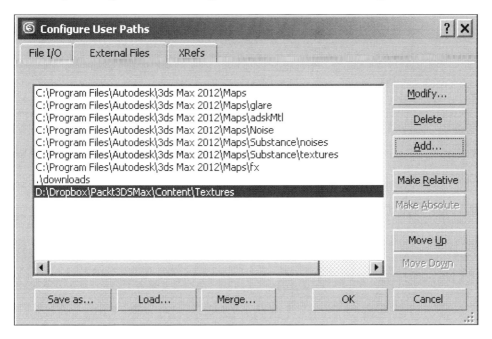

Syncing Custom Brushes

On the topic of syncing files, for textures you want to assign as **Custom Brushes** in **Viewport Canvas**, the default folder path is a local one and there isn't a direct method of changing it. It is possible to shift the location above by copying the application data for 3ds Max (everything in the \ enu folder in the long path below) to a new location (such as your local Dropbox folder) and then editing the original `C:\Users\UserName\AppData\Local\Autodesk\3dsMax\2013 - 64bit\enu\3dsmax.ini` so all the entries including a `C:\Users\...` path are set to the custom Dropbox path; for instance, `D:\Dropbox\3dsMax\`. Then your Viewport Canvas' Custom Brush directory will be located there and will be easier to sync.

Once Viewport Canvas is open, you'll probably want to drag it to the left-hand side of the viewport to dock it.

Note that even if the model has a material on it with textures assigned, if the texture is not found in the correct folder, Viewport Canvas will prompt you for a new texture. When you do wish to paint an entirely new texture, you must set a width and height value appropriate for the paint session, before setting the directory and file format. This can be done by clicking on the (**...**) button beside the **Save New Texture To:** field.

Channel selection

Simply put, for a model without textures, if you choose a channel to paint, you'll be prompted to assign one; if the model has a texture already, to start painting click on the icon ✐ in Viewport Canvas, then from the rollout list select the texture that will show in the channel you want to paint, as shown in the following screenshot:

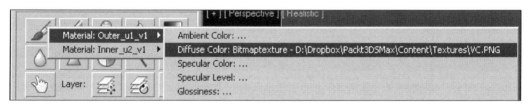

Now all the directory and file settings preamble is dealt with, let's move on and begin to paint.

In this topic we're interested in the 2D View mode, and this can be set to automatically open when you begin to paint by editing the configuration file `Default.txt` in `\2013 - 64bit\ENU\plugcfg_ln\ViewportCanvas\Settings` so the last line reads `View2DOpen=true`, as shown in the following screenshot:

Otherwise, you can click on **2D View** in the Viewport Canvas panel.

In 3ds Max 2013, you can move the 2D View to a second monitor. It's a good idea to paint a model in the **Isolation** mode (right-click in the **Quad** menu and select **Isolate Selection**) so other models don't obstruct the view as you orbit.

 To make the 2D View have more screen real estate, mouse over the side border until the cursor changes to an arrow icon and then drag it outward.

Apart from having the **2D View** window open, it is good to situate the **Layers** panel somewhere unobtrusive, and straight away add a new layer to the paint session. Viewport Canvas layers work the same as Photoshop layers, with **Composite** type choices, **Opacity** slider, and simple **Adjustments** and **Filters**. In the **Layers** window, from the **File** menu you can select **Save PSD As...** to convert your session to a layered file (instead of the flat .psd assigned to begin with) as shown in the following screenshot. Once you are painting a layered **PSD** (**Photoshop Document**), and that's assigned to the model, there's no problem, but you can't assign a .psd from scratch when beginning to paint.

When you select the paintbrush icon 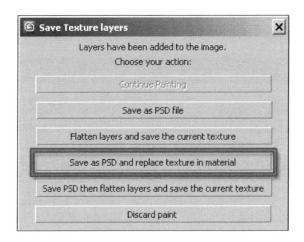 to complete the session, you'll be prompted with a variety of options. Usually, you'll want to select **Save as PSD and replace texture in material**. I usually do this even before I start painting to be sure the .psd is placed on the model, since after that it's enough just to go to **File | Save as PSD** to commit changes. The option shown in the following screenshot is also helpful if you are saving textures incrementally:

Shortcuts and 2D View painting

So far we've opened and closed a paint session without doing any painting at all. Well, we're really just warming up. The next steps show ways to indirectly paint the model, adjusting the application of texture, and basic Brush settings.

1. Create a new layer by clicking **Add New Layer** icon 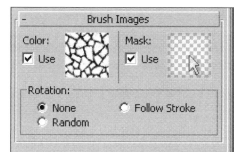 in the **Layers** window.

2. Make sure that **2D View** is open, and in the Viewport Canvas tools click on the color swatch next to **Color** in the **Brush Images** section, then select the last item in the **Mask Presets** row, as shown in the following screenshot:

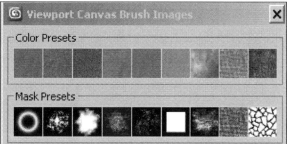

3. With the default brush stroke in the 2D View make sure the model is oriented so you can see, for the most part, where the paint is applied. Notice the stroke contains the active Brush Image confined within the radius of the brush.

   You can adjust the Brush Settings using typed values or the spinners, but you will probably find it faster to learn the following shortcuts:

   - *Ctrl + Shift*: Hold and drag vertically to change the brush radius. Note that the brush is actually spherical, so when painting thin geometry you may wind up painting both sides.

   - *Alt + Shift*: Hold and drag vertically to change the paint opacity.

   - *Ctrl + Alt*: Hold and drag vertically to change the hardness/softness of the brush edges. 100 is sharp, 0 is fuzzy.

   - *Shift*: Erases parts of what you have drawn during the current activation of the tool. This mode uses the **Opacity** setting of the Erase tool, rather than the standard Opacity setting used by the other tools.

   - *Space bar*: Hold and click to draw a straight line from the last painted point to where you click. This works with all stroke-type painting tools, including Paint and Erase.

- ○ *Ctrl*: If you are not using a Brush Image, just a color value, holding *Ctrl* and clicking the model surface samples color from the pixel under the cursor.

- ○ RMB: Should you right-click in empty space you will commit the paint session to the currently active texture.

- ○ MMB: Scrolling the mouse wheel zooms in and out in the 2D View, and holding-and-dragging *MMB* pans, as with any view. You can also use zoom shortcuts available at the top of the view.

4. Expand the **Brush Image Settings** section in the **Viewport Canvas** tool panel, and set the values as shown in the following screenshot so that instead of being confined to the brush radius, the image is projected onto the canvas (the UV mapping square in effect), and again paint in the view with a reasonable-sized brush. Notice that this time the texture acts as a kind of stencil (something similar to the stencil tool in Mudbox but fitted to the entire 2D View).

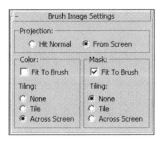

In particular, what makes a difference here is toggling off **Fit to Brush** and setting the **Tiling** radio button to **Across Screen**.

5. Paint an area of the model to compare the difference to the first stroke, as shown in the following screenshot:

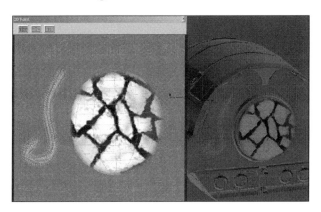

6. Now set the option for **Projection** so it uses **Hit Normal** instead of **From Screen**. Paint again, and compare the look of the stroke, which should appear finer.

7. Now hold *Ctrl + Alt + Shift* and drag in either the 2D View or perspective view. This moves what you have painted across the surface until you release.

8. Now zoom into the 2D View using *MMB* scroll and paint again. Observe that as the UVs scale up, the relative resolution of the brush increases on the model surface, while you can still paint on the model without changing the brush radius. After each zoom with the scroll wheel, you'll see the brush preview - the look of the texture in both the 2D View and the perspective view. In the perspective view, since we have **Fit to Brush** toggled off in the **Image Brush Settings**, a change in brush radius won't change the projected texture. Delete the layer you've painted so far and then discard the paint session by right-clicking in the Perspective view.

9. To paint only on a selection of UVs, a part of the model, or a single UV island, add a new **Unwrap UVW** modifier and click on **Open UVW Editor ...**, and in the **Edit UVWs** window select a likely section, which you might want to paint in isolation. Note, you just need to click one polygon in each UV island and then you can use the **Grow** icon 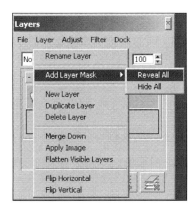 in the **Edit UVWs** window to fill the selection out to the green UV seams. Convert the model to editable poly, and in polygon mode (the polygons selected in the collapsed **Unwrap UVW** modifier will remain current and you might want to create a **Named Selection Set** using them to keep the selection at hand later) go to **Render | Render Surface Map** in the main menu bar. This will expose a dialog to set the size of the rendered map and type of map. In this case, select the **4096 Size** preset, dial down **Seam Bleed** to 0, and select **SelectionToBitmap**. A render will be produced that you can save to the file as a .png. Now turn off polygon mode, and restart your paint session in **Viewport Canvas**. Click on Add a new layer icon 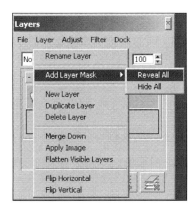, right-click on it, and select **Add Layer Mask | Reveal All**.

10. This will create an empty mask and automatically make it active (its border is highlighted). Click on the left-hand side thumbnail of the layer to make that active, then go to **File | Load Bitmap into Curent Layer**, and browse to find the render of the **SelectionToBitmap** file you made before. An example is provided in this chapter's content: `UV_SelectionToMap_MaskExample.png`; you can use this if you prefer. Once the image is loaded, right-click on the mask thumbnail and select **Apply Image**. When you start to paint, you'll affect either the layer or the mask depending on which is active. In the following screenshot, yellow has been painted on the layer, which is active, and the mask is only showing the color where the UV islands were rendered.

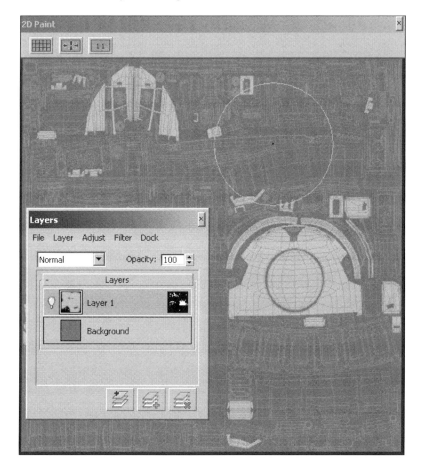

More about the layer masking features is shown by Louis Marceux in his Autodesk Area blog: `http://area.autodesk.com/blogs/louis/3ds_max_2011_s_viewport_canvas_tips_and_tricks`.

Note that because the UV mapping of the spaceship mesh used in the example actually spans two UV squares, you will see yellow on the second part of the model even though it uses a different texture. It will display like that until you hit commit, whereupon the display updates to show each texture correctly.

One thing to remember when painting in 3ds Max is that saving the texture used in the mesh material is independent of saving the 3ds Max scene. If you save changes to a Viewport Canvas texture painting session and then decide to quit 3ds Max without saving, next time you load the scene, the model's texture will reflect the newest saved from Viewport Canvas.

In this topic, we dealt with **SelectionToMap**; it's worth noting the **Render Surface** tool (found in the **Render** tab) can also be used to easily generate cavity and ambient occlusion maps from the model, which can then be loaded into a Viewport Canvas layer as a reference, mask, or texture content.

Brush Images and Custom Maps

Textures used as **Custom Brushes** must be `.tif` files, and you can manage them by opening the folder directly from inside **Viewport Canvas**, after clicking on one of the swatches under **Brush Images**. Click on **Browse Custom Maps Dir**. If you are in Photoshop and want to add an image to the `Custom Maps` folder, rather than ferreting through many subfolders to find the right location using Explorer, simply save to the desktop or to your textures folder. You can then copy and paste the required file via the 3ds Max **Browse Custom Maps Dir** route, as shown in the following screenshot:

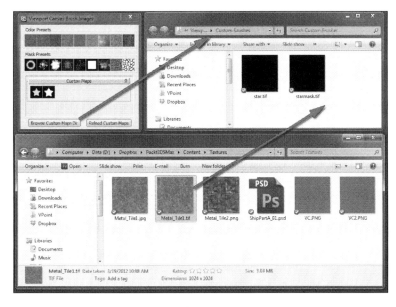

Using an added Custom Map `Metal_Tile1.tif` as a Brush Image, I used the Paint Bucket tool ✎ to cover the entire ship with an undercoat, and then layered over the top an **Occlusion** map set to **Multiply** in the layer properties. The AO map was derived using **Render | Render Surface**, as discussed earlier. More or less, the rest of the process of painting is a matter of artistic taste, but it is a good approach to begin painting with a generalized base texture, and work from larger features of the model down to smaller details, just like with the modeling process. It can also be helpful to do up a small section of the model to finished quality early on to set some direction for the rest.

Using the Clone brush

If you want to clone areas of the texture, the **Clone brush** ⛨ is a handy tool, so long as you remember to set the **Clone Source** options in the **Paint Behavior** section of Viewport Canvas. This matters because frequently the area you want to clone is on a different layer than the layer you are painting. You can choose either to sample the **Current Layer** or **All Layers**, much like in Photoshop. You can also use the viewport as a source, the entire screen, which helps a lot if you are using the 2D View to paint. In the following screenshot, on the left-hand side, is a detail painted by holding down *Space bar* (to get a straight line). Using the **Clone** brush, sample by holding *Alt* to click the area, which will be the clone source, then brush with the **All Layers** option set in the **Paint Behavior** options to achieve the strip on the left-hand side reasonably quickly. In 3ds Max 2012, a new option to sample from the entire screen, the **Screen** radio button, was added as **Clone Source**, which is great if you want to sample from an image not in 3ds Max.

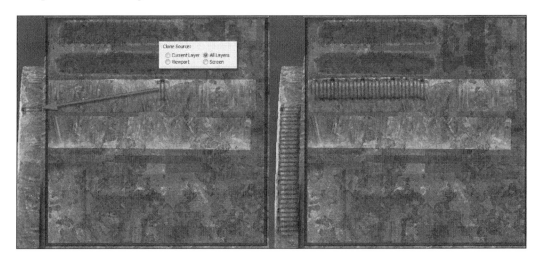

Keep in mind the default Brush setting for hardness is 0, which is very soft. If you want to have sharp lines in your texture, besides using a tiny brush, you can raise the hardness so the brush edges are sharper.

Also, to save time while doing the base texture, before detailing the model to have unique qualities on both sides, the **Mirroring** options in the **Paint Behavior** section of Viewport Canvas will allow you to assign X, Y, or Z symmetry.

Configuring Light and Shadows

Viewport shadows are often quite dark, and it is helpful to dial their **Intensity/Fade** value down when painting so the internal or cast shadows on objects aren't so strong that you can't see what you are painting. To set viewport shadows, go to the **Views** menu, select **Configure Viewports**, and adjust the **Lighting and Shadows** values in the **Visual Style & Appearance** tab. This was also discussed in *Chapter 1, First Launch: Getting to Know 3ds Max*. Alternatively, you can set the **Ambient** color on the model's Material to white so the texture appears fully lit everywhere.

Direct painting using spherical and depth brush settings

The biggest advantage of painting on the model is that you can paint across a mapping seam with perfect paint deposition. In the following example, the two joining sections were painted in 2D view, which leaves a visible texture discontinuity at the seams. To fix this is just a matter of painting directly in the viewport over that area, as shown in the following screenshot, where two stripes converge at the bottom of the circular drum on the front of the hull:

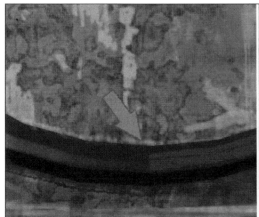

In most painting applications the surface will most accurately receive the brushstroke when it faces the camera, and the paint deposition will be less accurate as the incident angle is less direct. Viewport Canvas compensates for this by using a **Spherical Radius** default for the brush where surfaces aren't directly facing you. The paint projects based on the brush's contact with the surface, not based on the camera. Note that the option to switch to a **Depth** brush type does not create a flat brush; it shoots the paint all the way through the model like a kind of energy beam, leaving paint wherever the surface is touched. Therefore, by using the **Depth** brush, you will get stretched strokes if your surface has a steep incident angle compared to the brush. On a thin-walled model, since the default **Spherical Radius** brush has a volume, you may find paint is deposited on both sides of the model if the radius is big. Using **SelectionToMap** masks, discussed in the 2D View section earlier, removes the overlap problem. In the following screenshot, the blue circle on the left-hand side is shown projected through the model on the right-hand side because depth brushing is turned on.

Layers

Layers can be used in two ways: you can mix the content by overlapping layers with reduced opacity or you can separate content cleanly between layers to keep content organized. You can use masks or the default transparency of layers to expose content below. This is the same as in Photoshop, but let's do an example in case you want to rehearse working with layers in 3ds Max.

1. Open from the provided content \Packt3dsMax\Chapter 8\Ship_ Quads_VP_Start.max, and in the Material editor (*M*) assign the texture LayersStart.psd to the Bitmap feeding the **Diffuse Color** channel of the **Standard** material Outer_u1_v1.

2. Launch **Viewport Canvas** from either the **Quad** menu (PacktUI.ui) or go to **Views | Viewport Canvas**. Make sure you paint on the Material by going to **Outer_u1_v1 | Diffuse Color: Bitmap texture | LayersStart.PSD**.

3. Click on the **Layers Dialog** button. This may be set to automatically turn on, shown earlier in the chapter. The **Layers** window should pop up and show a **Background** layer. Note, you can paint directly on the background layer, but you can't erase from it (you have to paint over a mistake on the background to fix it or undo). It's generally a good idea to straightaway select **Add New Layer** icon when you paint and merge down the layer when you're done. To do so, right-click on the layer and select **Merge Down**, but there's no need just now.

> You can also merge all the layers by selecting **Flatten Visible Layers**. This is a simple flatten and is not selective of what layers are chosen or currently showing. Unlike in Photoshop (which preserves hidden layers when you select **Merge Visible**), layers that are hidden when you select **Flatten Visible Layers** are discarded completely, so it's more akin to Photoshop's **Flatten Image**. It is possible to Undo the deletion and collapsing of layers using *Ctrl + Z*.

4. Layer handling is not very difficult. You can drag-and-drop to reorder layers. Create four layers above the Background layer and on each right-click. Now click on **Rename** and enter front, back, left, and right respectively. For each layer, in a different color paint the words on the ship in the appropriate spots as shown in the following screenshot:

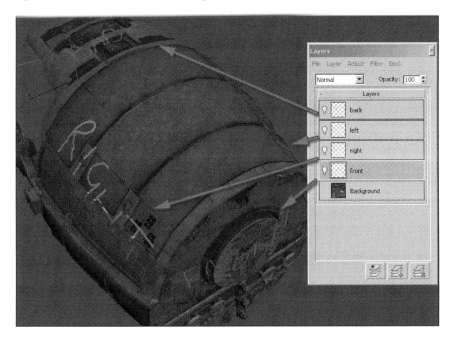

5. Next, adjust the colors of the paint strokes layer by layer so they are all the same using the **Hue** option present in the **Brightness/Contrast/Hue/ Saturation** dialog box of the **Adjust** tab. Try making them all yellow for instance. There are other adjustment types, in the **Adjust** menu, such as **Color Balance**, **Auto Levels**, and **Invert** that you may be familiar with from using Photoshop for texturing.

6. Set the **Opacity** value for the layers to 75 so you can see the underlying Background layer.

7. Select the Background layer and click on **Add New Layer**. Notice that this will appear above the Background layer rather than at the top of the layer stack. In this layer, draw in black under the words to create a border for them, as shown in the following screenshot:

This simple task will exercise your layer adjusting skills. Let's say you wanted to combine the lettering and black border layers all together without combining them with the Background layer. From the top layer down, keep choosing the right-click option **Merge Down** until only the merged layers and the Background remain. This might present some problems if each layer had very different composite types (such as Multiply, Color, and Overlay). You would probably find it more reliable to extract the merged layers in Photoshop if you want to kill off the Background layer and have an alpha for transparency.

Loading maps into other channels

Textures can be used to map into other channels in the material, for instance, Bump, Specular, Opacity, and Self-Illumination, all of which can support colored or monochrome bitmaps to drive the intensity of their influence. Normally, where the texture is brightest, the effect of the respective channel is strongest. One thing to watch for is whether white is 100 percent opaque or 100 percent transparent. Standard materials have an Opacity channel, so there white is 100 percent opaque. Some materials, such as MentalRay or VRay, have a Transparency channel, so there, white is 100 percent transparent. Sometimes you will need to invert a texture's values so it works appropriately in these cases.

A critical downside to Viewport Canvas is that you can't paint two channels simultaneously (which is why Mudbox has a distinct advantage over Viewport Canvas besides its sculpting capabilities). However, you can drop the image from one channel into another to use as a reference while painting, and then at least you can track where to paint to match the content used in a map in other channels. In this example, we paint a bumpy decal on the front of the ship and also give the front disk of the ship hull a strong reflective value:

1. With the same scene as before opened with **Viewport Canvas** ready to go, select **Add New Layer** for the Diffuse channel and paint a big, red X on the front disk of the ship. Name the layer BigRedX.

2. Under the BigRedX layer, add a new layer and fill it with black color.

3. In the **Layers** window, go to **File | Save Bitmap (Flattened) As...** and name the file X.png.

4. After saving, delete the black layer, and click on the **Paintbrush** icon to finish painting the Diffuse channel.

5. You will notice that in the **Options** section of Viewport Canvas the **Paint On:** button is available and currently set to **Diffuse Color**. Click on this and select **Bump** from the list. Set the created image settings to 4096x4096 and Black. Save it as ShipBump.png, and once it loads, click on **Paint**, and then click on the **Layers Dialog** button and then on **Add New Layer**. Highlight the new layer and go to **File | Load Bitmap into Current Layer**, and when prompted click on the X.PNG file, which should then display on the front of the ship.

6. The red color will give you about 50 percent bump, if converted to gray values. There's no point in trying to paint a Normal map in this channel, though presumably it is possible. Use the **Brightness/Contrast/Hue/Saturation** dialog box (present in the **Adjust** tab) to set the X to be a lot whiter. Watch the black value doesn't bloom up either.

7. Save the paint session, and make sure the map you've just adjusted is assigned in the Bump channel of the material `Outer_u1_v1` on the ship. Render to check its influence shows.

8. Currently, you would be hard pressed to keep painting more bump, since the black value covers most of the ship and you can't see where to paint. To reveal ship detail, create a new layer called `Reference Diffuse` and select **Load Bitmap Into Current** and click on the `Flat.png` image, which is the partial texture for the hull from the content provided for this chapter.

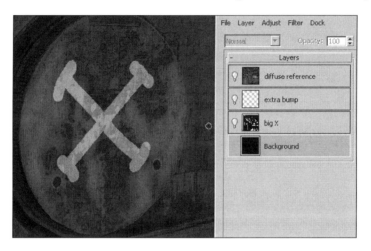

9. On a new layer `Extra Bump`, paint some more bump detail with white and shades of gray, then turn off the `Flat.png` layer so it doesn't contribute. Save, making sure you assign the changes in the material channel correctly, and render again.

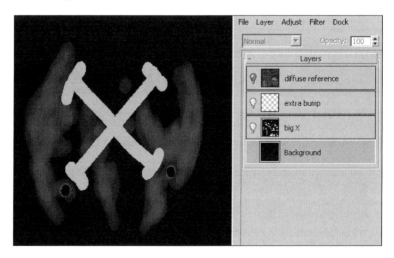

10. The following screenshot shows the contribution of the bump. You could undertake a similar referenced painting process for the specular contribution, or just hook the same map into multiple channels to compare the difference.

In the preceding screenshot, the left-hand side shows the material rendered with its Bump channel contribution set to 333, and the right-hand side shows a contribution set to nothing. The frames were rendered using NVIDIA iray, using default render settings.

Note that black and white bump images are not so much supported in real-time engines, which typically use Normal maps for bumpiness. You can always convert a black and white bump map to a Normal map using a program such as CrazyBump or NDO.

Tablet user's guide

It takes a while to get used to painting with a Wacom tablet, but Viewport Canvas does offer some enhancements, making use of the grip-pen pressure. Expand the **Tablet Pressure** options in the **Viewport Canvas** UI and you'll notice that pressure can be selectively toggled between controlling any or all of **Brush Radius** (size of the stroke), **Opacity** (heaviness of the stroke), **Hardness** (which controls the brush edge falloff), and **Scatter** (which creates noise in the Brush Image distribution). These functions have analogs to Wacom tablet used in Photoshop and most other painting programs.

In the following screenshot, the brush stroke examples are as follows:

- **A**: Default moused stroke
- **B**: Wacom pressure, using **Radius** only
- **C**: Wacom pressure, using **Radius** and **Hardness**
- **D**: Wacom pressure, using **Opacity** only
- **E**: Wacom pressure, using **Opacity** and **Scatter**
- **F**: Wacom pressure, using **Scatter** only and with a **Random Scatter** (22-33) range

  The **Randomize** section allows us to set arbitrary ranges for the brush controls. These are useful for creating brush noise.

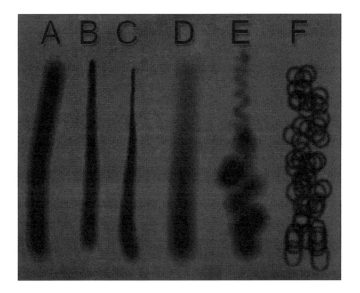

Swapping material types using Slate

Once you have used Viewport Canvas for a while, you will notice it accepts the material channels of other renderers such as NVIDIA iray, Vray, and MentalRay (while Mudbox only lets you use a Standard material if you want to transfer content back and forth using **Send To**). In the Material Editor, if you right-click on a Standard material such as the ones applied to the ship model we've been examining, you can select **Change Material/Map Type** in order to change the material used on an object. The replaced material will keep its name, and it will still participate in a **Multi/Sub-Object** material if it was previously assigned to one, but it will lose the maps assigned to it.

A nice feature of the Slate editor though is that all the previous maps will still be present right next to the material for easy reassignment. In the following screenshot, the Standard material has been changed to a **VRay Mtl** and the bitmap is about to be rejoined to the Diffuse channel, where it is labeled `Replace`. Unattached nodes can be deleted by pressing *Delete*.

Using Slate you may notice the **Controller Bezier Float** nodes that are added every time you add a map to the material can be expanded by clicking on their + icon. The 1.0 float value is the default contribution of the map, akin to the 100 values in the Maps list in the Material's parameters. If you don't like to see these, right-click on the **Additional Params** part of a given material node in the Slate editor and toggle **Hide Child Trees**.

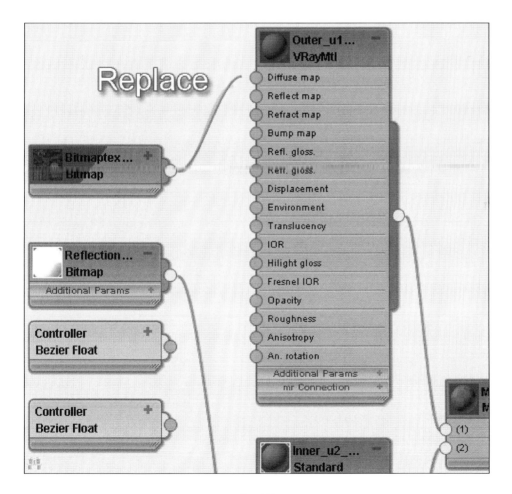

Substance procedural textures

In recent versions of 3ds Max, support for Allegorithmic's Substance Ecosystem has been included. Substance is a set of procedural texture generation tools that allow textures to permeate the surface and volume of an object, driven by a node-based creation interface that allows very complex maps to be created. To get started with Substance, it's a good idea to look at the Allegorithmic website, which introduces users to how it works in 3ds Max `http://www.allegorithmic.com/content/substance-3ds-max`.

In Slate, if you right-click you can browse a list of default maps. Selecting **Substance** from this list provides you with the base node for building or loading Substance content.

A further product enhancement related to this is B2M, which lets you extrapolate in one-click operations seamlessly tiling material elements (normal, specular, height map, and so on) from one source image, but it costs $150. Information for this can be found at `http://www.allegorithmic.com/products/b2m/overview`.

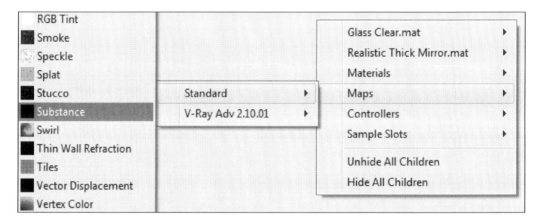

The **Substance** map starts empty, and you can apply content from the parameter dialog, which lets you browse assets stored in `C:\Program Files\Autodesk\3ds Max 2012\maps\Substance\textures` or from the massive Internet repository run by Allegorithmic (similar to micro-transactions in your 3D editor instead of your games). The following screenshot shows our model ship with a Substance preset applied to it:

A simple connection between the material and the substance map would be set up as shown in the following screenshot. The **Map Output** nodes are created automatically. Also, notice that the Normal connector is fed through the intermediary **VRayNormalMap** map type to the material's **Bump** map channel. This you should do yourself if you are using **VRay**. The actual textures involved are entirely derived within the **Substance** map's preset, in this case the **Aircraft_Metal** preset, according to the values set in **Aircraft_Metal Parameters**. For the rendered example shown here, the defaults were left alone:

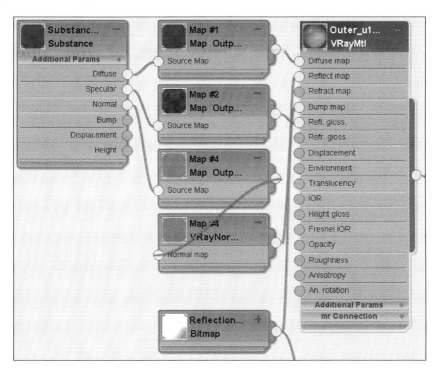

The previous screenshot shows the node network typical of a substance material, and the next screenshot shows the base parameters every Substance map has (not including the specific parameters of the preset, which control its look), where the size and source for the Substance are defined. The default **Engine** is **Software Rendering**, changed here to **Hardware Rendering**.

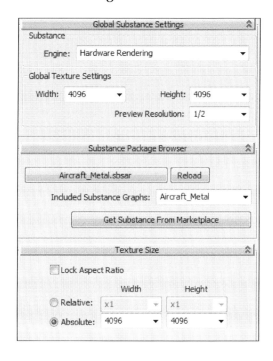

Clicking in the channel next to **Reload** lets you browse for local **Substance Packages**, such as `Aircraft_Metal.sbsar`. In the following example, the resolution was cranked up to an absolute setting of 4096 x 4096. Note that when changing between **Relative** and **Absolute** the preview of the map has to be recalculated and isn't always snappy. Be mindful of the fact that the viewport preview of the Substance texture will be much less detailed than the rendered frame.

If you wanted to paint on top of a Substance map, you could use the **Composite** material type, whereby the ViewPort Canvas painted material is layered above the Substance bearing material using a mask. The following example shows the Viewport Canvas texture masked against the Substance map using **SelectionToMap** image present in **Render | Render Surface**. In the following screenshot, the Substance map sits in the **Base** material of the **Composite** material, and the **Material 1** layer (a layer above the Base) is the painted and masked texture. The mask sits in the **Opacity** channel of the **Material 1** layer. An example of this scene can be found in the content provided for this chapter: `\Packt3dsMax\Chapter 8\Ship_Quads_VP_SubstanceDEMO.max`.

In the previous chapter, we UV mapped the model in preparation for texturing, and now we've followed that up using Viewport Canvas to explore painting methods that make use of its layered, multi-channel features. By now you should feel comfortable throwing a texture into the Diffuse, Normal, Specular, and Opacity channels and using the brushes in Viewport Canvas to paint with color and image brushes, clone areas from the object and from the screen, set your own custom content as a Brush Image, and render masks and surface properties for use in the texture layers.

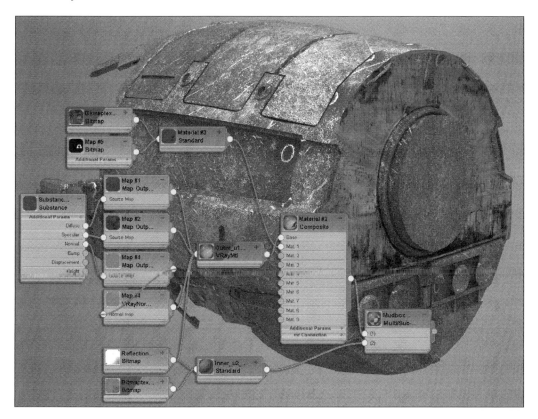

Asset texturing walk-through

The final section of this chapter shows a walk-through of a texture painted for the spaceship model by Ajay Choudhary. Quite often when you work on a project you wonder about how it would look if somebody else took your model and painted it (as well as your own hopefully if not better). I decided to find someone (via the `www.udk.com/forums` community) who would be available to paint this model with game quality in mind. The task I set was to provide diffuse, emissive, normal, and specular maps. Ajay Choudhary offered to take this on and came up with the following work, during which we exchanged 20 e-mails, discussing the direction and features I needed. The following screenshots are available at 4096 x 4096 with the `.max` scene in `\Packt3dsMax\Chapter 8\Ship\....` Notice the textures are named according to their use on each part of the model.

First, here is the final result of combining the maps in Autodesk Generic iray materials, through a Multi-SubObject network.

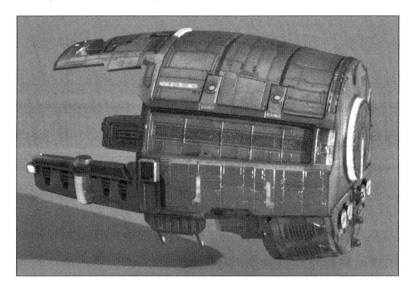

I adjusted the color of Ajay's emissive and also toned down its brightness, then added a little noise detail too. Not every creative decision a freelancer makes will match your own ideas, so you have to choose what to direct and what to let go. If you trust their artistic ability, you can get back some surprising results you wouldn't have come up with. Contractually, you can only expect what you specified in the project brief, so while the freelancer's work may give you a lot of further ideas, you may have to extend the agreement if you want to take things in another direction, or be ready to add to the work yourself. Really make sure the folio work of the artist shows strong signs that the artist will be able to deliver in excess of your actual needs. The following is the original job ad:

tomacmuni ●	📄 One off texture paint - Spaceship model

tomacmuni ●
MSgt, Shooter Person

Join Date: Nov 2009
Posts: 218

Hi

EDIT: -- artist has been hired.

I have an already UV-Mapped spaceship model that needs a lick of paint.
There is a fly round of the base model at : http://youtu.be/Jq9DOo1CMfY
Textures for the Material are spread over two 4096x4096 textures.
Must have paypal - fee is 400 USD.
Delivery date negotiable, but looking at mid-April/start of May max.
I don't mind what software is used to paint the texture. Would be nice to have bump/spec/dirt/reflect maps separately.
If you are interested, please show your past texturing work via UPL in email to : ipad4tom@gmail.com or @tomofnz

Regards,
Tom

This is the artist's early work in progress. It's incomplete but good to show it early because they can get valuable direction from the client before they get deep into it.

The following is some of the feedback to the artist, and after that, their response (in the art):

```
tomofnz: By and large, avoid decals and large areas of bright color
-- because they reduce scale. Instead, do panels and machinery/
engineering guts -- also try zooming in and noodling more close up
features.The glowing ring around the front is fine, but maybe make it
the only glowing part -- all the other glowing parts would be better
as machinery detail.
Let me show you a version I was working on.
*** tomofnz sent Ajay_detail example.png ***
tomofnz: You know the Millenium Falcon - how its surfaces are covered
with panels and nothing is flat... sort of along those lines. The
inner part of the ship looks interesting as being very dark, and the
little emit lights on the cylinder arch look promising. Negate the
bright blue LEDs to armor plating - those four disks on the front need
lots of detail. On top of that, I'd suggest just drawing features
with a black brush - cut lines, panels, cavities, vents, frames,
infrastructure, and so on.
```

The artist took this on board and progressively made some enhancements. When I replied, I made sure to focus on the positives and keep the requests brief and on topic:

```
I like how the added panels are vertical/horizontal, which contrasts
nicely against the big circle on the front... just be mindful of the
way the two meet or join around the border of the circle. If they just
butt together it exposes the Photoshop-like nature of the texture;
a fix is just to paint some extra complication at those points to
'explain' the join. I marked letters to correspond with areas that
stood out to me:
A - Make more of this feature. Frame/border the area around it to lead
into it.
B - Put borders or some other integrating detail around the two
features where they join.
C - These bolts on the rim are too large, just cover over them or
'square' them so they look like panels or coverings. Check for 'scale'
problems.
D - These look shiny, which should be done in the specular layer.
Also, the blue color pops too strongly given it is surrounded by drab
tones... so make it drab too. Pick out the edges from the geometry
too on the gray rim.
E - Here it would be nice to see exposed engine innards.
F - Too white... just let the front disk have white... I'd suggest
layering more detail over the top too, kind of like those bits the
repeat on the underneath of the hull (those are really nice), that I
marked G.
```

G - These look good - also detail a border for them using some of the
mesh edges on the outer part...

H - This is a good base, but I think it needs to be detailed/broken up
since the geometry there is fairly plain... but it's a good progress.

I - These areas need more detail -- mostly cut lines will probably
look fine. And the decals are too simplistic. You'll have to noodle in
closer to the model there I guess. Maybe you just didn't get round to
that back end as much yet, but it should have about the same level of
finish as the front does.

A lot more of the vent/scaffold/duct stuff like at G would be good.
That bottom/front part looks sweet.

Ajay's continued efforts follow. Notice that each time the model is shown from
several representative viewpoints:

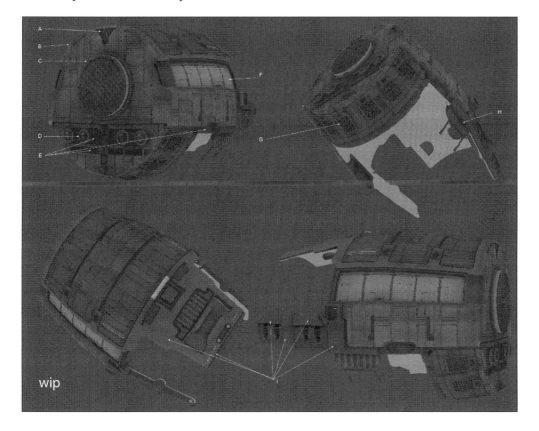

The **A**, **B**, and **C** markup is where I added some requests to the work in progress. Another option is to paint over the submitted work in progress directly, and then mark where the changes are. It's not a good idea to paint in some art direction without also stating in writing what changes you made or want. Try not to overwhelm the freelancer; it's important to keep them engaged and let them have fun while performing the task. A good artist will take ownership of the task and invest a lot of their personal energy into making it great. Over time, artists who perceive value in the artwork itself and believe in delivering to their utmost just to make you happy can be identified among those who are motivated only by being paid. You'll just take work in future to those who deliver the best. I thought that in this case, I got what I specified, felt my requests were acted upon, and had a good time and no difficulties talking to the freelancer, Ajay (`http://gambitcreativeworld.daportfolio.com/`).

The final textures are supplied in the this chapter's content at `\Packt3dsMax\Content\Chapter 8\Ship\Ship_DiffuseOuter1.tga`.

Summary

In this chapter, we ran the gauntlet of texturing as a pipeline step in creating the game. We covered setting up the document, painting over the UVs, creating additional texture channels for use in the model's material, and how different renderers tend to take different material types. It takes some time to get used to Viewport Canvas, but hopefully you'll find traction with it. Painting with a graphics tablet makes texture creation in Viewport Canvas a great deal easier.

In the next chapter, we move on to a different stage of asset creation, which deals with reducing the complexity of sculpting models so their polygon count is not so high and their wireframe structure is clean. This is known as retopology, and in 3ds Max the Ribbon offers several powerful tools for this process.

9

Go with the Flow Retopology in 3ds Max

This chapter shows ways to get a highly detailed model down to a useable polygon count, without losing the key detail from the original.

The following topics are covered in the chapter:

- High poly model import
- Retopology
  - ° Exploring the Freeform/Polydraw tools
  - ° Pinch/Spread
  - ° Using Quad Cap Pro to generate meshes to conform
  - ° Filling stubborn polygons

- Topology concerns for animation
- Manual polygon reduction
  - ° End corner building and turning edges

- WrapIt by The Pixel Hive
- Finalizing the retopologized model

Introduction

This chapter is about **retopology**, the process of reducing the polygon count of a high-resolution mesh tidily, without losing key detail. Quite often, sculpted meshes have polygon counts in the millions and it is messy to decimate or optimize them automatically. There are specialist tools for retopology, such as Topogun and 3D-Coat, but 3ds Max does include its own retopology tools, found in the **Freeform** section of the Ribbon.

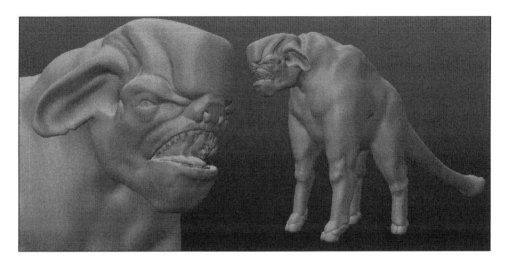

High poly model import

Different applications are biased to different file formats and may therefore have different import procedures. In the previous chapter, we looked at the **Send To** functionality between 3ds Mudbox and 3ds Max (which is possible as both are Autodesk products). This is essentially a `.fbx` transfer. If you are using ZBrush, you will want to get used to the **GoZ** equivalent transfer feature. Note that **GoZ** must be run from ZBrush to 3ds Max before it can go in the other direction. **GoZ** also works the free, mini-modeler tool from Pixologic (who make ZBrush too) called Sculptris, which is available at `http://www.pixologic.com/sculptris/`. In the following example, we'll directly export from Sculptris, a model made from a sphere (so it needs retopology to get a clean base mesh). We'll export it as a `.obj` and import it to 3ds Max in order to show a few of the idiosyncrasies of this situation. With a model that is sculpted from a primitive base, such as a sphere or box, there are no meaningful texture coordinates, so it would be impossible to paint the model. Although many sculpting programs, including Sculptris, do automapping, the results are seldom optimal.

Importing a model into Sculptris

The following steps detail the instructions on importing a model into Sculptris:

1. Install Sculptris 6 Alpha and run it. Note that the default scene is a sphere made of triangle faces that dynamically subdivide where you paint. Use the brush tools to experiment with this a while.

2. Click on **Open** and browse the provided content for this chapter, and open \Packt3dsMax\Chapter 9\Creature.scl. The file format .scl is native to Sculptris.

3. To get this model to work in 3ds Max, you will need to choose **Export** and save it instead as Sculptris.obj.

Importing the Sculptris.OBJ mesh in 3ds Max

After we have imported a model into Sculptris, we'll move on to see how we can save this file into 3ds Max. The importing part is fairly easy.

1. In 3ds Max, choose **File** | **Import** and browse to Sculptris.obj, the mesh you just exported from Sculptris. You could also try the example .obj called \Packt3dsMax\Chapter 9\RetopoBullStart.obj. The import options you set matter a lot. You will need to make sure that the options **Import as single mesh** and **Import as Editable Poly** are on. This makes sure that the symmetrical object employed in the Sculptris scene (actually a separate mesh that conforms to the model) doesn't prevent the import.

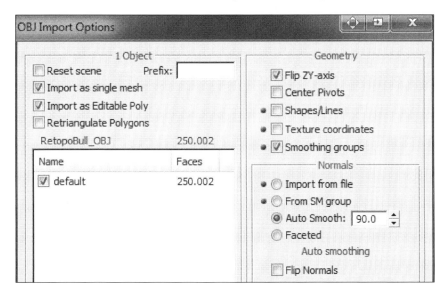

2. While importing, you should also swap the **Normals** radio button from the **From SM group** to **Auto Smooth**, to avoid the triangulated mesh looking faceted. A model begun in Sculptris won't contain any smoothing information when sent to 3ds Max and will come in faceted if you don't choose **Auto Smooth**. After importing, another way to do the same thing is to apply a **Smooth** modifier. The **Auto Smooth** value should be **90** or so, to reduce the likelihood of any sharp creases.

3. Finally, once the model is imported into the 3ds Max scene, move it in the Z plane so it is standing on the ground plane, and make sure its pivot is at 0,0,0. This can be done by choosing **Edit | Transform Toolbox** and clicking on **Origin** in the **Pivot** section. Note that the model's edges are all tiny triangles. This is a result of the way Sculptris adds detail to a model. Retopology will help us get a quad-based model to continue working from. The idea of retopology is to build up a new, nicely constructed model on top of the high-resolution model. The high-resolution model serves as a guide surface.

4. If you are curious, apply an **Unwrap UVW** modifier to the model and see how its UV mapping looks. Probably a bit scary. A high-resolution model such as this one (250K polys) is virtually impossible to manually UV map, at least not quickly. So we need to simplify the model.

5. If you can't see the Ribbon, go to **Customize | Show UI | Show Ribbon**, or press the icon in the main toolbar.

6. Then click on the **Freeform** tab.

7. With the creature mesh selected, click on **Grid** in the **Freeform** tab. This specifies the source to which we'll conform the new mesh that we're going to generate next. We don't want to conform to the grid, so change this to **Draw On: Surface** and then assign the source mesh using the **Pick** button below the **Surface** button, shown in the following screenshot:

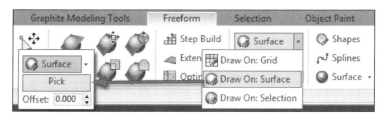

8. Each time you relaunch 3ds Max to keep working on the retopology, you'll have to reassign the high-resolution mesh as the source surface in the same way.

9. You could also use **Draw On: Selection**, which would be handy if the source was, in fact, a bunch of different meshes.

10. There is an **Offset** value you can adjust so that the mesh you'll generate next will sit slightly above the source mesh that can help reduce frustration from the lower-resolution mesh, which is likely to sink in places within the more curvy, high-resolution mesh. If you're just starting out, try leaving the setting alone and see how it turns out. An additional way to help see what you are doing is to apply a semitransparent material or low **Visibility** value to the high-resolution model (or press *Alt + X* while it is selected).

11. Next, in a nested part of the Ribbon, we have to set a new object or model to work on (that doesn't exist yet). Click on the **PolyDraw** rollout at the bottom of the **Freeform** tab.

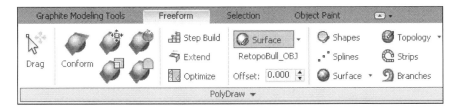

12. Having expanded **PolyDraw**, click on the **New Object** button ⫶ and we're ready to start retopologizing. I would strongly suggest raising the **Min Distance** value in the **PolyDraw** section, so when you create the first polygons they aren't too small. When using the **Strips** brush, usually I set the **Min Distance** to around 25-35, but it depends on the model scale and the level of detail you want. Just like with modeling, when you retopologize, it is best to move from large forms to small details.

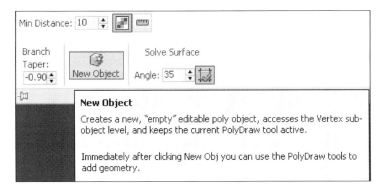

The object will be called something like Box001, an Editable Poly beginning in the **Vertex** mode. You can rename it to Retopo or something more memorable.

13. Turn on the **Strips** mode and make sure **Edged Faces** is toggled on (*F4*) so you can see the high-resolution model's center line. Starting at the head, draw a strip of polygons along the symmetry line so that there's an edge on either side. As this model is symmetrical, we only have to work on half of it.

> If you hold the mouse over the **Strips** mode icon , you'll get a tool tip that explains how **Strips** are made, and if you press *Y*, you can watch a video demo albeit drawing on the **Grid**. Note that the size of the polygons, as you draw, is determined by the **Min Distance** value under **PolyDraw**. Bear in mind that apart from the **Min Distance** value, the size of the polygons drawn also depends on the current viewport zoom. This is handy because when working on tighter detail, you'll tend to zoom in closer to the source mesh.

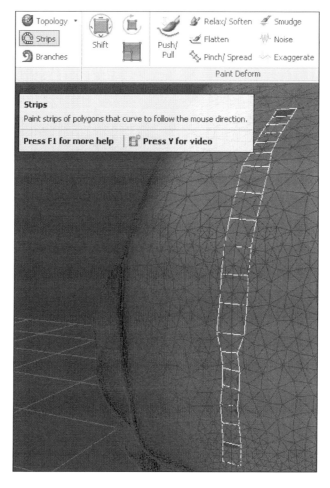

Retopology

There's no rush to do everything at once. You can edit what you've done to your liking, and then continue adding more strips. Strips can be joined at their ends using **Step Build** or **Bridge**, or **Target Weld**. You can also use the **Drag** brush 🔆 to slide the points of the strip on the high-resolution model surface.

I like to use the **Strips** method to establish the symmetry line as much as possible all the way round the model. You may want to skip over areas of tight detail like the mouth, saving them until later. Sometimes the strip's edge distribution will be a bit fine, as in the example shown below. Consider using Dot Ring to grab every second edge and choose *Ctrl + Remove* to lighten the mesh.

You will notice that since we're adding the strip along the symmetry line, there isn't a good fit to the actual middle as the polygons don't have a center edge. We can add a center line by making a **Ring**, selection around the strip, then **ConnectEdges** to make a new loop. To force this loop to be centered and absolutely flat, use **Align | Align X** found in **Graphite Modeling Tools** of the Ribbon.

Using `Packt3dsMax\PacktUI.ui`, right-click and choose **Convert to Vertex**, which makes the edge loop a vertex loop and puts us in the **Vertex** editing mode. After that, using the **Conform** brush tool 🖌 provides an easy way to make the edge loop fit to the high-resolution mesh's symmetry line. The **Conform** brush when active shows an options palette that, when expanded using the arrow icon ▸, lets you toggle **Use Selected Verts** 🖰, which in this case makes sure you only affect the added loop. Due to the fact that the strip runs around the back and front, you may want to also toggle on **Ignore Backfacing** 🔆 below **Use Selected Verts**. Set the **Conform** value to **100** so verts jump immediately to the high-resolution mesh surface.

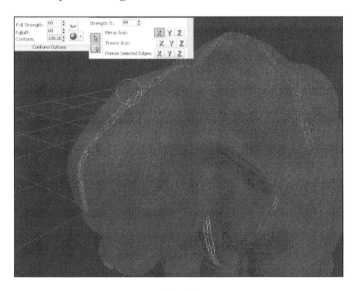

There are several ways to slap new polygons on top of the source mesh, including **Step Build**, which is a kind of one-at-a-time method that is good for detailed areas as you will have the most control. Also, there is the **Topology** tool that lets you draw guidelines on the surface and generates a polygon for each quad the drawn guidelines create, as they cross each other. Let's look at both of these methods in turn.

While this model isn't so very high poly that it will overtax the viewport, having set a strip of polygons to make a loop around the center line, you could now delete half the model down to its symmetry axis via **Select by Half** in the **Polygon** mode.

Exploring the Freeform/Polydraw tools

Open the scene RetopoStrip.max to begin from here, with the strip already running around the symmetry line of the monster.

1. The **Step Build** mode ⊞ lets you add verts and polys aligned on the surface of the high-resolution mesh. There are more hotkey combinations for the various possibilities.This tool offers us more hotkey combos then there are in Tekken, so it pays to rehearse them. You can view the tool tip list of key operations if you hold your mouse over the **Step Build** icon.

2. The basic idea is to click to add points, and then hold *Shift* and drag the mouse within a quad of points to create a polygon. You can create rows of points and then drag across them all in one sweep, holding *Shift + LMB*, as shown in the following screenshot:

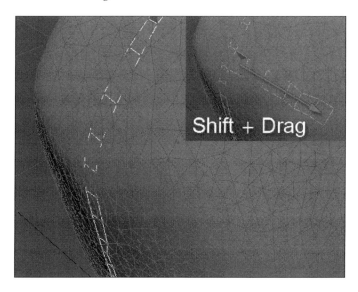

3. If you want to check for quads you might have missed, you can apply a **Shell** modifier with a sufficient **Outer Amount** thickness value, and turn on **Show End Result** ▌ in the modifier stack while working with **Step Build** at the **Editable Poly** level. Remember that the **Shell** modifier used this way is only meant to provide a visual guide and should be removed later.

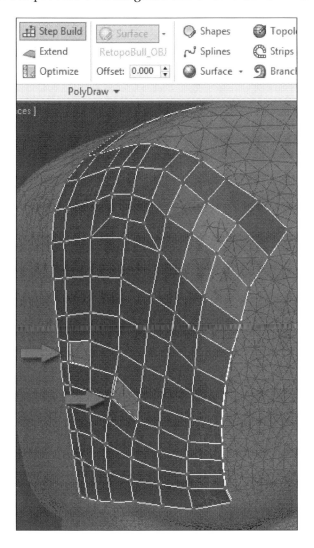

4. Enter the **Drag** mode ⊮ to shuffle points that you've added around on the surface, so the edge loops you're creating flow nicely.

5. The **Topology** tool lets you draw a series of interlacing lines in a grid over the high-resolution mesh surface, and where the lines overlap to form quads, it creates polygons. The nice feature of this tool is that you can explicitly control edge loop shapes. In the following screenshot, smaller lines help form end corners:

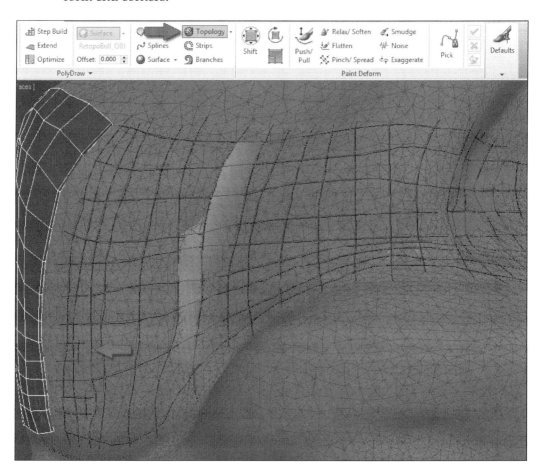

6. After creating a lattice of such lines, right-click to commit them. They show a surface while you are drawing the lines, but you have to commit them to include the result in your object. Once you do so, you'll notice that the **Shell** modifier kicks in (if you are using it). In the following screenshot, the first section made with **Step Build** and the new section made with **Topology** have been joined together. To join the pieces, select the facing edge loops and use **Bridge Edges**. Make sure there's the same number of segments on both sides.

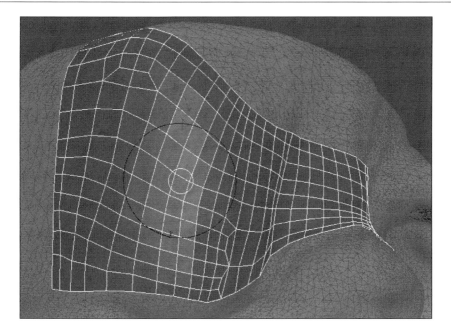

7. After joining the pieces, I used the **Conform Relax** brush, highlighted in the following screenshot, to help smooth the edge loops created so far. There's also a **Conform Scale** and **Conform Move** brush in the same section of the Ribbon. If you try them out on a section of your mesh, it'll be clear enough how each brush affects the mesh

8. If you want to continue from here, you can open the provided scene at `\Packt3dsMax\Chapter 9\RetopoExtendStart.max`.

9. The **Extend** tool ✎, below **Step Build**, allows you to quickly drag out a new strip. The best way to use this is by holding down *Shift + LMB* and dragging an existing edge. The leading edge of each new polygon has the same relative shape as the edge you drag it from. It's similar to extruding an edge while modeling, by using *Shift + LMB* in the **Move** mode, except the points conform to the surface of the source mesh. Skewed edges that you drag out can be adjusted in the **Drag** mode ▹ or **Extend** mode ✎ by holding *Shift + Ctrl + Alt + LMB* and nudging the points. This key combination may seem a bit annoying at first, but you'll get used to it. Think of it as "mash all the command keys at once".

10. Note that there are other shortcut combinations for **Extend**, which allow you to do even more. You can reproduce entire loops in one go by dragging while you hold *Ctrl + Shift + LMB* and then nudge the new polygons around until you release. You can effectively bridge between two edges by dragging while you hold *Ctrl + Alt + LMB*.

11. Try dragging a strip of polygons using **Extend** (*Shift + LMB* and drag an edge) along the length of the creature's ear. Also, try it using the **Strips** tool. Note that the **Strip** mode polygons have an even size and spacing based on the tool settings we discussed earlier, whereas the **Extend** mode polygon size is up to you, since each polygon will only be created when you release after dragging.

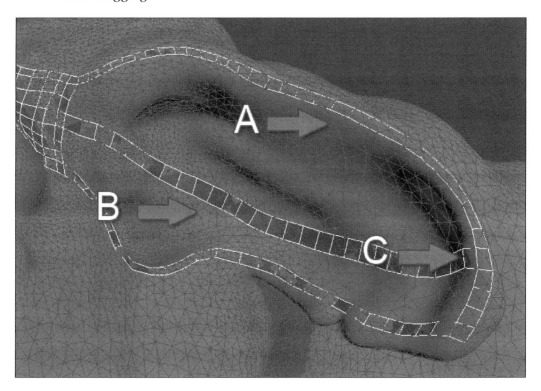

12. In the previous screenshot, **A** was made using **Extend** (plus nudge), **B** was made using **Strip** (set to **Min Distance** = **25**), and the join at **C** was made in the **Extend** mode using *Ctrl + Alt + LMB*.

Pinch/Spread

When you use **Extend**, you may notice that the strips you generate may tend toward being thinner than they need to be, especially if you're starting from an area of detail and moving out towards a broader surface. To solve this quickly, we can use the **Paint Deform** tool **Pinch/Spread** ✎. To use this, set the brush radius to be a bit bigger than the strip you added (around **0.55** was fine for the example in the following screenshot), and hold *Alt* while stroking over the polygons to spread them out (not using *Alt* will shrink them to be even tighter). This is very similar to the **Scale Conform** brush 🖌 and works well alongside it.

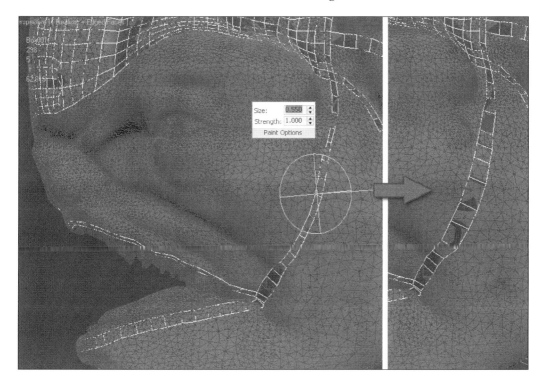

Using Quad Cap Pro to generate meshes to conform

The highly worthwhile commercial script called **Quad Cap Pro** can be used to generate a quad-based mesh from an extruded Spline or border. The script is available on Marius Silaghi's website at `http://www.mariussilaghi.com/products/quad-cap-pro`, and there's a video example there about capping splines. The script allows us to fill an area bounded by polygon strips, as shown in the following steps:

1. In the following screenshot in step **A**, an open border that frames an empty area we want to fill has been selected. Using `Packt3dsMax\UI Settings\UI.ui`, you can right-click and choose **Create Shape From Edges**, or you can find it in the **Graphite Modeling Tools** by expanding **Borders**. We used this tool in *Chapter 4, Mod My Ride: Extending upon a Base Model*, so you may want to review it. Be sure to set **Linear** in the **Create Shape** options. After creating it, at **Top-level** select the new `Shape01` object and add an **Extrude** modifier with its **Amount** set to **0.5**. You can use **Quad Cap Pro** directly on the **Border** selection of the model, but I like to break it off to be safe.

2. In step **B**, the extrusion has been created by giving a large single polygon on top. If you have the **Quad Cap Pro** script, you can run it and choose **Preview**, then **Apply**. The default options should be fine in this case, but you may want to use the **Rotate** function to adjust the result, which works a bit like the **Twist 1** function in the **Bridge Polygons** tool. The result is shown in C.

3. In step **D**, finally, the new surface has been detached from the extrusion. Since the polygon selection to which you applied **Quad Cap Pro** remains selected, you can press *Ctrl + I* to invert it and delete the rest of the extruded shape. Then you should **Attach** and **Weld** the result to the retopology object. This should be easy since the border you're rejoining it to is the same. Then you can use the **Conform Relax** brush to ensure the newly added polygons fit to the high-resolution source mesh. If you find that the welded borders don't join properly, it is probably because the extruded face that gets capped needed to be flipped. Also, you will find from time to time that **Quad Cap Pro** asks you for a border with an even number of segments, so you have to add an extra edge (or remove one).

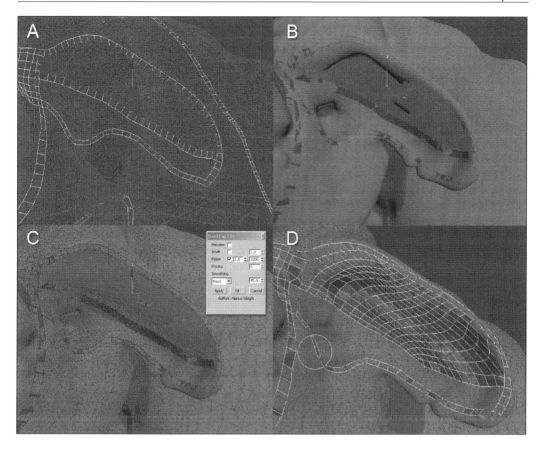

Filling stubborn polygons

To fill a quad using **Step Build** ⬚, dragging while you hold *Shift + LMB*, make sure you drag it out from the middle of the space you want to fill toward the unclosed gap. From time to time when you use **Step Build** and want to fill a polygon, it may not want to be your friend. So, you have to use another mean. In cases like the one in the following screenshot, in **Step Build** mode hold *Shift + Alt* and glide the mouse over the four points you want to surface, and then left-click in the middle of them after they're highlighted. If you are working inside of a cavity or on a surface with a lot of existing surface behind it (even with **Ignore Backfacing** ◌ turned on), you may find that this method is the easiest way to get a result even though it's more or less manual polygon building. For this tool to work without glitches, it is best to orient the current section you are working on so that there are no polygons behind it, and it even helps to hide polygons that you have already constructed from time to time while working on a really complex part, such as the inside of a mouth.

To hide a polygon selection, use **Edit Geometry | Hide Selected** in the Command Panel or **Graphite Modeling Tools | Visibility | Hide Selected** in the Ribbon.

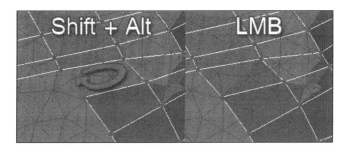

Topology concerns for animation

If you compare the source files `Retopo01.max` to `Retopo12.max` and `RetopoBodyStart.max` from `\Packt3dsMax\Chapter 9\`, you will notice that the process first shows the build-up of the quad-based mesh, and then there's a second pass where the flow of the edge loops is cleaned up to maximize the potential of the model; this is done, in particular, so that deforming areas like the skin around the eyes and mouth and neck get tidy, uninterrupted loops.

In the cleaned-up version, the key and secondary edge loops are marked by assigning differently colored materials to the polygon selections. Shading the loops can help you analyze and clean up the initial pass. It's advantageous also in that it helps you isolate edge loops that aren't contributing a lot to the form, which you can then remove using **Remove**.

The following screenshot shows a before and after of the retopology pass and the clean-up pass.

In the top frame, an edge loop around the eye is not closed, and in the lower frame it has been flowed by using **Cut** and **Target Weld** and regular edge editing steps, so that it is closed.

Also, in the top frame, the arrow points to an overly dense area. The same area has been cleaned up in the lower frame. The arrow in the lower frame shows that the cheek edge flow is tidier too.

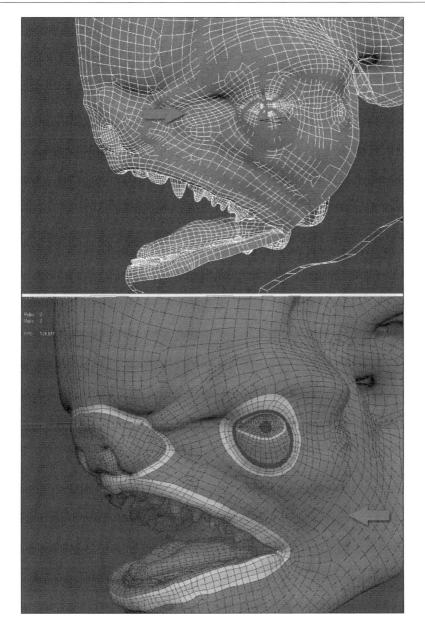

Around the corner of the mouth, the edge loop flow simulates a muscle flow around the lips. Flowing loops are helpful in highly flexible, deformable areas of a model. Around joints like the elbow, knee, ankle, and wrists, distribute clean edge loops so they are evenly arranged on either side of the rotation point. In an area such as the skull, there is no movement of the polygons themselves during animation, so you can turn the edges and include less detail.

One of the simplest explanations of edge loop topology that I've come across is shown on the Blender forums (okay, it's not 3ds Max but polygons are polygons) at `http://blenderartists.org/forum/showthread.php?93651-Poles-and-Loops`. A similar reference is the blog tips compilation at `http://gotwires.blogspot.com`.

It's worth noting that if you work on the model in parts, you can approximate some topology automation using **Conform** and regular primitives, for example, setting up cylindrical meshes for the legs and conforming them into proper place:

1. Create a Cylinder on the ground under the leg, as shown in the following screenshot in **A**. Drag this up to the height of the inner part of the leg.

2. Add an **FFD 4x4** modifier, and turn on the **Control Points** mode via the Command Panel options for the modifier. Select and move the control points so the Cylinder better fits the shape of the source mesh, as in **B**.

3. Delete the top and bottom of the Cylinder, as in **C**. We don't want the capped end because we'll be joining the surface to the rest of the retopologized mesh later.

4. Use the **Conform** or **Relax Conform** brush in the **Freeform** section of the Ribbon to quickly wrap the Cylinder mesh to the source mesh, as in **D**. Remember to set the source mesh as the **Surface** in the **Freeform** options. You may also want to add additional edge loops using **Swift Loop**.

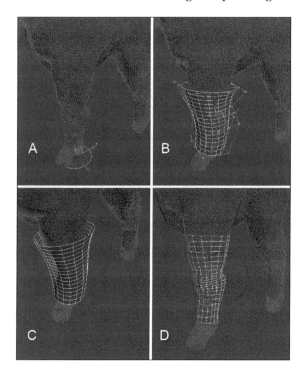

WrapIt by The Pixel Hive

Unlike in software such as 3d Coat, Modo 601, or ZBrush, there is no automatic retopology tool in 3ds Max. It so happens that a third-party company — "The Pixel Hive" — has written a commercial plugin **WrapIt**, which fills this gap. Matt Clark has updated the plugin to 3ds Max 2013.

To see what this offers, check out the demonstrations at
http://www.matt-clark.co.uk.

WrapIt has two primary advantages over the methods we've looked at so far. One is **QuadGen**, which automatically shrink wraps a target quad mesh over the source mesh according to user settings. The other is **AutoWrap**, which gives you a live mesh update as you use **Branch Paint** for new loops around the form, bridging to the previous loop or to a border selection. It includes a **Spacing** tool, which redistributes loops evenly, and a **Relax** tool. There are certain limitations with shrink wrapping a mesh onto another. **Automatic** edge loops may miss nuances in the flow of forms that handset loops will allow you to achieve; and more importantly, cavities tend to be ignored, so for example, the mouth of our current creature would be a bit unresponsive to that approach. Also, extreme spikes in a mesh, such as branching horns, tend to stretch the wrapping mesh and are better conformed in parts. A logical workflow would be to work on the finely detailed areas of your creature by hand, and use **WrapIt** for larger volumes like the body, tail, and legs to get those out of the way quicker.

A quick walkthrough of **QuadGen** to get a base primitive to wrap to a high poly source mesh follows. After you install **WrapIt**, you can access it via **Customize UI** and assign it to a shortcut or **Quad** menu entry. Activate it, and a pop-up dialog will show the **WrapIt** options and tools.

1. In the scene, create a Box01 primitive with **1 x 1 x 1** segments that fits to the bounding box of the high-resolution model. The segments value is not at all important, as the final conformed mesh is a freshly generated object with segments determined during the procedure; so we just need a starting volume, as shown in the previous screenshot.

2. Press **High Poly** and pick the source mesh from the objects list that pops up.

3. Press **Low** and click on the Box01 object.

4. There is a vertical slider in the **Select Objects** panel, shown in the previous screenshot, that lets you vary the relative opacity of the high and low resolution meshes in the viewport.

5. Next to the picker button **Low** there's a button **>**, which opens the **QuadGen** dialog. Here, set the **Quad Size** to be **0.25**. This value is much smaller than the default **10**. A value of 10 gives a quick result, but usually much too chunky to be useful. The smaller value means the calculation of the mesh will take a while but have better fidelity.

6. Make sure the **Optimize Quads** checkbox is ticked. If you click on **Hide Target**, the high-resolution source mesh will be hidden after calculation. You may prefer to leave it unchecked and calculate in wireframe mode to see everything, as, after all, all the meshes overlap each other. In this case, you don't have to worry about projecting UVs or Materials. Skip down to the big **Generate** button, press it, and wait for the **Status** bar to complete.

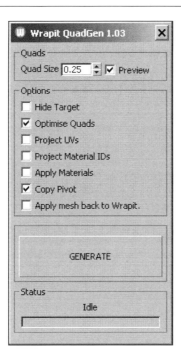

7. If you don't like the result and want to try different values, close the **QuadGen** dialog to pop up the **WrapIt** dialog and start again, and adjust the **Quad Size** value in the **QuadGen** dialog.

Note in the following example that the quad mesh tends to align vertically and horizontally, not at all based on the flow of forms in the source mesh. This is particularly evident in the tail, as indicated by the marked lines where the loops might be better aligned. Also note that the mouth is not properly concave; rather than fussing around trying to get that to work, it would be easier to join the body to a better version of the head. Also note that the feet details are a bit smoothed out. You can select the mesh faces, delete them, and then go ahead and manually build the faces for the detailed areas.

In conclusion, **QuadGen** is good for quickly deriving a base mesh to sculpt on (a mesh made from evenly sized, evenly distributed quads that will subdivide well). It isn't so good for a final, animation-oriented retopology mesh, where the flow of loops should be sensitive to the possible deformation during animation. Note that **QuadGen** is just one part of the **WrapIt** toolset, and the plugin does include other manual polygon creation tools similar to those in the **Freeform** tab of the 3ds Max Ribbon.

Finalizing the retopologized model

Suppose that you have manually reconstructed the head, used Cylinders as the base for the legs and tail and conformed those, and used **WrapIt** for the bulk of the body; you could attach the pieces together and use **Quad Cap Pro** on the borders between them to seal up gaps, and then relax the result using **Conform Relax**. The final check on the model is that its symmetry is okay and that there are no stray triangles or N-gons, which is easiest to do using **Selection | Select by Numeric** in the Ribbon. An example is provided in \Packt3dsMax\Chapter 9\RetopoBodyWrapItJoins. max (you don't need the **WrapIt** plugin or **Quad Cap Pro** script to open the resulting mesh).

As a final note, it is possible to automatically reduce the polygon count in a mesh while retaining its texture mapping using the Pro Optimizer modifier. Nice topology will generally be tossed out by this modifier, but it can produce a result very quickly. The usefulness of this might be to generate a very low-resolution proxy or collision mesh, or to create a mesh that's easy to bind to an animation rig using the **Skin** modifier (and then transfer the weights via the **Skin Wrap** modifier to the original mesh automatically). This process is discussed in the next chapter.

Summary

In this chapter, we've examined quad-based mesh retopology, and you should understand the difference between retopologizing a sculpted base mesh (for UV mapping and for further high-resolution sculpting) and retopologizing for animation so the edge loop flow is good for mesh deformation. You should also feel more comfortable about using the **Freeform** tools in the Ribbon, for modeling in general.

10
Pushing the Envelope – Model Preparation for Animation and Games

In this chapter, we will complete our modeling round by readying a model for game production through **level of detail** (**LOD**) creation, rigging, and skinning.

This chapter is not about modeling; instead, it aims to take you one step further towards animation. Many people learn modeling with the aim of doing animation, but the intermediate steps can prove a daunting obstacle. The first step we'll take involves model simplification (as it is easier to skin a low-resolution mesh than a highly sculpted one). After that we rig the creature using CAT, skinning the mesh to the rig, which is also known as binding or weighting, and examine some animation used to test the result.

The following topics are covered in this chapter:

- ProOptimizer
- Rigging the creature with CAT
- Rig naming and selection
- Rig display and access via layers
- Skinning the creature
- Skin advanced parameters
- Adjusting envelopes
- Painting blend weights
- Weighting per vertex
- Saving the rig and storing a setup pose
- Transfer of low poly skinning to a high poly character
- Testing the animation and making a preview
- 3ds Max 2013 CAT data transfer to MotionBuilder
- Game readiness check

ProOptimizer

The model used in the previous chapter will serve our purpose. It has 28K polys and could be skinned directly, but it's a nice trick to first skin a low-resolution version and then copy the skinned data to the high-resolution model. For this we'll use **ProOptimizer**, which is a modifier that decimates unnecessary polygons according to the user's specification.

Creating a low-resolution model prior to skinning

This section takes us through the workings of the ProOptimizer modifier, which is useful for polygon decimation of a mesh so that you can quickly give it a target poly count.

1. Open the file `\Packt3dsMax\Chapter 10\Creature_SkinStart.max` and select the main mesh `Creature`. Press *Ctrl + V* to paste it in a clone and be sure to set the **Copy** and not the **Instance** option. Hide the new model.

2. Convert the model in the scene to an Editable Poly, and in the Ribbon click on the **Selection** tab, and at the **Polygon** sub-object level (press 4) click on **Select by Half** (using the symmetry axis). After you have selected half of the mesh, press *Delete*. What working on half of the mesh does for us here is to ensure that after reducing the polygon count, both sides are identical despite the decimation.

3. Go to the modifier list in the Command Panel and select **ProOptimizer**, or go to **Modifiers | Mesh Editing | ProOptimizer**.

4. When reducing polygons you can select **Keep Material Boundaries** (on meshes that use more than one material), and you can also select **Keep Textures** and **Keep UV Boundaries** (which means there is no reduction in mesh density around the mapping seams, so UV islands will still hold their intended texture).

5. For what we're doing, which is generating a low-resolution mesh to make skinning easier, we don't need to worry at all about UV mapping. Eventually this model, once we've skinned it, will be discarded as soon as our original mesh shares the skin data from the optimized mesh. For now, what's more important is to be sure **Protect Borders** is on, since we've cut the model in half and we need to keep a clean symmetry mirror line.

6. In the **ProOptimizer** main parameters, you have to select **Calculate** before you can enter a lower vertex count. How long that takes depends on the mesh density. The result returned will at first be 100 percent, and the mesh will triangulate. Note that changing the parameters for **Optimization Options** after you have selected **Calculate** will invalidate the current solution, and you'll have to select it again to update the solution.

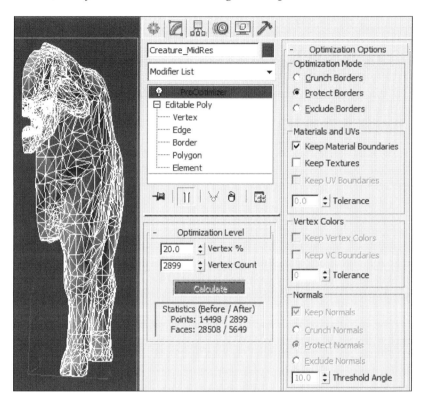

7. Enter 2500 in the **Vertex Count** field. You could also enter a percentage value around 15 to 20 percent, but the result is going to be about the same. That's all we need to do, except add a **Symmetry** modifier and then collapse the mesh to Editable Poly.

Rigging the creature with CAT

Character Animation Toolkit (CAT) was originally intended to be a platform for developing multi-legged skeletons, as opposed to 3ds Max's native biped tool. It was originally written as a plugin for 3ds Max by Phil Taylor, who I worked with in my hometown of Dunedin, New Zealand, before it was acquired as a plugin by Softimage (since Phil went to work there). Now integrated into 3ds Max, CAT itself is still being developed. The newest version of 3ds Max 2013 sees some better CAT integration with MotionBuilder. On the Autodesk Area forum, you may notice Louis Marcoux in particular has posted some great demonstrations of CAT in action. So let's look at how CAT works.

1. Open the scene `\Packt3dsMax\Chapter 10\Creature_CATStart.max`, or continue from where you left off. In the provided file, the different creature meshes have been set to different layers named after their resolution. Select `Creature_LowRes` and right-click and select **Hide Unselected**.

2. Notice the mesh has its pivot at the origin and it uses X = 0 for its symmetry line. This will make rigging and skinning a lot easier.

3. Go to the Command Panel and click on **Create** , then **Helpers** , and then expand the list, and instead of **Standard** helper select **CAT Objects**. This will expose the **CAT Parent** helper object. Highlight it and click in the scene on the Grid. Move it to (0, 0, 0) after you have created it.

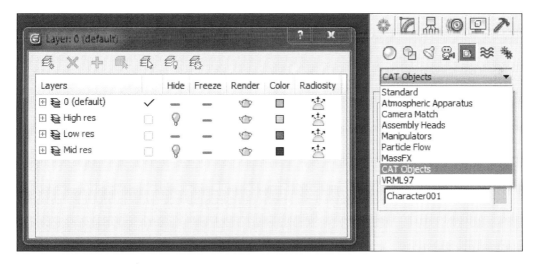

4. CAT comes with a set of provided rig templates, but here we really need to start from an empty one, so first off, in the modifier panel give the rig a name; `Bull`, for example. Every bone added to the rig will have this as its prefix, so a short, descriptive name is best.

5. Set the **CATUnits Ratio** value to `1` and then click on the **Create Pelvis** button, as shown in the following screenshot:

6. This should give you a box geometry floating above the **CAT Parent** helper object, which contains parameters that let us extend off new limbs. Since we're making a custom skeleton, the name of the geometry will be `Hub001`. Rename this in the Command Panel to `Pelvis`. You can scale the pelvis in the viewport or set its **Length**, **Width**, and **Height** parameters in the modifier. It doesn't matter much what you set, so long as the pelvis location is at the groin (between the hind legs) of the creature, on the center line at about the height a pelvis would be for this kind of creature. The last step to making the pelvis is to make its width span the distance between the back legs, since the leg bones generate with their pivot on the sides of the pelvis. A width of `50` units should be sufficient.

You may want to select the creature mesh and press *Alt + X* to enable X-ray mesh shading so you can see where bones from the rig will certainly be buried inside the model (as is the nature of bones).

7. With the `Pelvis` bone selected, click on **Add Leg** in the modifier panel section **Hub Setup**.

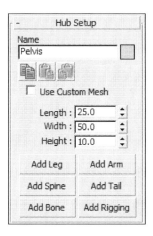

8. The created leg will have a square shape called a **platform** at $Z = 0$. The leg bones are generic, so will probably be overlong. Set the viewport coordinate system to **Local**, as this means when you scale and rotate the bones they adjust according to their own space, not the scene grid (View). To do this quickly, hold *Alt* and right-click in the viewport to expose the **Animation** Quad menu. You will have to do it for each of the transform types (unless you set the **Constant** coordinate system in the 3ds Max Preference Settings dialog).

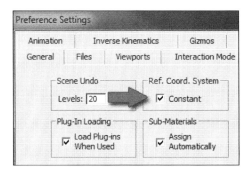

9. Scale the leg bones and move the foot platform so the foot sits where the mesh back foot is, and also make sure the knee joint is about where the mesh knee is located. Besides using **Scale** to adjust the bones you can also set their length in the modifier panel **Limb Setup**, or just use **Move** to locate the joint where you want it to be. After you're done with the limbs, experiment with moving the foot platform to see how the solver for the leg handles its overall motion. Don't forget to **Undo** to reset the location after you move the platform. Having taken the trouble of making one leg fit, we can now just select the `Pelvis` bone, and in **Hub Setup** click on **Add Leg** again to add an identical leg on the flip side of the creature.

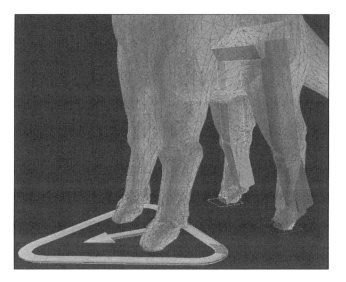

10. Next, click on **Add Spine**. This creates a chain of bones with another hub at the top. This is vertical, aimed at human-like skeletons, but we can move it around however we like. Fit it so the second hub is where the top of the creature's ribcage would be, on the center line between the two forelegs. Note, you can either move the hub or move each spine bone individually. At any time you can set the number of links you want to have in the spine, though the default 5 links should be fine in this case. Rename the hub as `Chest` — which will be the chest. Rotate it, and possibly the `Pelvis` bone as well, so the spine follows the right curve for the creature, as shown in the next screenshot. The spine of an animal goes just on the inside of the back, as shown in the next screenshot. You can move the bones of the spine a bit away from the pelvis bone to make this easier; their linking won't change.

11. Adding the tail is fairly easy. In the **Hub Setup** panel, click on **Add Tail** and then rotate the foremost tail bone into position and press *Page Down* to step down the chain of bones and adjust each one to suit. You can also select them all together and rotate them in a curling fashion. If you double-click on the top of the chain, it automatically selects dependent bones further down as well. It doesn't matter what you set as **Width** and **Height** of the tail bones so long as their Length is the longest dimension, as **Skin** envelopes tend to align to the longest bone.

12. Next, click on the Chest hub and again click on **Add Spine** in its **Hub Setup** panel. Except, we're going to use this as the neck and head. Select one of the new spine bones and change the link count for the spine to 2, then rename the new hub as Head. Rename these newly added spine bones as Neck.

The foreleg

For the foreleg, it would be handy to add a clavicle bone even though we're making another leg. Luckily, there's a checkbox in the leg properties that will insert the extra bone into the preset chain. Add the forelegs off the Chest hub.

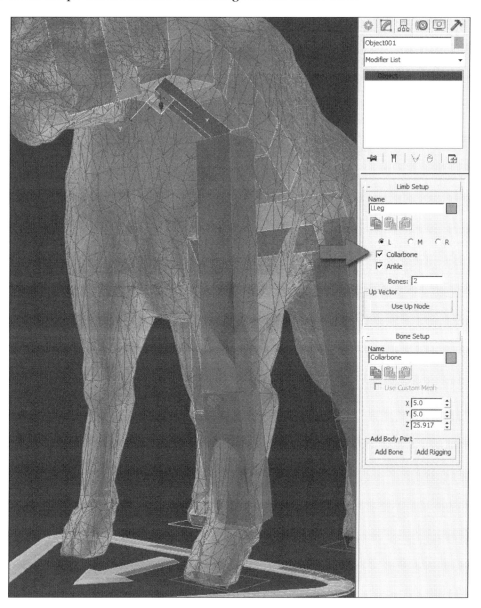

Rig naming and selection

Remember to appropriately name the joints of your character. In some cases you'll want to follow a naming convention established by a TD you're working with, or to match the naming convention in another rig type to make retargeting easier. As we've seen, CAT doesn't distinguish between a hub used as a pelvis and a hub used as a chest or head. Likewise, a leg can be an arm. With many characters you will want to add an arbitrary bone, such as the one that is linked to the head, used as a jaw. Whether it's a jaw or floppy ears, you'll need to name the bone yourself to make the rig easy to parse. To add floppy ears, while we're here, select the head and click on **Add Bone**, and locate the bone where the ear is on the mesh. With the new bone selected, click on **Add Bone** again to extend another link from it. Then, with the upper-most ear bone selected, click on **Copy Bone Settings** and select the head. Click on **Add Bone**, then select the new bone, and also click on **Paste/Mirror Bone Settings** in the **Bone Setup** panel, which will ensure both the ears are the same on both sides of the body, as shown in the following screenshot:

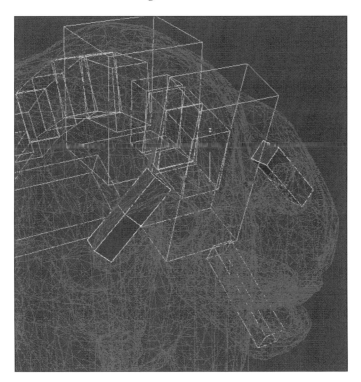

Once you have named the bones, copy each one's name and paste it in the **Create Named Selections field**, and press *Enter* to commit it. This will add the bone to a list you can pull down to access quickly, where many parts of the rig may overlap or be buried inside the mesh, or may be quite small. In the case of the creature we've rigged, named selections should be added for `Pelvis`, `Chest`, `Head`, `LeftEarUpper`, `LeftForeLegFOOT` (platform), `LeftHindLegFOOT` (platform), and possibly `LeftForelegShoulder`, `LeftHindlegShoulder`, and so on for the right-hand side of the body.

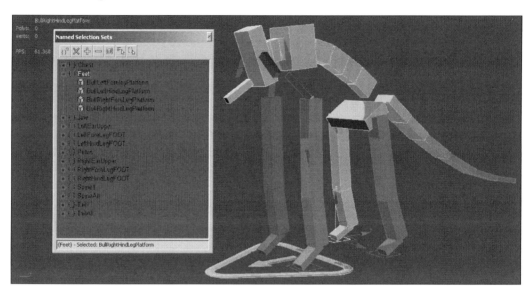

CAT has a shared field in its modifier properties for entering the name of an entire limb, which then prefixes each involved joint, and each joint has a field for its own specifics. I tend to name bones for their rotation point (putting shoulder and elbow rather than upper arm and forearm). You may also want to set a shortcut for the selection of the entire spine and the entire tail, as well as the first bones for each. While you can *Ctrl + LMB* click multiple named selection entries, you may find it can save time to set a single named selection also for the feet.

Finally, don't forget to name the neck bones as `Neck` instead of the default `Spine` they get, because they are generated from a hub (the renamed `Chest`). This is important because when you **Skin** the model, the bones are accessed by their name and it can be confusing to have two `Spine1` entries in a list.

Rig display and access via layers

The rig is made up of brightly colored boxes. It is possible, though often not worth the time, to substitute these with custom meshes (or pieces of the target character mesh) so the rig looks more interesting. Animators often use a rig made with optimized pieces cut from the mesh that are linked to the bones (or used as bones), so they can hide the mesh itself while doing the rough stages of animation. It's just a matter of selecting the polygons, clicking on **Detach**, naming the piece, and hitting (in CAT) the **Use Custom Mesh** checkbox in the **Bone Setup** panel. You may have to set the pivot of the mesh to match the bone you're replacing first.

To change a bone's color, you can use the color picker next to the bone's name. Often, animators use blue for the right side of the body, green for the left, and yellow for the middle. In some cases, it can be nice to make long chains of bones gradient from one end to the other, as is the case with the provided rig's tail bones and spine.

Whether you use custom geometry or the default boxy bones, at times it is handy to set them to be less obtrusive. You can do this in a variety of ways. Collectively or individually, in their **Object Properties** you can set **Display as Box** (which makes them display as a box wireframe) or **See-Through**, or set a low value for their **Visibility**.

Often you'll want to hide the rig entirely. When rendering a viewport preview to a file, for example, the bones may be visible even if they have **Renderable** toggled off. A convenient way to do this is to assign a layer to the CAT elements and just toggle the layer hidden in the **Layer Manager** rollout 🔲. Since all the rig elements are prefixed with the same rig name, it's easy to select them and assign them to a layer. Select the entire CAT rig by selecting **Select By Name** (press *H*) and typing the rig name in the select field. Another way to hide the rig is to toggle **Bone Objects** and **Helpers** in the **Hide By Category** list in the **Display** tab of the Command Panel.

Saving the rig to a file

If you want to populate your scene with several versions of the same rig and also want to include the mesh with the rig, you can select the **CAT Parent** helper object, and in the modify panel under **CATRig Load Save** click on the **Add Rigging** button. This pops up a selection dialog, which is empty. Select **Add** in this dialog, then click on Creature_LowRes showing in the **Pick Extra Nodes** window, which pops up after that; then click on **Pick Nodes** and close the **Extra Rig Nodes** window. Now click on **Save** 🔲 above **Add Rigging** and you'll be able to browse to a location for your new CAT3 Rig Preset (.rg3). In future, when you create a **CAT Parent** helper, you'll be able to select the new preset, which includes the bones, controllers, and the mesh if you have added it.

Skinning the creature

From here you can load \Packt3dsMax\Chapter 10\Creature_SkinStart.max, which includes a ready CAT rig and the low- and mid-resolution meshes. Note that before you start, it is worthwhile to check for and delete empty objects in the scene or stray vertices floating in the model (tiny polygons that aren't attached to anything or other weird geometry glitches). This should be done before skinning or it can lead to corruptions of the vertex weights.

1. Select the Bull CAT Parent, and in the modify panel note the **CATUnits Ratio** value is **1.0**. This is important because if the mesh was scaled very small and the **CATUnits Ratio** value was **0.1**, for instance, you might get problems if you were to load save motions onto the rig (which we'll be doing later). It is better to size up the mesh than size it down. Remember to apply **Reset Xform** on the mesh if it does need scaling. You can do this quickly from the menu bar by clicking on **Edit | Transform Toolbox**, and then selecting the **R** button in the Toolbox. In the provided scene at hand, this has already been done.

2. Select Creature_LowRes, and in the menu bar go to **Modifiers | Animation | Skin**. In 3ds Max you have the option to first add the modifier **Turn to gPoly**, which converts the model to the hardware mesh format used internally by 3ds Max, something you couldn't do before 3ds Max 2013. It results in a performance improvement when bones deform it. You can convert an editable poly object permanently to gPoly format if you right-click on its modifier stack and select **Deformable gPoly**. This might make sense for a higher-resolution model, but it won't be a big deal for this case.

3. In the Command Panel, you'll see in the **Skin** modifier's **Parameters** buttons called **Add** and **Remove** (currently grayed out) in the **Bones** commands. The **Edit Envelopes** button at the top doesn't do much until you have added bones to the list. Select **Add**, and from the dialog that pops up filter **Helpers** ▒ to be off, then add everything starting with Bull and then click on **Select**.

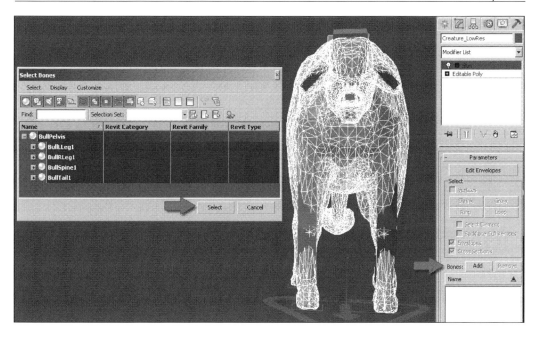

4. These should then show up as entries in the list below **Add** in the modifier. In 3ds Max 2013 you can reorder the list using the icon ▲. You don't want to add **Helpers** to the bone list because it would include the **CAT Parent** and the foot platform controllers, which would not contribute effectively to the skin result

Skin advanced parameters

Once you've added bones, the mesh will already have some kind of weighted solution but it probably will be far from perfect, and we'll examine what needs attention and fix it. Work from the larger issues to the smaller ones, and just work down one side of the mesh. It's not time to start animating or moving the rig around just yet though. First, expand the **Advanced Parameters** section of the **Skin** modifier parameters.

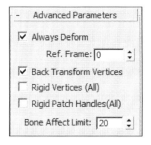

The main thing to change here is the **Bone Affect Limit** value. Few parts of a real body would be significantly influenced by more than four joints, let alone 20. For performance purposes too, the more bones you allow to affect a vertex, the more intense the calculation. Some game engines limit this internally, so it's best to skin with that in mind so the solution in 3ds Max isn't broken once you export for gameplay.

Under the **Bone Affect Limit** value you'll also notice a section where you can **Save** to file and **Load** from file your **Skin** solution, using the `.env` format. Once you have set up the **Skin** weights successfully, it can be helpful to save it, just in case something goes wrong in the `.max` file and you have to reapply the **Skin** modifier. Many times this has saved me pain; in particular, I suggest saving the `.env` file before using the Mirror vertices tools, which sometimes produces a result you may not like but which you can't undo. At the very bottom of the **Advanced Parameters** section is a checkbox **Weight All Vertices**, which is used to ensure every vertex in the mesh has some influence from a bone so it isn't left hanging in space when the rig is animated. This is on by default. Below that, there's a button **Remove Zero Weights**, which prevents a vertex having a bone assigned to it with no influence (which can occur if you shift the weights yourself from one to another). Normally, I hit this near the end of the skinning process.

Adjusting envelopes

To actually start adjusting weights then, it's normal to start with **envelopes**, which are a guide object with controls attached to each bone that you can scale to set how much coverage of the mesh the bone will have. To get started, click on the **Edit Envelopes** button in the **Skin** modifier. You'll see gray lines appear where each bone is, and the first bone in the list will have a red wireframe around it that looks like a capsule. You can directly select the gray lines in the viewport, but this is often tricky if they overlap or if you are not sure whether you're selecting the correct one.

Go to the bottom of the **Bones** list and select `Tail6`, and pan the viewport to show the end of the creature's tail. A tail is pretty easy to weigh, and the defaults may even be fine as they are. For now, let's just look at the structure of the envelope. There are two parts, an outer and an inner influence. The inner influence is stronger and bright red. The outer influence represents a falloff from the inner influence and is dark red. Each of these has, by default, two cross sections that have four small gray handles you can move around in the scene, and moving them scales the cross section and thus changes the shape and scope of the envelope. When you click on one of these handles the cross section involved goes pink, as shown in the following screenshot:

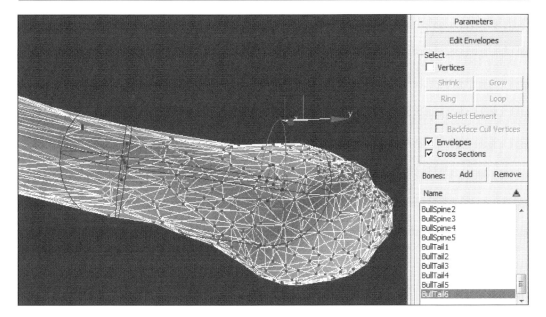

You can scale the cross sections, which is usually sufficient since most of the time you just want to decrease or increase the effect range of the bone. Sometimes though, you'll need to reposition the start and end of the envelope itself. There is a thin yellow line with gray handles at either end that you can select and move to change the envelope length, as shown in the following screenshot:

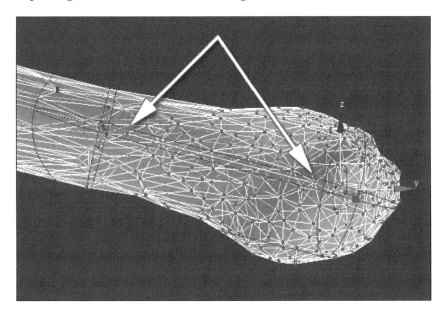

Note that you can copy envelope settings for cross sections and paste them to other bones, but you can't copy and paste the altered locations of the bone length handles. In the current rig, a good case where you might want to move the bone length handles is in the neck and head, which are not lined up along the length of the bone but instead are perpendicular.

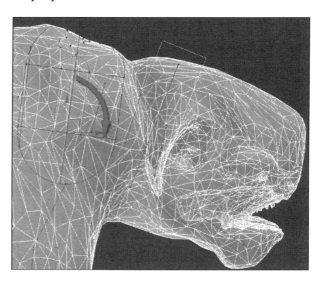

Where two bones connect there's usually an area of the mesh that will share the influence of both bones.

Envelope cross sections and properties can be changed in the modifier itself or in the viewport. You can **Add** additional **Cross Sections**, or **Remove** them (there's a minimum of two). The **Radius** value is what changes when you move one of the cross section handles. From inner to outer falloff there's an interpolation type you can set. The default is **Falloff SlowOut**. Often **Falloff Sinual** gives a more pleasant result, but can be time consuming to set for every bone.

Under the falloff setting there's also an **Abs. Effect** value and spinner you can use to set the weights of selected vertices to the current bone. This is only available when you have **Vertices** mode ticked in the **Select** parameters just under **Edit Envelopes**. We're not quite at the stage of editing individual vertex weights yet though. It's normal to set the weights as much as you can using envelopes first, because it's fast, and once you start editing by vertex the envelopes may become unresponsive. The order of changes made to skinning is best done as **Envelopes**, **Paint Weights**, and then per vertex using the **Weight Tool** dialog 🖉, then if you want to get really granular you can use the Weight Table (but we won't in this case). For information on using the Weight Table, refer to `http://goo.gl/4Kv7M` (link shortened).

While adjusting envelopes, you may wonder what is the difference between **Absolute** weights ᴬ and **Relative** weights 🅱 for each envelope. **Relative**, which I never really use, gives you full weighting within the inner envelope and calculates falloff from the inner and outer envelope. **Absolute**, the default, discards the inner strength and just calculates from the middle of the envelope to its outer limit.

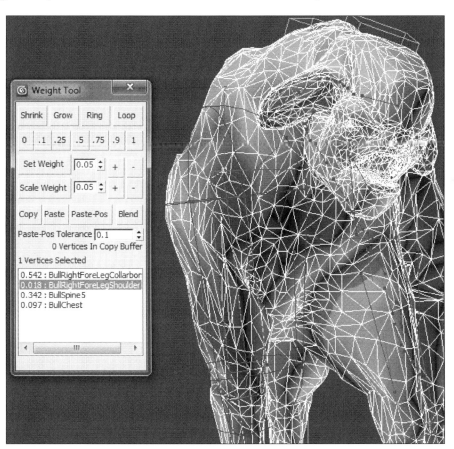

Checking skin adjustments

Now you have started changing weights, you'll need a way to see the effect of the changes. This is usually done in production by making an animation that tests the extreme rotations of the joints through a series of representative key poses. You can also rotate, check, and undo each joint bone by bone. As long as you save a Setup Pose you can reload on the CAT rig if you overdo the rotations testing things out. A weighting animation has been provided for this example called `\Packt3dsMax\ Chapter 10\BullAnimTestClip.clp`. To load this, select the **CAT Parent** helper, then go to the **Motion** panel, and in the **Clip Manager** rollout click on the **Browse** icon 📝 at the bottom. Browse for the file, and once you locate it click on **Open**. Go with the default loading options, and then you should see the animation layer getting a range of keys from 0 to 100 with distinct joint rotations for testing the creature's skinning. If you are in the **Setup** mode ●, click on the icon to switch to **Animation** mode 🔲 so you can see the animation playback. Don't test skinning in the **Setup** mode, as you may mess up the base structure of the rig. Using this animation you can check the effect of changing the envelopes to the point where you'll know what areas will need to be further adjusted by hand (using vertex methods).

Weighting per vertex

Typically, I'll skip directly to using the **Weight Tool** dialog 🖌 after setting the easiest of the envelopes. After that I'll use the **Paint Weights** brush to blend the weights by brushing on the mesh in areas I want to smooth.

The **Weight Tool** dialog is small but packed with functionality.

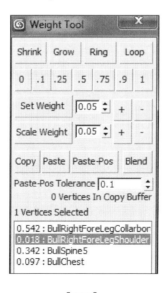

Let's have a look at how it works. The first few buttons let you **Shrink** and **Grow** a vertex selection you make in the viewport. If you use the **+** button to increase the current weight of the selection, then grow it. Now press **+** again and grow it again, and so on; you can easily create falloffs. If you click on a vertex, then by pressing *Ctrl* + clicking on a vertex in the same loop you can select the entire **Loop** or **Ring** using the respective buttons in the **Weight Tool** dialog. Underneath, there's a row of incrementing preset weights from **0** (nothing) to **1** (fully weighted) that are handy time savers. You can also type in a weight in the field under that and click on **Set Weight**. The **+** and **-** buttons increment the current value by the value in the **Set Weight** field. So if you enter 0.05 in the field you can fine-tune the vertex value up or down after clicking on one of the presets.

You can copy and paste weights from one vertex selection to another using **Copy** and **Paste**. Also, there's a more esoteric command called **Paste-Pos**, which according to the documentation, "Assigns the weight values currently in the copy buffer to the selected vertices based on the distance between them and the copied vertices." This is determined by the **Paste-Pos Tolerance** value defined in a field underneath **Paste-Pos**. Using **Paste-Pos** would be useful when you need to match weights between two superimposed skinned meshes sharing a common bone. I've never had a cause to use that command, but I can imagine it might be handy to fix up slight discrepancies in a skinning solution that's been created using the Skin Wrap modifier, which we'll be looking at shortly. I do use the **Blend** command right next to **Paste-Pos** all the time. This will more or less relax or smooth the weights of the selection among the bones that also affect it, if there are more than one.

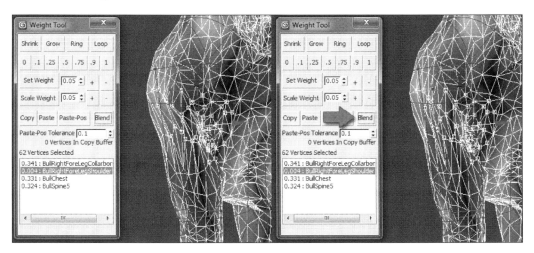

Below **Blend** there's a list of bones involved in the current vertex selection and the value for their weighting, which ranges from 0 to 1.

Painting blend weights

Apart from using the Blend tool we just mentioned, you can also brush the model in Paint Weights mode to either add or subtract weights using a set value, or else blend the weights based on the radius as it captures and averages the currently selected bone's influence based on the surrounding area and the other involved bones. The brush settings are accessed via a **...** button next to the **Paint Weights** button in the **Skin** modifier's **Weight Properties** section.

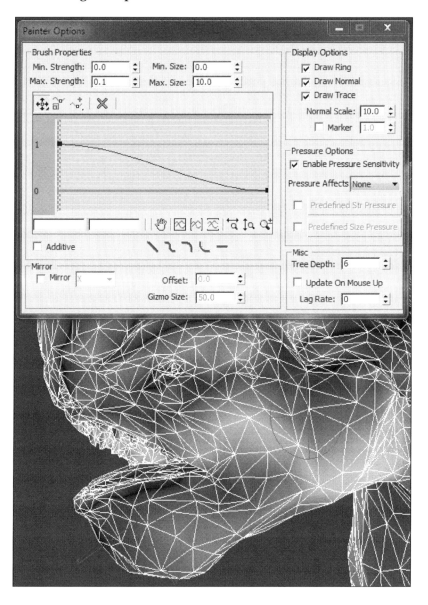

It helps to set a radius that's not too massive using **Max. Size** in the **Painter Options** window. In **Display Options**, the checkbox **Draw Ring** shows the radius, **Draw Normal** shows a line representing the surface normal where the cursor is, and **Draw Trace** dynamically draws the trajectory of your brush stroke. **Normal Scale** sets the length of the **Draw Normal** line. **Pressure Options** are relevant only if you are using a Wacom tablet or equivalent device, rather than a mouse. By default, pressure has no influence, but you can set it so **Pressure Affects** each stroke's **Brush Strength**, **Brush Size**, or both together, as seen in the previous screenshot. In certain cases you may also want to turn on symmetry for the brush by checking **Mirror** and setting the mirror axis.

The primary brush properties to set are **Min. Strength** and **Max. Strength**. If you set either to 1 then when you paint it's pretty sure your strokes will max out. To make the strokes build up less aggressively set the **Max. Strength** value to 0.05, for instance. This would make sense when you have **Paint Blend Weights** turned off and want to paint additive values stroke by stroke over the surface of the model.

The default setting for the **Paint Weights** tool is that **Paint Blend Weights** is checked, so the **Strength** value then influences the blending setting if it's on. Essentially you're going to be toggling between additive weight painting and smoothing.

Note that while the **Paint Weights** mode is active, you can't alter the vertex selection. The paint weights tool is indifferent to the current vertex selection and uses the surface of the model and the currently highlighted bone. You can change bones while painting by clicking entries in the bones list, but you can't change bones by clicking in the viewport.

When you are painting weights and using the **Blend** command found in the **Weight Tool** dialog, and setting weights vertex by vertex or adjusting envelope cross sections, remember to scrub the timeline to other poses to see how the changes affect the actual deformation of the mesh as the bones rotate. Also, if you can't manage to select vertices or brush into a tightly folded area of the mesh, try changing frames to where the opposite rotations of the bones make the folds less troublesome. The test animation poses, since they are focused on checking the range of distortion, may include extreme poses for the limbs that are unlikely to be seen in normal animation sequences.

Mirror Mode

It pays, if the model is symmetrical, to skin on a primary side of the body and then mirror the vertex weights when that side is working well to the other side. To do so, save your scene before continuing (or load `\Packt3dsMax\Chapter 10\ SkinMirrorStart.max`) and expand **Mirror Parameters** in the **Skin** modifier for `Creature_LowRes`. Activate **Mirror Mode** and note that green and blue points display on the model on either side of the **Mirror Plane** field, which defaults to **X** (which is what we want). In the provided scene, the blue vertices should be pasted to the green side, though this may differ if you have been doing your own version. Click on the appropriate option **Paste Blue to Green Vertices** 🔳 or in the other case 🔳, if that's what you need. The result should look similar to the following screenshot, after which you can deactivate **Mirror Mode**:

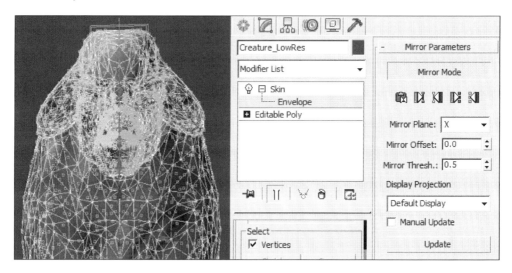

Be sure to check whether this mirror flipping of vertex allocations gives you a nice result. An easy way to check this is to grab `Feet` from the **Named Selection** list (or select all the foot platforms of the CAT rig) and transform them together, and see if both sides of the model behave in the same way.

Transfer of low poly skinning to a high poly mesh

Once you are happy with the low-resolution mesh skinning, you may want to apply it to a high-resolution version. The whole point of skinning a low-resolution version of the model is it is more effective than trying to skin the high-resolution mesh, because the lighter mesh performs faster and is easier to control while skinning.

In the scene `\Packt3dsMax\Chapter 10\Creature_SkinWrapStart.max`, go to the **Manage Layers** window 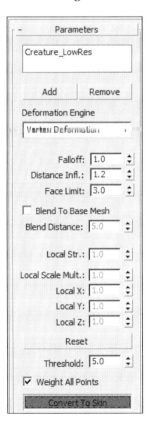 and unhide the `Mid_Res` layer to reveal the mesh `Creature_MirRes`. Click on `Creature_MidRes` and apply the modifier **Skin Wrap**. In its parameters, click on **Add**, and directly click on `Creature_LowRes` in the scene. At the bottom of the screen, in the status bar, you'll see a running calculation of the skinning solution as it is applied to the new mesh. After this is complete, drag the time slider to check everything looks alright. Check the **Weight All Points** checkbox at the bottom of the **Skin Wrap** parameters, and then click on **Convert To Skin**.

You will notice a new **Skin** modifier is added above the **Skin Wrap** modifier, which itself is automatically disabled and can even be deleted. You'll also be able to delete the low-resolution skinned mesh if you want to, though you may prefer to animate with the low-resolution mesh (saving the animation layers as clips using the **Clip Manager** rollout in the **CAT Parent** helper object) because the low-resolution mesh will likely perform better in the viewport. Remember in the case of the mid-resolution mesh, for its **Skin** modifier, to set the **Bone Affect Limit** value to 4 in the **Advanced Parameters** section, and as a precaution to **Save** the weights to an `.env` file.

Testing the animation and making a preview

This isn't a book about animation, but once you add an **Absolute** animation layer 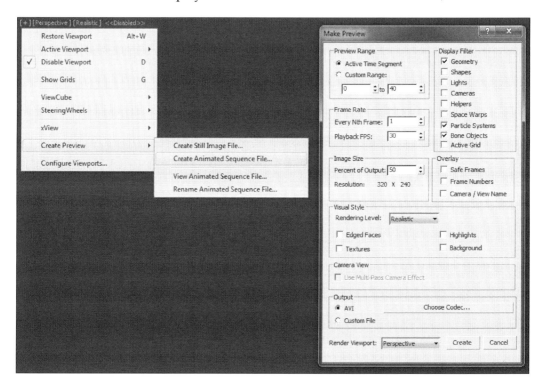 to the CAT **Layer Manager** rollout in the **Motion** panel, and press *N* to turn on the **Autokey** mode, you can readily start setting key poses at different frames in the timeline; you'll find it's not hard to get underway.

The provided \Packt3dsMax\Chapter 10\Creature_Walk.max scene shows the skinned model ambling along in a 40 frame loop, and even with the medium-resolution creature model the playback is pretty nice. The model in the provided scene has the **Turn to gPoly** modifier added to it, below the **Skin** modifier, which doubles the frame rate for playback.

Still, playback in the viewport is subject to the performance of the computer you're using, and you will want to be able to at least view the real-time playback via a preview. In the viewport, go to the + label and from the drop-down list select **Create Preview | Create Animated Sequence File...**. In the dialog that pops up turn off **Bone Objects**. You may also want to hide the CAT layer in the scene via the **Layer Manager** rollout. Set the preview's **Image Size** to 100 percent. 3ds Max defaults to 50 percent preview size, since a preview that's smaller renders faster and has a default render size of 640 x 480. However, the preview calculation is generally fast enough to get a speedy preview at full size. Much of the rest is a matter of preference. You want to toggle on **Highlights**, **Textures**, and **Background**, though in the current scene there aren't any to worry about. If you are rendering to show off your model topology, you might want to turn on **Edged Faces**. You have a choice whether to render a movie file format (AVI) or an image sequence, using still image formats such as .jpg or .png. You should also make sure your **Playback FPS** matches your output goal, either 30 fps, 24 fps, 25 fps, and so on.

In the case of an image sequence, you have to specify the output location for the frames, while for an AVI preview besides setting the video compression codec you prefer, you just have to look in the C:\Users\~\Documents\3dsMax\previews_ scene.avi folder. If you plan on keeping these, just rename the file and move it to another folder of your choice.

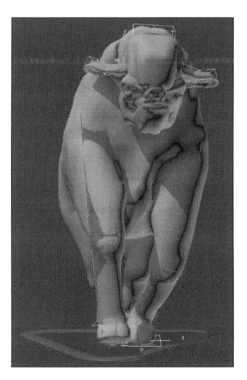

3ds Max 2013 CAT data transfer to MotionBuilder

If you are the proud owner of a Kinect sensor (an accessory for your Xbox), you will be able to use MotionBuilder to record yourself moving around using an open source software such as Brekel Kinect, which creates a live capture session you can then characterize and save out as an FBX skeleton or apply to a CAT rig. MotionBuilder is able to adapt or retarget the different proportions of the captured skeleton to a skinned CAT skeleton you need to animate. This is a little bit of fun and is documented by Autodesk's Louis Marcoux (`http://louismarcoux.com/`) on the Area website where he conducts a great blog (`http://area.autodesk.com/blogs/ louis/3ds_max_and_motion_builder_workflow_and_a_bit_of_kinect`), and in fact, one of the great new features in 3ds Max 2013 is the better interoperability between MotionBuilder and CAT, which can make motion capture data handling much speedier than before. All you need to do is select a rig's **CAT Parent**, and in the **File** menu go to **Send To | MotionBuilder**, supposing you have MotionBuilder 2013 installed.

Kinect motion capture – setting up with Brekel Kinect and MotionBuilder

For this you need a PC with a DirectX 11 capable graphics card. You will need a Kinect sensor (camera), MotionBuilder 2013 preinstalled, and a human actor so you can easily operate the software while they perform.

1. To install Brekel on a 64-bit Windows 7 machine, plug in your Kinect to a USB 2.0 port (not USB 3). It should autoinstall PrimeSense motor and camera drivers. Go to `http://www.openni.org/Downloads/OpenNIModules.asp`. Click on **OpenNI Packages** and then **PrimeSense Package Stable Build for Windows x64**. After completing the download, run the `primesense-win64-fullinstaller-dev.exe` installer. This adds OpenNI and NITE.

2. Run the web installer for the Brekel Kinect main application at `http://www.brekel.com/?page_id=160`.

3. Check **Kinect Camera** and **Kinect Motor** in your **Device Manager | Prime Sense**.

4. Install the MotionBuilder device plugin from `http://www.brekel.com/?page_id=160`.

5. Run MotionBuilder and Brekel Kinect (from the desktop icon).

6. Ensure the **User Tracking** panel has **PrimeSense NITE** checked on. Then ask your actor to walk in front of the scene and wait for the app to register you with a skeleton. If you are having trouble with the automatic tracking, ask the actor to move out of frame. Click on **User Tracking | Clear Calibration Data** and redo.

7. If you want to, increase the **Smoothing** amount to reduce capture jitter. Below **Clear Calibration Data** adjust the **NITE Skeleton Smoothing** to `0.6` or so.

8. In MotionBuilder, go to the **Asset Browser** panel and open **Devices**, and you'll see **Brekel Kinect**. This was installed by the MotionBuilder device plugin.

9. Drag this into the **Navigator** panel where it will show up in **I/O devices**. In the **BKD** panel, click on **Online | Live |Model Binding |Create...** to add a skeleton based on the Brekel Kinect session.

10. Ask your **motion capture** (or **mocap**) actor to take a stance as close to a T pose as possible. In the **BKD** panel, click on **(Re) Create Character Nodes**. This adds controls for the captured bones.

11. In the **Character Controls** panel of MotionBuilder (the one with the T-shirt guy), you'll see nodes for a character called `Kinect`. In the **BKD** panel, click on **Recording**.

12. In the **Transport Controls** panel of MotionBuilder, click on the red **Record** icon and also on **Play**. Ask your mocap actor to do some groovy moves. When ready, click on **Stop** in the **Transport Controls** panel of MotionBuilder. When prompted click on **Overwrite Take**. In the **BKD** panel, turn off **Live**. This allows you to play back the take using the **Play** icon in the **Transport Controls** panel.

13. Save the motion as `.fbx` by clicking on **File | Motion File Export ...** as `Move01.fbx`, for example.

Matching a CAT rig to an FBX in MotionBuilder

For this stage you need a PC that has both 3ds Max and MotionBuilder installed. What we'll do is to ensure our 3ds Max CAT rig can accept the motion captured movement.

1. In 3ds Max, assuming you have already made your CAT rig to match an existing model's proportions, ensure the CAT rig's hubs are named `Hips`, `Chest`, and `Head`.

2. Adjust one of the `Spine` bones (in the modify panel) so it is not set to the **Procedural** mode but set to the **Keyframed** mode. This sets the whole spine. Do this for the neck too since it probably started out as a `Spine` type.

3. Select all the CAT bones, including the CAT parent, and go to **File | Export**. Use `.fbx` as the output format. There's no need to turn on export animation in the `.fbx` export options. Set the filename as `CAT to MB.fbx`.

4. In MotionBuilder, go to **File | Merge** and browse to your exported `CAT to MB.fbx` content. Use the default merge options.

5. In the **Asset Browser** panel, grab the **Character** icon and drag it into the Viewer (Perspective = P). The character will show up in the the the **Navigator** panel as **Characters | Character**. Rename it to `FBXCAT_`, and in the **Navigator** panel click on the **Character Definition** tab.

6. Switch the Viewer from Perspective to Schematic (press *Ctrl + W*). Go to the **Navigator** panel, and in the **Character Definition** tab assign the CAT parent to the Reference channel using *Alt+ LMB*, and drag it from the **Schematic** view hierarchy to the **Mapping List**. Add all bones. The correspondence depends on bone names in your CAT rig, but the following table shows a general approach for a bipedal rig:

MB RIG	CAT RIG	
Main Section		
Reference	CAT Parent	
Hips	Pelvis	
LeftUpLeg	L_Thigh	(hip joint for the leg)
LeftLeg	L_Calf	(knee joint)
LeftFoot	L_Ankle	(ankle joint)
RightUpLeg	R_Thigh	(hip joint for the leg)
RightLeg	R_Calf	(knee joint)
RightFoot	R_Ankle	(ankle joint)
Spine	Spine1	(base of the spine)
LeftArm	L_UpperArm	(shoulder joint)
LeftForeArm	L_LowerArm	(elbow joint)
LeftHand	L_Palm	(wrist joint)
RightArm	R_UpperArm	(shoulder joint)
RightForeArm	R_LowerArm	(elbow joint)
RightHand	R_Palm	(wrist joint)
Auxiliarysection		
LeftShoulder	L_Clav	(clavicle joint)
RightShoulder	R_Clav	(clavicle joint)
Neck		
Spine Section		
1	Spine1	(already added above)
2	Spine2	
3	Spine3	
4	Chest	(ribcage)

7. When done, highlight the FBXCAT_ character, and in the main UI go to **File | Save Selection**. In the options for this, turn off everything except **Characters** in the list. Turn off **Export Animation** as well. Note that for future work, open the **Schematic** view (press *Ctrl + W*), select all the CAT bones, and *Alt + LMB* drag them for auto-remapping. So step 6 only needs to be done once for a given CAT rig.

8. Go to **Navigator | Character | Characters | FBXCAT_ | Character Settings**. Select **Characterize** and then go to **Create | FK/IK**. A control rig for the imported CAT content shows in the **Character Controls** panel.

9. In the **Asset Browser** panel, find Move01.fbx you made earlier using the Brekel Kinect device capture process. Right-click on it and select **FBX Merge**.

10. On your CATFBX character in **Character Controls**, go to **Edit | Input | Move01.fbx**. Also in **Character Controls**, go to **Edit | Plot Character**. This bakes the animation from one to the other. When prompted, select **Skeleton**. And again in **Character Controls**, go to **File | Save Character Animation** and call it CAT_FBX_ANIM or something similar.

Brekel motion capture tips

A wide-open background behind you, like a gym, won't be detected by the Kinect, so you will be tracked better against it. Otherwise, wear dark, tight clothes on a light background. The Kinect camera appears to have some trouble tracking knees in baggy jeans for example.

Make sure the capture area you'll perform in is clear of clutter, has no competing detail in the background, and is large enough for the moves you want to perform. Also, ensure the camera is capturing all of the actor.

The Kinect is not very good at registering bone rotations during crunched or side-on poses.

 Orient your Kinect at a fairly high level off the floor; about chest or head height should be fine. Also, make sure the ambient lighting is not too bright.

Kinect doesn't capture finger motions or facial expressions. In CAT you can adjust fingers into custom or preset poses to make hand animation easier. Also, you can use **Adjustment Layers** in CAT to nondestructively adjust the captured animation.

Try to design your character model around the proportions of the mocap actor who will be performing during the animation capture sessions.

You can use **Reduce Curves** in the **Curve Editor** to simplify captured animation data. MotionBuilder also has strong filters to improve common problems that occur in mocap animation, such as smoothing and spike detection.

Matching a CAT rig to an FBX in 3ds Max

This section covers how to handle the captured animation in 3ds Max on the original CAT rig. For this you need a PC with 3ds Max installed and the `CAT_FBX_ANIM.fbx` file from the previous section.

1. Import the FBX file. Go to **File | Import | CAT_FBX_ANIM.fbx**. In the import options go to **Include | File Content: Add to Scene**. Don't click on **Update Scene Elements**, because there's nothing to update the first time. Also in the options, tick on **Animation**. Go to **Bone Creation | Bone Conversion | Convert as Dummy** (although this doesn't seem to matter).

2. In the main 3ds Max UI, go to **Animation | Animation – CAT | Capture Animation**. A dialog pops up in which you need to match the original rig with the animated bones you imported.

3. In the dialog, **Set Target** as CAT Parent rig. **Set Source** as FBX rig, starting from the `Pelvis` bone.

4. Match **Target** entries to **Source** entries in the list by clicking the source entry and the appropriate target entry. You can *Shift* select to chain together a bunch of entries in the sequence, such as arms and legs.

5. Make sure, as before, that the `Spine` bones in the CAT rig are set to **Keyframed** and not **Procedural**. When this is completed, click on **Save** in the **Mapping** options in the **Capture Animation** dialog.

6. In the **Motion** panel, under **Layer Manager** (with a CAT bone selected), make sure **Available** is the highlighted layer (an empty one).

7. In the **Capture Animation** dialog, click on **Capture Animation**. It transfers over the motion and adds a new layer to the **Layer Manager** rollout. Note that as you have already run this process, the next time you import an FBX animation from your saved MotionBuilder CATFBX template to this CAT rig in 3ds Max, you can choose **Update scene element** in the import options, since all the required mapping has been done.

8. In the **Layer Manager** rollout, next to **Add Abs Layer** there is a **Move** icon ◈ you can click that reveals a ghost skeleton for the CAT rig with a controller below it. You can drag it to (0, 0, 0) and rotate as required. Note that this doesn't generate a walk on the spot effect; it just relocates the start of the animation to the origin.

Game readiness check

Throughout the book, we've already covered some ideas that contribute to a model's game readiness, such as creating good UVs, and setting a good object location in the scene. Since we're wrapping up the whole process we've been through, from preparing to model to making a base model to mapping and texturing the model, retopologizing it as required and even skinning it for animation, all we have to worry about is export. Should your model be required as an asset in a game, you will want to confirm all the features it has are correct, so the export and import into the game editor go as planned. The following is a list of important points to check over, to establish you are indeed done:

- For export, the model pivot should generally have its pivot located at (0, 0, 0) in the world space. The rig pivot should align with the rig at the origin as well.

- Before you skin it, your model should have its transforms reset so it doesn't scale strangely, for instance. If this wasn't done, you can save the skin data to a file, reset the model, then load the skin data back on. Or copy the skin data to a cloned version and paste it back after resetting.

- The scale of your model should be worked out so it isn't unreasonably tiny or huge in the world space of the game editor.

- The model might not export properly if it is part of a larger group.

- Some modifiers, such as Symmetry, may need to be collapsed to ensure the model works well external to 3ds Max.

- STL Check should be run on the model to check it doesn't have glitches such as doubled faces or unwelded vertices.

- Smoothing groups are often discarded during export or not read by other applications. If your model depends on them, you may face additional modeling work to compensate. General smoothing should also be checked so no curved surfaces in the model are faceted where they should be smooth.

- Texture coordinates or UV mapping should be checked they are correct, have no overlaps, and in some cases have the correct Material IDs.

- Morphs applied to the model should be checked, particularly that their weights be set to 0.0 before export. Sometimes you will need to export the morph targets themselves, and sometimes they'll be interpreted from the Morph modifier.

- The model's polygons should have appropriate materials assigned to them, particularly if you want to have different materials for different polygon groups. If the materials are meant for a specific renderer, it can be good to note this in file documentation and in the names of the materials.

- The model and the materials should be named, because once exported and imported to another application you may not be able to edit the names.

- The model may need to be in its setup pose or bind pose (the pose it has before animating). If you are exporting from an animated mesh, make sure the time slider is on frame 0, or you can specify the appropriate frame range to export.

- Hidden parts of the model, particularly if your model combines multiple elements or meshes, should be unhidden if you want them exported too.

- In most cases you will only export the skinned mesh, not the bones directly. Sometimes you will export the rig as a .fbx skeleton and load it separately in an editor, then assign it to the exported character geometry. Some editors may require animation driven by skin deformations or morph deformations to be exported as a point cache file.

- Some editors, or more likely sculpting software, can't handle open edges in the model; for instance, around eye sockets.

- In some cases you may want to save a thumbnail render or even a turntable animation of the asset so as to make it easier to stay organized when managing many files. If your asset includes a custom rig or custom controllers, it can be helpful to write some notes about their usage.

- Save a backup file of your completed 3ds Max asset even after it's been sent off into the game world and is there working nicely.

Summary

This chapter provides a fairly short overview of how to prepare a model for animation in terms of skinning and provisioning a rig. The intention is to round off the modeling process so there are no obstacles between modeling and animation. As we've observed chapter by chapter, each discrete topic in the model pipeline may at first seem bewildering, but practice really is the ingredient that leads to real fluency. Most of the processes are repetitive and predictable, and once you understand the basic idea you'll no doubt build upon what you know, and as you go you'll frequently stumble on a gem of new knowledge that makes your day. Hopefully, this book offers you a stepping stone, and I hope before long what we've been concerned with and been through step by step is the kind of thing you're taking for granted and can whip through without any trouble at all.

Index

B

base model
creating 86
fitting, to artwork 104, 105
forming 93, 94
image reference, adding 86
model forms, generating with Cloth
162, 163
parts, attaching 114-119
parts, detaching 114-119
poly loops. marking 126-128
Quad menu's editable poly tools 94-100
round forms, generating from quad-based
geometry 106-113
sculpting 119-123
shapes, generating from edge selections
139-141
smoothing group 156
soft modeling 129
Sub-Object selection, modifier applying
136-139
Sweep modifier, comparing with Loft object
153-156
values, setting with Autodesk style caddy
101-103
Basic Wheels 29
blend weights
mirror mode 386
painting 384, 385
Booleans
cleaning 250-253
creating 248-250
Brekel Kinect and MotionBuilder
used, for setting up Kinect motion capture
390, 391
Bridge Edges tool 112
Brush Images 319
By Polygon 102

C

caddy 101
capping splines 352
CAT
about 367
used, for rigging creature 367
working 367-371

CAT rig
matching, to FBX in 3ds Max 394
matching, to FBX in MotionBuilder 391, 393
CGSociety forums
URL 9
Character Animation Toolkit. *See* CAT
CheckMate Certification 266
Clear command 296
Clone brush
using 320, 321
Clone to Element option 112
Cloth modifier
about 162
used, for generating model forms 162-164
Cloth modifier parameters
setting up 164-166
cluster 267
ConnectVertex tool 260
content
searching, in scene 38, 39
Copy 66
creature
skinning 376, 377
creature, rigging with CAT
about 367
foreleg 372
layer manager 375
naming convention 373, 374
rig display 375
selection 373, 374
Customizable Workspaces, 3ds Max 2013
setting up 231
Custom Map
using 320
custom mapping texture
applying 283
custom selection sets
creating, with Named Selections 40, 41
custom UI scheme 17
Cut and RemoveLoop tools 129
Cut tool 180 258
Cut tool, 3ds Max 2013 231

D

default preferences, 3ds Max
changing 42-44

Ribbon tools
  about 258
  Cut 258
  optimize 262
  Paint Connect 258
  Quickslice (Qslice) 258
  Set Flow 258
  shift 261
  SwiftLoop 258
  using 258-261
  Vertex 259
round forms
  generating, from quad-based geometry
      106-112

S

scene
  organizing, Groups used 73
Screen space 132
script
  setting up 292
sculpting workflow
  about 119
  features 119
  UV mapping 119
Scuptris.OBJ mesh
  importing, into 3ds Max 341-344
SelectEdgeLoop command 94
Set Flow 258
shadow casting
  disabling 54, 55
shapes
  generating, from edge select 139-141
Shift brush
  about 132, 261
  Freeform tab 132
  Mirror Axis value 133
  Screen space 132
Show Frozen in Gray, Object Properties 51
skin advanced parameters
  about 377, 378
  envelopes, adjusting 378-381
  skin adjustments, checking 382
  weighting per vertex 382, 383
smoothing groups
  about 156

  editing 156-161
Snapshot
  about 66, 69
  capturing 69
soft modeling
  about 129
  relaxation techniques 136
  with Free-Form Deformations 134, 135
  with Shift brush 132
  with Soft Selection 129-131
Soft Selection
  about 129
  parameters 130
  using 130
Soft Selection tool 289
Spacing tool 357
spare parts
  2D graphic component, progressing to 3D
      component 172-185
  Greeble factory 186
Standard Tessellation Language. *See* **STL**
star ship
  building 192-195
  building, from primitive 192
  outer space, building 195-206
star ship construction walk through 206-225
Star Wars 186
Steering Wheel
  about 28
  Basic Wheels 29
  Full Navigation Wheel 29
  Mini Tour Building Wheels 29
  using 29-31
  View Object Wheels 29
Step Build mode 346
STL 205
STL Check modifier 203, 205
Sub-Object editing
  in Manipulation mode 244-247
Sub-Object level editing tools, via Ribbon
  about 236-238
  dot selection 243
  edge loop control 239
  edge loop, growing using Grow Loop icon
      239
  live select mode 242

Thank you for buying
3ds Max Speed Modeling for 3D Artists

About Packt Publishing

Packt, pronounced 'packed', published its first book "*Mastering phpMyAdmin for Effective MySQL Management*" in April 2004 and subsequently continued to specialize in publishing highly focused books on specific technologies and solutions.

Our books and publications share the experiences of your fellow IT professionals in adapting and customizing today's systems, applications, and frameworks. Our solution based books give you the knowledge and power to customize the software and technologies you're using to get the job done. Packt books are more specific and less general than the IT books you have seen in the past. Our unique business model allows us to bring you more focused information, giving you more of what you need to know, and less of what you don't.

Packt is a modern, yet unique publishing company, which focuses on producing quality, cutting-edge books for communities of developers, administrators, and newbies alike. For more information, please visit our website: www.packtpub.com.

Writing for Packt

We welcome all inquiries from people who are interested in authoring. Book proposals should be sent to author@packtpub.com. If your book idea is still at an early stage and you would like to discuss it first before writing a formal book proposal, contact us; one of our commissioning editors will get in touch with you.

We're not just looking for published authors; if you have strong technical skills but no writing experience, our experienced editors can help you develop a writing career, or simply get some additional reward for your expertise.

Unreal Development Kit Game Design Cookbook

ISBN: 978-1-84969-180-2   Paperback: 544 pages

Over 100 recipes to accelerate the process of learning game design with UDK

1. An intermediate, fast-paced UDK guide for game artists

2. The quickest way to face the challenges of game design with UDK

3. All the necessary steps to get your artwork up and running in game

Cinema 4D R13 Cookbook

ISBN: 978-1-84969-186-4   Paperback: 514 pages

Elevate your art to the fourth dimenstion with Cinema 4D

1. Master all the important aspects of Cinema 4D

2. Learn how real-world knowledge of cameras and lighting translates onto a 3D canvas

3. Learn Advanced features such as Mograph, Xpresso, and Dynamics.

4. Become an advanced Cinema 4D user with concise and effective recipes

Please check **www.PacktPub.com** for information on our titles

Google SketchUp for
Game Design

Create 3D game worlds complete with textures, levels,
and props

Beginner's Guide

Robin de Jongh

Google SketchUp for Game Design: Beginner's Guide

ISBN: 978-1-84969-134-5   Paperback: 270 pages

Create 3D game worlds complete with textures,
leavels, and props

1. Learn how to create realistic game worlds with
   Google's easy 3D modeling tool

2. Populate your games with realistic terrain,
   buildings, vehicles and objects

3. Import to game engines such as Unity 3D and
   create a first person 3D game simulation

Cool projects that will push your skills to the limit

Unity 3
Game Development

Eight projects specifically designed to exploit Unity's
full potential

HOTSHOT

Jate Wittayabundit

Unity 3 Game Development Hotshot

ISBN: 978-1-84969-112-3   Paperback: 380 pages

Eight projects specifically designed to exploit Unity's
full potential

1. Cool, fun, advanced aspects of Unity Game
   Development, from creating a rocket launcher
   to building your own destructible game world

2. Master advanced Unity techniques such
   as surface shader programming and AI
   programming

3. Full of coding samples, diagrams, tips and
   tricks to keep your code organized, and
   completed art assets with clear step-by-step
   examples and instructions

Please check **www.PacktPub.com** for information on our titles

3827691R00233

Printed in Great Britain
by Amazon.co.uk, Ltd.,
Marston Gate.